What does the Sermon on the Mount reveal about true human freedom?

In *Into the Darkness*, Gene L. Davenport probes the Sermon to its very core, demonstrating what the Sermon reveals about our humanity and examining the Sermon's implications for those of us living in contemporary Western society.

Using Light and Darkness as guiding metaphors, Davenport shows that the Sermon is not a new legalism, an ideal ethic, or an impossible goal. Rather, he asserts, it is a description of true freedom. It is a guide for God's people as they carry out the primary task of bearing testimony to the character of God.

Into the Darkness—with its unsparing criticism of contemporary Western society and the Western church—is certain to spark heated debate. It challenges positions held by both the theological right and left, but its value is in helping serious Christians re-examine their own understanding of Christian witness.

Though not an exegesis in the ordinary sense of the word, *Into the Darkness* is based on a thorough exegesis of the Sermon on the Mount and includes numerous exegetical insights that will be of interest to New Testament scholars as well as to pastors and serious lay readers.

(continued on back flap)

INTO THE DARKNESS

Also by Gene L. Davenport:

What's the Church For?
King Jesus: Servant, Lord, Soul Brother
The Eschatology of the Book of Jubilees

INTO THE DARKNESS

DISCIPLESHIP IN THE SERMON ON THE MOUNT

GENE L. DAVENPORT

ABINGDON PRESS
Nashville

INTO THE DARKNESS

Discipleship in the Sermon on the Mount

Copyright © 1988 by Abingdon Press

This book is printed on acid-free paper.

Library of Congress Cataloging-in-Publication Data

Davenport, Gene L.
  Into the darkness: discipleship in the Sermon on the mount / Gene L. Davenport.
    p. cm.
  Bibliography: p.
  Includes index.
  ISBN 0-687-19462-8 (alk. paper)
  1. Sermon on the mount—Criticism, interpretation, etc.
  I. Title.
  BT380.2.D34 1988   88-19039
  226'.906—dc19   CIP

Scripture quotations noted Phillips are from J. B. Phillips, *The New Testament in Modern English,* Revised Edition, Macmillan. Copyright © J. B. Phillips, 1958, 1959, 1960, 1972.

Scripture quotations noted RSV are from the Revised Standard Version of the Bible, copyright © 1946, 1952, 1971 by the Division of Christian Education of the National Council of Churches of Christ in the USA. Used by permission.

Scripture not identified paraphrases the RSV or is the author's translation.

MANUFACTURED BY THE PARTHENON PRESS AT
NASHVILLE, TENNESSEE, UNITED STATES OF AMERICA

For Charles W. Mayo

Whose courtesy, wisdom, and integrity
bear eloquent testimony to the Light,
in the face of the Darkness

CONTENTS

FOREWORD

Will D. Campbell

Thirty-one years ago a boy preacher named Gene Davenport got in some trouble in Alabama. He had a run-in with the Ku Klux Klan. He wasn't trying to get into trouble, just trying to be a good Methodist preacher and live like they taught him at the church in Sylacauga where he grew up. They had taught him to sing "Red and yellow, black or white, they are precious in His sight." And he believed it. He had also taken to heart the words of Isaiah, Micah, Jeremiah, and Jesus' Sermon on the Mount. He had listened to sermons by Methodist pastors like Dan Whitsett, powerful sermons, on justice, freedom, and judgment.

Now he was nineteen years old, a student at Birmingham-Southern College, and pastor of the Pelham Methodist Church, twenty-five miles outside Birmingham. His training had been good training. But not even fine teachers like Professor Francis Christie had told him what to do if a unit of the Ku Klux Klan came to church on a hostile mission. So he had to go on instinct.

In 1957 the Ku Klux Klan in Alabama was an organization few chose to engage, in any but a friendly fashion. It was three years after the U.S. Supreme Court had ruled that segregated public education was unconstitutional. White political, civic, and many religious leaders had led the vanguard in opposing any such change in Southern mores. In the capital city of Montgomery, not many miles to the south, a successful boycott had been waged against segregated city buses. And it was not long before police dogs in Birmingham would be snarling at children singing "O Freedom." The force of water from fire hoses would soon knock peaceful demonstrators to the sidewalks and roll them along like beach pebbles at high tide. Martin Luther King, Jr., was a name synonymous with Satan to many. There was anger in the land. And there was violence in its wake.

The church at Pelham was not a sought-after prize among appointments in the North Alabama Conference of The Methodist Church at the time (maybe something like Bethlehem of Judea). If it had been, a college student in his teens probably would not have been sent there. But it was not the size of the church nor the age of the preacher that accounted for the interest of the Klan. It was the ideas of the preacher.

In a discussion with his youth group, he discovered that not one of them had ever met a black person socially, someone who was not a servant or laborer. Together they decided to invite some students from nearby Miles College, a Methodist school for blacks, to meet with them. When a meeting of the Official Board of the church was called without his sanction or knowledge, he attended, knowing from the Methodist *Book of Discipline* that it was his right and duty to do so. He expressed his views on the matter, but the Board voted that the interracial meeting could not take place. When all of the parents indicated that their children would not be allowed to attend he had no choice. The meeting was not held. But by then the pastor was well marked by his sermons anyway.

On a balmy February night, Race Relations Sunday, he was five minutes into his sermon from Ezekiel, talking of sin and righteousness, of bones drying in the sun. A procession of Klansmen in full regalia began marching down the center aisle. Each one was carrying money in his hand. As the first one reached the altar and dropped his biased alms on the table, the little preacher stepped over the Communion rail to face them directly.

"We don't want your money," he said. The robed and hooded men continued their planned ritual without answer. As the last one placed a dollar on the table the pastor scooped it all up, held it above his head, and tore the money to shreds.

As they were recessing from the church he called after them. "I wish I had not torn your money up. I wish I had sent it to the NAACP." They were not words courting longevity in 1957 Alabama.

In not many days a call came to his college dormitory. "Are you Reverend Gene Davenport?"

"Yes sir."

"Are you the pastor of the Pelham Methodist Church?"

"Yes sir."

"And were you preaching last Sunday night when some visitors came and made an offering to the church?"

"A threat is not an offering," he replied. "But who are you? The joke is over." He thought it was a prank by one of his friends.

But it was not a joke. The caller was an agent with the U.S. Secret Service field office in Birmingham. Before the conversation ended the Reverend Davenport had been instructed to come to the Federal Courthouse the following day.

"Should I bring a lawyer?" he asked.

"No, there's no need for that," he was told.

In the Secret Service office he told the story as it happened. When he was through, the agent asked him to sign the transcribed copy. Then he was told that the Federal Grand Jury would meet in three months and that he would be notified when to appear. The penalty for defacing U.S. currency, he was informed, was a substantial fine, two years in prison, or both.

"The Federal agent was polite and gracious," the pastor later reported to some of his ambivalent parishioners.

The boy preacher was never indicted. But apparently he was a slow learner. He didn't master the lesson the Ku Klux Klan and the U.S. Secret Service sought to teach him. For now comes a book far more radical than defacing Caesar's image, although in many places that is precisely what it is.

Into the Darkness is not a book for timid Christians, for patriots who equate nationalism with righteousness. (Or maybe it is!) It is not a book to bolster self-image or tickle surface emotions. Those who know Gene Davenport as the gentle man he is will be surprised at some of the passages they find.

The boy prophet is all grown up now. He is as principled, tough, and courageous as the lad who stepped across the Communion rail to meet the Ku Klux Klan on their side of the railing and by doing so took on the state of Alabama, and Caesar's coadjutor, in 1957. It is not easy, whether at nineteen or fifty, to take issue with your own people; with those who nurtured you and whom you love. But he did not cower, did not use the sanctuary of his mahogany pulpit as he might have. In stepping across the railing he brought his understanding of truth into the world. He has done the same thing again. (One thinks of Jesus in the Temple at twelve. And again at thirty.) With *Into the Darkness* the professor has stepped from behind the lectern, out of the Academy, and into the world, to our side of the railing, bringing with him words of prophecy, words of warning. Also words of ultimate hope for those who have ears to hear and use them well.

His words now are buttressed by decades of meticulous scholarship. Although Professor Davenport dismisses any scholarly intent in this work the reader will soon disagree. A man who mastered the Ethiopic language in pursuit of the scholarly, who holds advanced degrees from one of the nation's finest universities, and who is widely respected as an authority on Intertestamental literature has no reason to make claims. His work here is scholarship at its finest; scholarship meant to teach. Whether he intended it or not, what he has given us is a commentary on the Sermon on the Mount the way commentaries ought to be written.

Many will thank him. I am honored to be first in line.

Will D. Campbell
January 1988

ACKNOWLEDGMENTS

My first taste of a rigorous, scholarly approach to the Sermon on the Mount was in a graduate seminar at Vanderbilt University under Leander Keck and Lou Silberman. In subsequent years, as teacher, preacher, lecturer, and just plain reader, I have dealt with the Sermon in just about every undergraduate academic, ministerial, and study setting imaginable. Across the years, I have entered into dialogue with so many of the major and minor treatments of the Sermon—from Patristic to Medieval to Reformation to modern, including even at least one Hindu treatment—that it sometimes is impossible to know whether an idea I have is actually my own or is an elaboration of one borrowed from someone and tucked away in the recesses of my mind. Frequently, I have read treatments in which the writer was treating a new idea, but one to which I had come already in my own work.

Although only here and there in this book will I lay out one or the other of the modern scholarly methods, untold hours of engagement using those methods precedes the approach that I have taken. Wherever I am aware of actually borrowing a fresh idea, I have credited my source. In general, however, the nature of the book makes footnoting irrelevant. The purpose of the book is not to present the fruit of academic research in the currently accepted sense of the term; my purpose is advocacy, and it hardly seems fitting to footnote a summons.

Although I have relied on the Revised Standard Version (first edition) as a basic reference, in numerous places I have modified that translation because I consider it to use words that cloud the meaning of the text. In some places, I have made a completely new translation from the Greek or Hebrew.

As the book began to take shape, Billy Vaughan, a former student and now close friend, helped by affirming, raising questions, and prodding in numerous lunch-time discussions. The observations and questions of Charles Mayo, colleague and trusted friend, helped immensely in the section on the beatitudes.

Most encouraging has been the dialogue I have been privileged to have with an adult class at First United Methodist Church, Humboldt, Tennessee. George Irvin Cooper, an unusual Christian layman, has turned me loose with the class on several occasions, and I was delighted to find that, whether they agreed or disagreed, they understood.

I owe a debt of gratitude to Michael Lawrence, of Abingdon Press, for prodding me at the right time and for shepherding the manuscript to final form.

The typing chores have been handled by several persons, and I hereby thank them publicly: my daughter Pamela Graf; Carol Watson, faculty secretary at Lambuth; and Charmaine Smith Wilkerson, my exceptional freshman student secretary.

Finally, I am indebted to Lambuth College for granting me a one-semester sabbatical so the book could move from the stage of scattered fragments to a unified whole.

AUTHOR'S PREFACE

The first hearers of Matthew's Gospel knew the end of the story before it was read to them. They did not have to wait for the final chapter to know that the infant visited by the magi and the teacher who spoke in parables was doomed to be executed, destined to be raised from the dead, and chosen to be elevated to the rank of cosmic Lord.

Matthew was not telling a new story for the first time, but was retelling an old story in a new way. He wrote so that his audience might hear the old story in a new way.

Those first hearers, therefore, did not hear the Sermon on the Mount as the instruction of a rabbi among rabbis, nor even primarily as the instruction of the Master Teacher, but rather, as the instruction of God's Anointed One—the one who had come as the true ruler of God's people, but who had been harassed, persecuted, tortured, and executed, the one God had raised, triumphant over Death.

When the first hearers of Matthew's Gospel heard Jesus' call to suffer rather than to inflict suffering, to accept death rather than to inflict death, to reject all efforts to save themselves from their plight by military action and to leave their deliverance to God, they knew that the one who gave such scandalous instruction had himself lived and died in accord with that call. The Jesus of the Sermon on the Mount is not one who extols an esoteric or naive or idealistic ethic—a way of life never tested or tried—but is one whose instruction sets forth the way of life which he himself embodied, the way of life that manifests God's own Light.

Matthew wrote so that his hearers might hear new emphases, new implications, new meanings and significance for them in their specific situations. The instruction in the Sermon on the Mount expresses and embodies the wisdom of God, a wisdom radically different from human wisdom. It is the wisdom of the cross, the wisdom of Light, the wisdom of the New Age, which undercuts the wisdom of common society.

It is important for the reader to understand at this point that the term *the New Age* as it is used in this book is in no way related to the New Age movements now so widespread. I will be using the terms *the Old Age* and *the New Age* in the sense that students of Jewish apocalyptic thought and of the New Testament have used them for several decades. The precise nature of that usage will become clear, I hope, in the course of the book. Nor do I plan to compare the two uses of the term *the New Age*. Those familiar with the current New Age ideas will recognize that at almost every point there is a significant difference between the two uses of the term, but the reader will also discover that my use of the term poses serious challenges to most of those who are in the forefront of attacks on the current New Age movement.

The wisdom of the cross appears foolish to the world—indeed, *is* foolish by the standards of the fallen world of the Old Age—but as the divine Wisdom, it is that which survives the chaotic destruction of the world.

That the Sermon on the Mount is to be understood as wisdom has long been recognized by certain scholars, and that view has been reemphasized by several writers during the last few years. Even before the recent renewal of interest in Matthew and wisdom, my own private research for purposes of preaching and teaching made it obvious to me that, at almost every turn in the Sermon, Matthew has recast his sources in traditional wisdom formulas and by the use of a variety of wisdom literary devices. The result is the portrayal of Jesus as the Anointed One, whose life embodies the same wisdom of God expressed verbally in his instruction. Moreover, his death and resurrection are the embodiment of that toward which his instruction pointed: God's power and the conquest of the Darkness. In Jesus' words, deeds, and death and resurrection, the Light of God, which penetrates the Darkness, has broken into the world.

Thus, Matthew portrays Jesus—perhaps even unintentionally—in terms entirely consistent with those of the apostle Paul (for whom Jesus is God's wisdom, according to 1 Corinthians) and the Gospel of John (which portrays Jesus as God's *logos,* or wisdom, incarnate). Paul and John both reflect the Hellenistic Jewish view that a great gulf separates God from the world of time and space and that God bridges this gap by means of his Wisdom—that expression of God which was active in the creation of the world, which provides a relative order for the creation, and which was manifested verbally in torah.

That is why Jesus' instruction carries, for Matthew, authority quite different from the authority of all other instructors in torah and from all others who claim divine sanction for their words. All other genuinely commissioned instructors and prophets bear witness to that which has been mediated to them from the Other. Jesus *is* the mediator. He begins neither with "My teacher got it from his teacher, who got it from his teacher, who got it from his teacher that . . . ," nor with "Thus says the Lord . . . ," but with "*I* say to you . . . ."

As God's wisdom in verbal manifestation, the Sermon on the Mount is instruction in those motives, attitudes, perceptions, and habits which are characteristics of God himself and which are the dynamics by which the universe itself, in the New Age under the sovereign rule of God, operates. Disciples are instructed, not under the assumption that by living in accord with those instructions they will know success and happiness in the ways of the Darkness, but precisely with the expectation that it will lead to failure in the eyes of the world of Darkness, to conflict with the world of Death, and—consequently—quite possibly to crucifixion. On the other hand, the cross of ignominy in the world's eyes is the cross of glory under the Reign of God.

PART ONE

THE BACKGROUND

Now when Jesus heard that John had been arrested, he withdrew into Galilee. Then, leaving Nazareth, he went and dwelt in Capernaum by the sea, in the territory of Zebulun and Naphtali—that what was spoken by the prophet Isaiah might be fulfilled:

The lands of Zebulun and Naphtali toward the sea,
    Across the Jordan, Galilee of the Gentiles,
The people who sat in Darkness have seen a great Light.
    For those who sat in the region and shadow of Death
        Light has dawned.

From that time, Jesus began to preach, saying, "Turn around! The Reign of God is at hand!"

Walking by the Sea of Galilee, he saw two brothers, Simon (renamed Peter) and Andrew (Simon's brother). They were casting a net into the sea, for they fished for a living.

And he said to them: "Follow me, and I will have you fishing for people."

At once, they left their nets and followed him.

Going on from there he saw two other brothers, James (the son of Zebedee) and John (James' brother), in the boat with their father Zebedee, mending their nets; and he called them. At once, they left the boat and their father and followed him.

And he went throughout Galilee, teaching in their synagogues, preaching the Good News of God's Reign, and healing every disease and every infirmity among the people. So his fame spread throughout Syria, and they brought to him all the sick—those afflicted with various diseases and pains, demoniacs, epileptics, and paralytics—and he healed them. And great crowds followed him from Galilee and the Decapolis and Jerusalem and Judea and from Trans-Jordan.

(Matthew 4:12-25)

CHAPTER 1

THE SETTING OF THE SERMON:
THE LIGHT OF GOD INVADES THE DARKNESS

Matthew's version of the Sermon on the Mount is instruction for disciples of Jesus in the New Age. It is not a new law code or a new set of rules and regulations, but is a description of the faithful assembly in the New Age, an assembly whose responsibility is to bear testimony to the Light of God in the midst of the Darkness of the Old Age.

The Sermon does not exist in a vacuum, but comes in the wake of Jesus' withdrawal into Galilee, his proclamation of the approach of the Reign of God, his call of disciples, and his works of healing and exorcising.

The withdrawal into Galilee is especially important, for Matthew has interpreted the withdrawal as a fulfillment of Isaiah's prophecy of the Light shining in the land of Darkness and Death. Jesus comes as the bearer of that Light, and the Sermon on the Mount is instruction for those who, hearing and embracing Jesus' call to discipleship, become themselves instruments of the Light.

The ministry begins in the wake of the imprisonment of John the Baptist. It begins with the withdrawal into Galilee, a land identified with the Gentiles, the land of the lost tribes, the land of Darkness and Death. The withdrawal is not a withdrawal of fear, but is Jesus' determination to act in accord with the age-old plan of God, a plan dimly perceived by Israel's prophets through the haze of the centuries.

The prophets had spoken of this scheme of God that their hearers might be established and built up in hope. Now, all human hope is gone. Israel is exiled in her own land. The last of the prophets—John, the one who has stood looking into the new promised land, unable to enter—has joined his people in imprisonment and soon will die at the hands of the self-styled pious ones. And now, in the determination of God, it is the right time! The Light can shine into the Darkness. New Life can displace the power of Death.

On one level, Jesus' opening words and John's opening words are identical. On a deeper level, they are radically different. For John the

Reign of God is at hand, outstretched, bending forward, strained to the breaking point. For Jesus that Reign is at hand, bursting forth in power and fury, lighting up the Darkness, overwhelming the powers that oppose God and corrupt history, bringing Death to heel.

FIRST TO ISRAEL

The Light comes first to Israel. In her history of inner struggle, defeat by Assyria, exile to Babylon, subjection to Persia, struggle with Greece, and restive acquiescence to Rome, however, Israel stands as a paradigm of all human history. Jerusalem, the capital, in its history, reflects the history of the entire world before God—a history of divine initiative, human pride, and divine judgment and promise. Israel's exile is a mirror image of the world's exile.

Moreover, neither for Jerusalem nor for the world had Persia's defeat of Babylon, in 539 B.C., spelled the end of exile. The exile, in 587 B.C., had not been a mere geographic dislocation; consequently, geographic relocation could not end the exile. Ezekiel had portrayed the exile as bones strewn across a valley—bones dried by the sun, abandoned without burial, having neither human hope nor human understanding. Isaiah of the exile had spoken of a suffering servant of God, a servant whose grave, made among the rich, was vulnerable only to the intervention of God. According to Isaiah, however, the only purpose for which Israel existed was to be God's light to the Gentiles. Just as her exile represented the entire world's exile from God, her release from exile would be instrumental in the entire world's release from exile. Through Israel, tne whole world would be delivered from the Darkness, which had engulfed it since the dawn of human history.

So, among the Gentiles, Israel—sometimes consciously, sometimes blindly—had awaited her own Light, that she might become the instrument of the universal dispersion of that Light, the means of God's Light to those very ones who had cast her into Darkness, the means of Life even to those who had consigned her to Death.

Now her Light has come. The one who is the unique bearer and the embodiment of the Light appears, stirs the ashes, and, finding no spark, kindles new fire from the unconsumed splinters. He calls disciples, disciples who, along with those who join their company and as long as this Age continues, become the nucleus of Israel's renewal.

THE NATURE OF THE DARKNESS

The Darkness of the Old Age is not a darkness of tint or color, but of blindness and hiddenness. It is one of the primary characteristics of the primeval Chaos—that formless, purposeless turbulence which God brought into being from nothing and from which God created life. As a primary characteristic of the Chaos, the Darkness shares in the power of the Chaos and at times seems to exercise the power of the Chaos. It is that Darkness into which God brought Light, but which God, in response to human rebellion and resistance, has allowed to threaten the very survival of the Light.

Ultimately, the Darkness is transcendent—residing outside the world of time and space—but it manifests itself in our world in a multitude of ways.

The Darkness is ignorance of the hidden working of God.

It is that veil which religion spreads over the face of God—the veil of ideology, dogma, morality, and practicality.

The Darkness is the consequence of God's own withdrawal, handing the world over to that corruption for which the world still foolishly longs, centuries after the revelation of the Light.

It is the silence of God, manifested in the Babel of religion, in the pride of science, and in the self-aggrandizement of the arts.

It is the source of that inevitable corruption of all human movements, noble or ignoble, humane or inhumane, enlightened or unenlightened, qualifying even the most laudable.

It is the origin of that pride which undercuts the liberating drive of the Renaissance, transforming the divine gift of freedom into the oppressive chains of secularity.

It is the character of the Chaos that churns the Reformation's prophetic reordering of the gospel into a disoriented secularism as debilitating as the technological spirituality of the Middle Ages.

It is the course of that thirst for power which turns liberators into the new colonialists, hurling a so-called Dark Continent into a different kind of darkness in the name of enlightenment; destroying inhabitants of conquered territories by genocide, economic tyranny, or cultural engulfment; displacing earlier idolatries with their own—justifying all accomplishments in the name of civilization, parading them in the guise of progress, or dressing them in the garments of eternal salvation.

The Darkness is the root of that drive for immortality which lies at the heart of space exploration and medical experimentation.

It is that spirit which masquerades as Light in the torch of Lady Liberty and in the evangelistic and missionary outreaches of churches engulfed in the values and perceptions of the Old Age.

It is the same Darkness that enshrouded Golgotha, and is the primary attribute of Death itself.

It is, then, the same Darkness that characterizes human civilization in every age and which will be overcome and banished only in the triumph of the New Age—the resurrection and transformation of the entire creation.

For a moment, the Darkness is hidden by its own nature, masquerading as Light to those under its power. Thus, those imprisoned by the Darkness actually perceive the Darkness as Light, a perception that can be overcome only by the Light itself. The Messiah was and is rejected because the world loves the Darkness rather than Light, because the world's deeds are evil, that is, are opposed to what God has approved.

THE DARKNESS AND HUMAN ACTIVITY

Matthew's portrayal of Israel as languishing in Darkness among the Gentiles indicates that the entire world is caught up in Darkness, and not merely a Darkness of poetic expression devoid of substance. Moreover, this Darkness characterizes the entire creation. Earthquakes and cyclones, psychoses and anxiety, senility and infirmity, deformity and disabilities, warfare and poverty, nationalism and racism, intolerance and bigotry, slavery and exploitation—all are expressions of the corruption by which the original goodness of the creation is threatened and thwarted. All are expressions of Death. Because this is the condition of the creation, all merely human accomplishments—as events in the creation—participate in the corruption. All, as human accomplishments, are works wrought in Darkness—flawed by self-will, characterized by opposition to God. When God adopts, affirms, and uses these for purposes other than our own, they become God's own work; but apart from that use, they are no different from any other human works by which the Darkness of the fallen world is manifested and perpetuated.

To be in exile is not to be inescapably determined to do evil rather than good. It is, rather, to be inescapably condemned to making decisions that are deeply corrupted by self-will and whose goodness, when it is present, is, from the human standpoint, accidental.

In the biblical narrative of the fall of the creation, the serpent told Eve that if she ate from the tree of the knowledge of good and evil, she would become like God—a knower of good and evil. Since Eve did not know that God's declaration of good and evil is a declaration rooted in his own knowledge of how to further his own purposes and intentions, the serpent was able to trick Eve into thinking that good and evil are values exterior to God, thereby reducing God to the role of messenger of eternal rules, a being bound by external realities. The serpent promised Eve access to the *true* Ultimate Reality: Cosmic Principle, Eternal Law! The fruit of the tree, according to the serpent, would put Eve on such intimate terms with what furthers and what inhibits the creation that she would be able to declare it herself, instinctively. She would become truly wise!

Eve did not understand that she already had that knowledge in the only manner, to the only extent, and on the only level that God intends human beings to have it—through direct and specific command (not revelation as this is properly defined). She knew only that she and Adam had received certain permissions, commands, and prohibitions directly from God. But why have to depend on God for knowledge of what is and is not productive, enhancing, and ultimately pleasing? Why not, by ingesting food that will make such knowledge not even "second nature," but primary nature, have that knowledge as spontaneous insight?

God's commands, however, truly are knowledge of good and evil only when they are heard in that freedom which God creates and sustains in us as confidence and trust, or as faith. To turn these into impersonal, eternal principles is to place them *between* ourselves and God.

Once Adam and Eve had eaten of the fruit, God, startlingly, declared to the heavenly council, "Now they have become like us, knowers of good and evil." Adam and Eve had become *more* than human, and God would not allow that. God expelled them from the garden, leaving them *less* than human. It is now the turn of the readers of the narrative to say, "Now they have become like all of us," which is but to say, "We are they!"

In the Genesis narrative, the expulsion of Adam and Eve from the garden is a specific rejection of divine wisdom as a human possession. To the extent that humans are to know good and evil, it can be only from the divine address. Outside the garden, we are *condemned* to do what Eve *wanted* to do—to declare good and evil—although we have no way of knowing whether our good and evil bear any resemblance whatsoever to what God declares good and evil. In the course of human history, God frequently reveals our light to have been Darkness.

THE DARKNESS MASQUERADES AS LIGHT

The Darkness frequently masquerades as Light. In the desert, Satan approached Jesus in a manner at least open to being perceived as friendly. The opening of the first two tests, "If you *are* God's son . . .," could easily have been heard as an effort to help Jesus keep his feet on the ground. "Should you trust your ears? And if your ears heard accurately, should you trust God?" The third test, the invitation to worship Satan, in effect suggested that Jesus affirm that Death, in all its manifestations, has the last word in this world. It was the call to affirm what the world calls realism, a realism that begins with a superficially accurate analysis of the present order of things, but then advocates a response born of the Darkness.

The realism born of the Darkness possesses a Siren's call: "Let us be realistic. Let us not romanticize about the world. Let us admit that Death in one form or another constantly seeks to destroy us. All the more reason to fight for human freedom from the Chaos. It is our responsibility as Christians! God has delivered into our hands the knowledge and ability to liberate the captives. Let us use our knowledge and ability to develop humane techniques by which to control our destiny as partners of God. We must protect humanity from itself!"

Responding to that lure, today's Western society, using behavioral psychology and various other techniques, attempts to manage itself, to control its own evolution. And always with the most reasonable, humane, even loving of arguments. In order to make our tinkering seem more sophisticated, we devise labels—"genetic counseling," "wellness," "parenting," "spiritual formation," and the like. One fully expects before long to be offered instructions on "friending," "husbanding," and "wiving."

In this obsession with efficiency, nothing must be left to spontaneity. Nothing! Never must we admit that a person learns to do things or learns to be human by trial and error. Even if one eventually learns from trial and error, it is so sloppy, so wasteful. To acknowledge that the outcome of spontaneity, unexpected as it is, might be at least as beneficial as the product of our efficiency would be to give up control of the future. It would be to place our destiny in the hands of stimuli and responses outside ourselves and, thereby, to surrender our responsibility. Indeed, if we have learned our lesson well, we know that spontaneity and freedom are mere illusions, mere wishful dreams. Such are the musings of those who, though engulfed in the Darkness, assume themselves to be moving into the Light.

This drive for ever-increasing efficiency has characterized Western society since the breakup of the Middle Ages. It was from pride, not from mere whimsy, that the intelligentsia of the fifteenth century called their age the Renaissance and the preceding centuries the Dark Ages and that a later generation called itself the Age of Enlightenment. Nor is it accidental that each succeeding age has defined philosophical and scientific change as progress, has equated intellectual learning with human goodness, and has equated intellectual achievement with moral excellence. The assumption that what can be done *must* be done has been not merely a technical imperative, but a moral and ethical one as well. If we can enable people to live longer and longer, it is assumed to be uncaring and immoral not to do so, even if this opposes the desires of those affected. If we can control the sex or condition of a person by manipulating the genetic material, it would be backward not to permit, if not encourage, parents to do so.

Such moral imperatives are not automatic, but are the next to last step in a distinct trail of reasoning: Once it is decided that something can *probably* be done, a rationale for attempting it is devised. After it has been accomplished, reasons are contrived to show that it *must* be repeated, regularly. The final step is to press the ethicists into service. Their role is to justify our desire by developing a rationale and an ideology that will show our actions to be the only moral or most loving course "under the present circumstances." Thus it has been with abortion, space exploration, nuclear energy, military weapons, computers, medical developments, "advances" in education, church management, and so on, and so on, and so on.

> [And] the LORD God said, "Behold, the man has become like one of us, knowing good and evil; and now, lest he put forth his hand and take also of the tree of life, and eat, and live forever . . . "
>
> (Gen. 3:22 RSV)

> And the LORD said, "Behold, they are one people, and they have all one language; and this is only the beginning of what they will do; and nothing that they propose to do will now be impossible for them."
>
> (Gen. 11:6 RSV)

Thus seeking to justify our disobedience, to validate our inescapable participation in the Darkness and our surrender to the power of Death, we deny our need for repentance. The call of Jesus is relegated (subjectively) to personal, inner piety or (objectively) to ancient history. In either case, it amounts to little more than imitation.

At the same time, the church, and individual Christians, busily engage in embracing and legitimating, in the name of the Light, structures and practices that are born of the Darkness. Because of the difficulty of escaping them, we hail and embrace them as expressions of freedom—either as conservative saviors of a romanticized past or as progressive liberators from a demonized oppression. The necessary act is declared good by virtue of its inescapability. Various wars are declared compassionate because they are supposedly the lesser of evils, and church programs are sanctified with pompous language because they are socially acceptable to a Godless world. The seeming inaccessibility of the perfect becomes the occasion for praising that which was inevitable.

THE CHURCH'S ATTEMPTS TO MANIPULATE THE DARKNESS

The church's tendency to bless the Darkness and to attempt to use it because of the popularity and supposed harmlessness of the Darkness is nowhere more evident than in the church's fascination with cultural fads and continuing activities such as motion pictures and television, pop music, and sports or athletics. Of course, when the last two terms are used with precision, there is a difference between sports and athletics. The word *athletics* comes from a Latin term that refers to competition in physical activities; *sports* comes from a Middle English word meaning "diversion." The verb form of the latter means "to divert." Frequently, athletics is used when we wish to designate the specific topic under discussion; the same topic, under other conditions, may be labeled simply "sport" or "sports."

I shall not bother here with the more obvious enslavement of the church to sports—the shifting of the schedule of worship and study for Monday night football, the Superbowl, and the like. Far more subtle problems arise in the area of evangelism. There is, for example, the use of sports stars as drawing cards (in the same manner that movie stars, beauty queens, and military heroes are used). Whereas the New Testament consistently commends the gospel through the cross and resurrection, and the apostle Paul's examples of God's power are the poor and lower classes—the nobodies God uses for purposes hidden to the world—much of the success of the institutional church, such as in sports, becomes a sales gimmick. Paul referred to reliance on the world's techniques as peddling the gospel, and he refused to have any part in it (2 Cor. 2:17).

Another surrender to sports is the growth of church sports leagues. If worship, study of the Word of God, and engagement in the history of the people of God cannot attract people or enhance faithful discipleship, basketball will. Bowling pins and a bowling ball will preserve the church against the gates of Death.

Finally, I refer to the building of gymnasiums and so-called activity centers for the avowed purpose of ministering to the neighborhood. I agree fully with those who say that the church must bear testimony to God's love for his creatures in every dimension of their lives, and it is not out of the question that here and there a recreation building might draw into a vibrant, faithful community persons who otherwise might be lost forever. I put this possibility in the same category with the possibility that some people may have been brought to the gospel by movies such as *The Ten Commandments* or *The Greatest Story Ever Told,* through comic book versions of Bible stories, or through the crassest preaching of a mob evangelist. This merely testifies to God's ability to use the superficial and even the crass to claim God's own and in no way vindicates the church's use of these. In fact, what quite often happens with regard to gymnasiums and activity centers is that the people of the neighborhood do not respond, feeling no more at home on Third Church's basketball court than they would feel in a Third Church pew. Consequently, the building is used by the members of the congregation who have driven back into town, by students enticed from local colleges and universities, and by other semi-constituents.

But there is an even deeper problem. Because the institutional church has become so captive to society, even if a congregation succeeds in attracting the "unchurched" from the neighborhood, the chances are overwhelming that it does not really draw the people to the gospel, but to a highly corrupted version of the assembly, institutionalizing them and insulating them from the gospel. It instructs them in a truncated gospel, teaches them about a domesticated Jesus, and guides them to worship idols in the name of God.

The problem is not that there is anything any more wrong with sports than with any other activity of the world of Darkness. The problem, rather, is the assumption that diversions can be humanly manipulated in such a manner as to make up for some imagined inadequacy of the Word of God. In the name of the gospel, the church capitalizes on the fallen condition of the human race by pandering to those very elements of human nature from which the gospel promises liberation—competition, desire for mastery over others, and violence. Whereas Jesus refused to turn stone into bread, we grasp the opportunity in the name of Jesus. No effort to exalt sportsmanship to the status of a Christian virtue can change the nature of the enterprise.

With regard to motion pictures and television as media for the Word, again we fail to recognize the central nature of those instruments. They have their own dynamics, their own rules—dynamics and rules that become barriers to the Word they are said to communicate. Television, for example, not only isolates the viewer, thereby destroying the essential community orientation of the gospel, but also depends on image rather than on substance. It is no accident that television preachers are always well-groomed, as though posing for a fashion ad. Mass evangelism has always relied on mob psychology for its impact, and television evangelism further relies on the packaging of the product. Content is smothered by personality and frills.

Motion picture film can never present the Bible, for no medium can reproduce another. Motion pictures present a visual image, yet the words of the Bible, those visual on the page, are more nearly a verbal medium. All efforts to film portions of the Bible are, by nature and of necessity, interpretations of the Bible. Thus, films about the Bible, though supposedly produced in an effort to make the Bible more accessible (which really means more *attractive*), such as cartoons that insert twentieth-century children into the story or sentimentalize their scripts and musical accompaniment, not only fail to be the means of the Word, but also, when they claim to be films of the Bible, insulate us from the Word.

Popular music has long been used to attract youth to the church, as musical settings for religious lyrics, as a means of recreation (or play), or simply as bait. Again, naively assuming that popular music (folk, rock, or whatever) is neutral, the church has believed it possible to use it in the service of the gospel.

Although until recently the more liberal mainline churches were more caught up in this method, the conservative and pentecostal churches and the parachurch movements have now taken over the method in an even more radical way. So-called contemporary Christian music, for instance, relies on soothing melodies, soaring strings, and grandstanding vocal calisthenics for its impact and, in its overall effect, substitutes *eros* (the Greek word that means aesthetic attraction, or love of beauty) for *agape* (the Greek word that means unqualified love, complete giving of oneself for the well-being of others). In other words, it mistakes feelings for faith, and equates rhythmic response with devotion.

Of course, some of our most traditional "religious" music was composed using popular forms of the day. Without the words, for example, the styles of Handel's *Messiah* and his *Water Music* are indistinguishable. The issue, however, is not the style of the music, but the extent to which the music, whatever its style, displaces the Word. My criticism is not a nostalgic gripe about the present in comparison with some supposedly purer period. One can easily show that musicians in certain eras of Western history have written religious music because that was where the money was, and we are as easily insulated from the Word by a performance of the *Messiah* as by any modern piece of fluff. One might make the argument that Gregorian chant and plainsong are more appropriate forms of music for genuine worship because they tend to call attention to themselves less often than do other forms, but even here it is a matter of degree, not of absolutes.

The use of prerecorded orchestras for solo or choir presentations surrenders to a superficial eroticism, the integrity of the Word thus being undercut by the desire for emotional pleasure. One need not necessarily argue that the Calvinists of the sixteenth century or certain denominations today are correct in rejecting musical instruments (and the Calvinists in rejecting singing) to acknowledge that, by and large, the history of the actual practice of music in the church has been as idolatrous with regard to instrumentation as any statues of bulls ever could have been.

Again, the question is not whether sports, movies, television, or pop music are evil, but whether the church, in its attempt to use cultural elements to attract and keep members, has abandoned the Word, failed to trust God to use our faithfulness *to* the Word, and become in every respect simply a cultural institution like every other cultural institution. In brief, the question is, Have we not become an atheistic church?

WAR AS A MANIFESTATION OF THE DARKNESS

Recent wars in which the United States has been involved are typical examples of the pull of the Darkness. No single individual, or the collective will of a nation, or the will of all the nations involved in those wars can alone bring an end to the hostilities. There are forces at work that lead us—through the more detectable realities of pride, political ambition, economic greed, racism, and fear—from terror to terror. Nor will we be clear of such wars until it pleases God to end them. When one considers that the land on which this nation is built was stolen from the ones the European settlers found living here, that in several instances there were efforts to wipe out entire populations of these inhabitants, that the economy of the nation was built through enslavement of millions of prisoners brought from Africa solely and specifically for the purpose of slave labor, that those slaves saw their families wrenched apart on the auction block or in deals between farmers and plantation owners, that the nation was itself wrenched from the possession of the British Crown by violence and bloodshed, and that this nation is the only nation in the era of nuclear weapons to use those weapons to destroy human cities and human lives (without regard for military or civilian identity), then it is not at all archaic or quaint to suggest that God has turned the nation over to the transcendent powers that drive individuals and nations to fiery destruction.

War, however, is only one of the more blatant expressions of the transcendent powers. Racism, poverty, fear, boredom, cancer, AIDS, and the common cold are also manifestations of the persistent, plundering activity of those transcendent forces as they focus both in human schemes, motives, attitudes, and infirmities and in the erratic movements of "nature." Natural and social scientists can describe and, with relative accuracy, predict certain dimensions of these manifestations, but they can never reduce them to the sum of their individual parts, for there is a dimension to these phenomena and events that eludes empirical examination. It is the dimension known only as a result of God's revelation of the existence and nature of the powers.

THE DARKNESS AND THE HOLOCAUST

The most vivid—one may even say the typical—modern expression of the Darkness is the Holocaust. Although the Holocaust does not stand completely alone as being absolutely unlike any other event in history (since it manifests the Darkness, which is expressed in all history), it is joined only by the crucifixion of Jesus as a typical manifestation of the Darkness, "typical" meaning a sign by which all other manifestations are to be understood. From a Christian standpoint, the crucifixion of Jesus is the one event in which the Holocaust itself receives its full meaning. The Holocaust, that is, was not simply one nation or group attempting to destroy an ordinary people. It was the manifestation of the powers of the Darkness attempting to destroy the people of God. It was an effort in which the entire world was implicated. Hitler simply expressed an antagonism that has smoldered throughout the centuries in the corporate breast of the world. Hitler's work was anticipated in and was the logical extension of all those expressions of anti-Jewishness which, across the generations, have echoed throughout the East and the West. Whether they are the subtle degradation of the

Jew-oriented joke, the discrimination of the social structure, the knee-jerk charge of Jewish conspiracy, the patronizing compliment about Jewish superiority in certain endeavors, or the outright attacks by the Medieval church or the modern Ku Klux Klan—all are subsumed and fulfilled in the Holocaust.

Although we must take care not to construct some nonexistent counterworld in that nebulous, elusive realm called the unconscious (or the subconscious), it is nonetheless true that our individual and corporate desires and motives frequently are other than what we believe them to be. We are always guided and influenced by motives and desires, fears and ambitions, which churn below the threshold of our awareness; and it is precisely in this realm of the unconscious that faith and distrust, love and hostility are most effectively rooted. Here lurk the secret sins of our inward parts, known only to God, who knows us better than we know ourselves.

The various attacks in which Jews have been singled out across the centuries are manifestations of that hostility to God which, as a part of our fallen nature, lurks in the unconscious, even in the unconscious of many who profess the utmost devotion to God. This hostility strikes out at God's representatives as a way of attacking God himself.

From a purely documentary standpoint it is evident that for Hitler the Jews were to be but the first to be exterminated. In fact, approximately five million non-Jews, of various categories, were killed in the Holocaust in addition to the six million Jews usually noted. Eventually, Christians were also to be exterminated. As the Gentile wing of the people of God, they were logical targets, for if one wishes to destroy Israel, one must destroy both the synagogue and the church.

The Darkness attacks Israel not simply because Israel represents God, however, but because Israel represents the human race, which, in the beginning, was itself God's representative on the earth. The Holocaust is understood in its full dimensions only when it is perceived not so much as the scheme of a raving maniac propelled by insanity, but as the Powers of Darkness and Death using the systematic efforts of intellectual, university-trained technicians and managers to destroy the people of the Living God and, thereby, to destroy the human race and defeat God himself. Their actions were those of cultured, civilized, and, by the standards of the Darkness, perfectly sane people. It was this high evaluation of them in the world's terms, however, that revealed once and for all the insanity of the world's sanity.

For those who deeply believe in the power and love of God, the Holocaust also posed anew the ancient question of the validity of their faith. How could a God both all-powerful and all-loving permit such suffering? If God were *able* to stop the Holocaust and did not, is he truly all-loving? If God *is* all-loving and would have stopped the Holocaust, does his having not done so mean that he is not truly all-powerful? And if we say that to have intervened would have robbed human beings of their freedom, we say that the freedom of the murderers was purchased at the price of the slaughter of millions.

In the Holocaust, not the heavens, the Pit was opened, and the Darkness of the Chaos rushed forth to engulf the world and undo the creation. This was the supreme effort of the Powers of the Darkness to prevent God from reversing the conditions of the Fall. It was Satan's supreme post-resurrection effort to maintain his sovereign rule over the creation. To thwart God's plan to restore the creation to his own dominion, the Powers of the Darkness must keep God's original representatives under subjection. In order to do this the Powers must destroy the ones God called into existence as a priestly assembly for the restoration of the integrity of the human race; and, in turn, this requires the defeat of the one in whom the priestly community's own renewal, integrity, and unity are secured—Jesus Christ himself. Since the Messiah is bound up in unity with his people, to attack the Messiah one may attack his people. The Holocaust, then, was the reenactment of the cross through the crucifixion of those most closely related to him who hung upon the cross. By crucifying first the Jews and then the Christians, the Darkness would undo the cross and resurrection, thereby undoing the creation itself and condemning the world to eternal Chaos, Darkness, and Death.

None of this is to suggest that ascribing the horrors of this world to transcendent malignant powers makes them easier to understand or to accept. That the powers have been essentially conquered in Christ does not clarify as much as it confuses. If they have been conquered, then how are they able to wreak the havoc in which children die and entire populations are consigned to oblivion? If they have been conquered, why are they allowed to spread such horror? The New Testament calls us to resist the powers, not to give in to them. Jesus instructs us to pray that we be delivered from them. Thus, the things that we affirm are the soil from which grow our greatest dilemmas of reason.

For Christians and Jews alike, the enduring question of the Holocaust is posed in the first line of Psalm 22: "My God! My God! Why have you abandoned me?" That this is the opening cry of a psalm of praise does not soften the cry, but merely deepens the mystery.

THE METAPHOR AND REALITY

One might ask at this point whether the persistent use of terms up to now reflects a narrow, literalist approach to the Bible. After all, do we not live in a world in which science has made concepts such as the powers and principalities, Satan, and the like old-fashioned? And if the author is not a literalist in his approach, why use such elusive language? Does not such metaphorical discourse obscure the author's intent? What sense can we make, for example, out of a description of the Holocaust as Satan's work if Satan is to be understood as a metaphor rather than as a literal personality?

Since the language of Darkness and Light and of the powers and principalities will be used throughout, it will be useful to digress for a moment and to clarify that use.

The language of Darkness is metaphor only in the sense that all human language is metaphor. Because God is transcendent, even our language about God is metaphor. Unfortunately, however, most of Western society today has lost any sense of God as transcendent. This is not to say that our problem is, as was said a few years ago, a loss of the sense of Transcendence as such. There *is* no such thing as Transcendence, for Transcendence is an attribute of certain "realities," not a reality unto itself. The problem of Western society is not a loss of a "sense of transcendence" or a loss of a "sense of mystery," as though these were larger categories under which to subsume the figure of God. Our problem is atheism. Just as Polycarp, standing in the arena about to be executed, regarded the Roman audience as atheists, despite their belief in the Roman gods, so we should regard as atheists those who, though professing a belief in God, worship a god essentially bound to human categories, all human categories being essentially temporal and spatial. Even a transcendent god is an idol if *transcendent* is asserted in spatial terms (God *out there* or *in my heart,* for example).

The loss of a sense of God's transcendent character has resulted in a distortion of our perception of biblical language and of symbol and metaphor. Since we distinguish between symbols and those things symbols represent, we assume that the biblical writers also made this distinction. We assume, for example, that the New Testament writers believed in Death or in Satan as cosmic figures. Because we assume that the writers believed in a literal Death and a literal Satan, we assume that Death and Satan therefore were not symbolic for them. The New Testament writers, however, perceived symbols as *means* by which Truth is conveyed. They never thought of symbols as "merely" literal. God, who is transcendent, that is, who cannot be enclosed in human thought, is present through those people and events through whom and through which he chooses concretely to manifest himself. Thus, Amos, in the Old Testament, could say to Israel with regard to the coming Assyrian destroyers, "Behold your God!"

The New Testament indicates that the demonic can manifest itself even in one's most cherished acquaintances and friends. Jesus' rebuff of Simon

34

Peter (Matt. 16:22-23), for example, uses the language of exorcism. First, Peter rebukes Jesus (*rebuke* being a technical word for "exorcism"). Peter has mistaken Jesus' willingness to go to Jerusalem to suffer and die as indication that Jesus has fallen under the influence of Satan. Jesus correctly perceives Peter's words to be the mark of Satan's influence and, for the moment, exorcises the demonic will from him. We do not, the apostle Paul reminds us, contend with mere flesh and blood, that is, with mere psychological madness, mere emotional disorders, mere chemical imbalances, mere laws of nature, mere genetic disorganization, or mere human ignorance; flesh and blood *are* among the temporal and spatial means by which the transcendent forces confront us. On occasion, the manifestations seem so goal-oriented, so flexible and ingenious that personal terminology (Satan, the powers, and so forth) is quite appropriate. On other occasions, sheer chaos seems to dominate. Chaos, however, is precisely the goal, for Chaos is utter destruction, the cloak worn by Death.

Only a people beguiled by excessive claims of rationalism and seduced into believing that only that which can be seen and examined is real could speak of such references as *mere* metaphors. For Ezekiel, Isaiah, and Matthew, the exile was a concrete manifestation of transcendent Death. Israel in exile was not merely *figuratively* dead. She was as truly dead as are the pharaohs and their courtiers in the desert tombs of the Valley of the Kings.

THE DANGER OF TRIVIALIZED METAPHORS

In no way does this nature of language and reality validate current fads such as exorcism (so-called) or the harangues of those who insist that Satan is responsible for all they find morally despicable, politically vile, or economically disastrous. Excessive biblical literalism is as naive an approach as that which speaks of biblical categories as merely symbolic. The latter trivialize the symbols by denying the cosmic realities symbolized; the former trivialize them by reducing them to mere literality. Both deny the transcendent nature of the realities and thereby undercut the truth about our cosmic situation. One loses the picture through a *rejection* of symbols; the other, through a *reduction* of symbols. Trivializing symbols and metaphors, they trivialize language itself.

Those who deny the reality of the symbols engage in self-defeating attempts to solve all their problems as though there were no cosmic dimension to them; they literally attribute demonic influence to those who disagree with their social, economic, or theological perspective. If the devil is merely literal, he must be located somewhere, and the opponent is the most logical and convenient place to look. If the devil is merely symbolic, we need not be alert to the danger and possibility that he might pitch his tent in our camp.

The devil is, in brief, a transcendent reality, created by God and manifesting himself in our ordinary experience as the magnetism of that which opposes God. (Later, in discussing the Lord's Prayer, I shall speak of the metaphorical use of our language about God.)

LIBERATION, DELIVERANCE, AND MIRACLES

Into this realm of Darkness and Death Jesus came, proclaiming the Reign of God: liberation, freedom to the prisoners, release to those who sit in the Darkness and in the shadow of Death. The Messiah's appearance initiates the liberation of the entire creation. The proximity of God's Reign in the work of Jesus undercuts all of Death's manifold expressions, for in Jesus, God is at work to restore, to transform, and to heal.

In the fallen world of the Old Age, obedience to God is impossible. All things are consigned to Death. The world's independence is, in reality, bondage. In the gospel, which Jesus proclaims and embodies, the creation is set free that it might be bound in perfect service to the Creator.

Jesus' preaching and teaching are accompanied by acts of wonder. He heals, exorcises, and gives strength to those who are victimized by the transcendent hosts of the Darkness. The miracles are visible manifestations of God's conquest of the transcendent forces of the Darkness. They are concrete expressions of his conquest of Death. The proclamation is the context of the miracles. Jesus' prophetic proclamation is the word by which the Reign comes. His teachings interpret the events through which the Reign is manifested and testify to the character of God as revealed therein.

The physical expressions of the Reign of God indicate that the Reign is not simply "inward" or "spiritual," but that it takes over time and conquers space. God's Reign is God's assertion of his power over nations, over empires, and over all physical and natural phenomena, as well as over the unseen dimensions of human nature. It is God's conquest of any and all those forces and powers which corrupt, distort, or seek to destroy his creation. To proclaim God's Reign as the liberation of the creation from the power of Death is not to proclaim independence, but to proclaim freedom to live in unthwarted obedience to God, in whose service is perfect liberation.

REPENTANCE: THE POSSIBILITY AND THE NECESSITY

For Matthew, the opening word in Jesus' proclamation is "Repent!" In other words, "Turn around! Change your ways! Come out of the Darkness! Live no longer by its values and standards!"

The proclamation is, at the same time, both invitation and command. The Reign of God makes repentance both possible and necessary. Those for whom repentance has been impossible—because of God's imposition of hardness of heart—now are free to turn around, to take a different path, to live under a new dominion, to step out of the shadows of Darkness and Death, and to walk in the Light. This freedom is made manifest in the act of repentance. Though theoretically we repent when we have been set free to repent, there is no chronological priority of either forgiveness or repentance. Freedom is manifest in the "works that befit repentance." Continuing to walk in the way of the Darkness manifests bondage and the absence of repentance.

True repentance is expressed in each and every act that the exhortations of the Sermon on the Mount urge on us. It is manifested in divesting control over others, in ceasing oppression, in acts of mercy toward the enemy, in refusing to retaliate or avenge oneself, in dependability in one's dealings with others, and in submitting to God's determination to bring peace and healing to the creation.

A nation that truly repents, for example, will dismantle its arsenal of weapons and turn its defense budget to aid and assistance programs for all nations in need—including those nations that have been the most dangerous of its feared opponents. It will do so without qualification, without reluctance, and without quibbling. It will do so spontaneously, because it is motivated by an abhorrence of the destruction those weapons would bring upon the beloved enemy were they used. Its motivation will be a burning desire that the health and safety of the enemy be made secure. Essentially, it will do so not because any external law requires it, not even the external expression of the will of God, but because it is impelled by the inner compulsion of an innate "law," which the Spirit will have made the central dynamic of its conscience. That inner compulsion will indeed be torah. It will indeed be law. It will be the very command of God. But it will be that rule over the heart which frees the heart from the power of the Darkness, setting the nation free from the power of death. Such freedom is realized in, and only in, unqualified work for the well-being of the neighbor, whether friend or foe.

In true freedom, therefore, the Word of God is both invitation and command, both these dimensions having been merged into their original unity, outside of which neither can be heard except in a distorted way. To the extent that we separate invitation and command in discourse and imagination, we reveal our own participation in the Darkness and the degree to which we still lack full expression of the freedom in which we essentially stand.

CHAPTER 2

THE LIBERATING CALL TO DISCIPLESHIP

The gospel comes into a world in which power and violence hold sway. Jesus' birth, ministry, death, and resurrection all take place in a world of violence and destruction. Freedom and light, therefore, are not simply ideas for contemplation, but are as real as violence and death. The gospel of Jesus Christ is no more concerned with the idea of freedom, the ideology of freedom, or the principle of freedom than with the ideas, ideologies, or principles of love, peace, or justice. The gospel is the proclamation of the presence of freedom, the reality of love, the movement of peace, and the establishment of justice. These are not to be contemplated, debated, or respected, but accepted, appropriated, lived, and manifested. Though not to be politicized, they bristle with political implications.

FREEDOM IN DISCIPLESHIP

The liberation the gospel brings is not to be equated with what society recognizes as political or economic independence—although, as Caesar correctly sensed, it is explosive with political and economic freedom of its own kind. It is a liberation, or freedom, found in *discipleship*. Freedom from the politics and economics of the Old Age, freedom from the politics and economics of the powers and principalities, liberation from the dominion of Satan, liberation from thralldom to Death, freedom from the Darkness: These are the liberation of the gospel. The primary person to whom we may look for a model of this freedom is Jesus himself. In Jesus we see the one truly free person, the one in whom all freedom is to be found. His appearance on God's behalf creates a new situation in the midst of the Old Age, evoking a response to the conditions of the Old Age quite unexpected in nature and form.

For Jesus, victory and rule are manifested in vulnerability, self-effacement, suffering, death, and resurrection. Heading for crucifixion, the

Ruler enters his own city in a manner reflecting solidarity with his people. He comes on a donkey, an event erroneously interpreted by most commentaries as an act of subjective humility, but more accurately perceived as a sign that the true Ruler has been subjected to the same affliction to which his people have been subjected. The Monarch comes to his own city, accompanied by returning exiles and members of the ancient northern tribes, the latter regarded by many as Gentiles. At first, those who now inhabit the city, including the pretender to the throne, are troubled (Matt. 21:10). Soon, they cry out for his death! Scandalously, while the apparent monarch, in hollow and troubled grandeur, holds forth in the palace, the true Monarch reigns from the cross. The scandal, however, manifests the glory, for the freedom of the Monarch is revealed in his giving of self for his people. The power of God is manifested precisely in that event which is perceived by those of the Darkness as weakness.

THE CALL OF THE FIRST DISCIPLES

The initial community of disciples consists of those Jesus directly calls. They, in turn, by their call to others, will be the means by which Jesus himself will enlarge the community of twelve until it includes all people of all nations. In this way, all disciples will continue Jesus' proclamation and teaching, which, by the gracious intervention of God, become the liberating Word of God to those who hear.

For Matthew, it is not important whether the fishers or the tax collector whom Jesus called had known or heard Jesus before that call. The decision to follow Jesus does not depend on some psychological preparation.

Of course, John's Gospel indicates that some of the disciples had known Jesus before the call; and the surprise that anyone would suddenly abandon family and job to follow a passing stranger has led some to use John's narrative to explain the Synoptics. Surely, it is said, Jesus must have spoken with the men, preparing them for the eventual call.

Perhaps what bothers us is the suspicion that we would not have followed Jesus at first call. After all, do we not, in our own preaching of the gospel, assume that the success of our activity depends on discovering the proper preparation, the proper motivational techniques? Surely, Jesus must have prepared *them*. In our own doubt, we seek to console ourselves with speculation born of logic and behavioral psychology.

Some writers glamorize the scene, imagining Jesus to have mesmerized the first disciples by his magnetic personality. They say it must have been his charisma. (Ironically, from a purely verbal standpoint, this is not a bad statement, for the possibility of the disciples' response was created by the work of the Spirit or the *charisma*, which empowered Jesus. This, however, is not what the romanticizers mean.)

Both psychologizing the call of the disciples and romanticizing it miss the thrust of the story. The story is concerned neither with the preparation nor with the absence of preparation of the disciples, nor with Jesus' personality, but with Jesus' demand that the disciples make a radical break with their past, their present, and their future. That break was made possible only by the freedom that swept over them in the call itself. Jesus did not just happen by. As the one in whom the Reign of God had drawn near, liberating the world from Darkness and Death, and by his presence and invitation, Jesus set them free to respond and to share in the proclamation of the Reign of God. They could have said no to the invitation and stayed with their nets. At that point, however, they would have been not merely rejecting a call to be followers of a wandering rabbi, but would have been saying no to freedom itself, falling back into bondage in the life of the Old Age. Turning aside from the Light, they would have fallen back into Darkness.

THE DISCIPLES AS MIRRORS

The disciples, throughout the Gospels, are models of appropriate or inappropriate reaction for all who claim to be followers of Jesus. Here, they are examples of the proper response to the call of Christ. Completely ignoring the values, mores, and traditions of the society in which they have been raised, they leave jobs and families to take up life in the new order Jesus brings on them by his word. Leaving their jobs, they become dependent on others for food, shelter, and clothing. Leaving their parents, they cast off their torah-rooted responsibility for their parents' future security.

They leave the dead to bury the dead; and in so doing they also die to the world and its expectations (even to those expectations traditionally said to be the command of God) and no longer have any identity other than that which comes from the one to whom they now are joined. They are now members of a new family. They now have a new job. Some of them even receive new names, Jesus' renaming being itself a sign of his authority and power over them. Just as all who come afterward die, in baptism, the only death worth considering, the first disciples, in casting off their former lives and joining themselves to Jesus, die to the Old Age and its Darkness and come into the Realm of Light and Life.

Any responsibilities that, for the disciples, coincide with former responsibilities merely *seem* to be the same. Although to the eyes of those still dominated by the Old Age they appear to be the same, as the result and expression of the peculiar dynamics of the New Age, all such actions and responsibilities are, in fact, radically different. One is an act born of the self-interest of the Darkness; the other, an act born of the self-giving of the Light.

THE FREEDOM TO RESPOND

Only the person God has set free can have any inkling of the possibility opened up for those first disciples. The person in bondage will either confess astonishment at the unhesitating, immediate response of the fishers or equate his or her own piety and moral determination with the life of freedom.

In every age, when the announcement of and invitation to God's Reign are truly spoken—not merely repeated as an intellectual acknowledgment, or used as a verbal ploy to add numbers to the church roll, or piously announced as an indication of one's subjective emotional condition—then that freedom which came to the fishers comes to the one who hears, bestowing the freedom to say yes! Of course, the announcement does involve intellectual acknowledgment, does call the hearer into assembly with others, and does have its emotional dimension, but the diversity of understandings of the assembly from one community to another rules out equating these with the reality they manifest.

The task of free disciples is to be witnesses, witnesses in both word and deed, to the liberating Reign of God in Jesus Christ.

CHAPTER 3

MANIFESTATIONS OF GOD'S REIGN

The word about Jesus goes out even into the region of Syria, to the North. Jesus is reaching out to restore the scattered people of God that they might themselves become the Light-bearers they were created to be. For the moment, they are harassed and helpless, like sheep without a shepherd (Matt. 9:36; Zech. 10:2). Jesus has come, however, to fulfill the promise made through Zechariah—the promise of restoration of the whole scattered house of Israel, the promise of return from the ends of the earth (Zech. 10:6-12). The restored people then will themselves become the means of the world's restoration.

Those who come to Jesus are representative of the scattered sheep coming to the voice of the true Shepherd. They come in response to the proclamation that God's sovereign Reign is at hand!

Jesus' ministry is rooted in that Reign, a Reign manifested in Jesus' own word—whether in the word that proclaims the nearness of the Reign, the word that calls for those who hear to turn around and come under the Reign, the word that asserts the Reign over those forces of Darkness which are manifested in the afflictions of the people, or the word by which he instructs with regard to the Reign. Language, that which distinguishes human beings from all other life forms, that gift the distortion of which was God's last act of judgment before the call of Abraham, now becomes the means by which the renewing, restoring, and transforming work of God enters the world. The disciples will themselves be given the authority, the power, and the responsibility to cast out the powers of Darkness, to proclaim the Reign, to baptize, and to teach in the name of Jesus the Anointed One of God.

The Reign of God is manifested in healing. Conversely, the so-called miracles are signs and manifestations of the Reign. None, therefore, are personal, private miracles simply for the benefit of the ones who are their objects, but are works intimately related to the appearance of the New Age on behalf of the entire creation. Just as God spoke and brought to life the original creation, bringing Light into the Darkness and order to Chaos, so now Jesus speaks, restoring the Light and banishing the Chaos which has been allowed temporarily to reassert itself. Jesus' instruction to some to go tell the priest indicates that the miracle is a sign that in the Messiah that complete renewal toward which the cult was a promise now is at hand.

Vast numbers of people are brought to Jesus, people in whom the Darkness is vividly manifested by way of various psychoses, neurological disorders, and other physical and emotional disorders. The Greek text should actually be translated, "They brought to him all those with some evil." That is, the disorders described are contrary to God's ultimate desire and plan for the creation. Evil, by definition, is a description of whatever is contrary to God's ultimate desire or plan. When God is said to plan evil or to bring evil upon someone or something, we are to understand this to mean that God has somehow been driven to act contrary to his basic character and intentions. The conditions that characterize the Old Age and that are vividly manifested in physical and mental disabilities, are evil in that they are characteristics of a world from which God has pulled back, a world God has allowed momentarily to fall under the domination of powers and forces to which ultimately he said *no!*

This manifestation of the transcendent opposition to God in various forms of mental disorder amply justifies the frequent use of insanity as a model for analyzing the world as we know it—oblivious to reality, swept up in a self-contained counterworld of its own invention, obsessed with trivia, driven by paranoia, dialectically absorbed in self-love and self-hate, driven toward self-destruction. The course of human history—seen from the standpoint of human drives and intentions—is characterized by nationalistic bravado, wars of conquest, craze for increasingly more powerful weapons, exaltation of suicide over submission to foreign nations, and blindness to the dynamics of violence. Creating in their minds a counterworld in which death can defeat Death, violence can overcome Violence, and deception is a feasible instrument of Truth, they deny the absurdity of these illusions, and all evidence of the absurdity is either ignored or twisted into an even more absurd proof of the validity of the tactics. Counterworlds that thrive on the trivia of class, race, sex, and physical charm replace worlds rooted in justice, honor, and gentleness. Suspicion and fear of those who in some way are different become the driving force underlying national and international policy. National defense is pursued at the cost of danger from the weapons with which the defense is attempted. And, through it all, we are charmed into the belief that our headlong plunge into Death is a race for Life. One of the most consistent habits of the powers and principalities is to convince us that Death is Life, that violence is justice, that power is benevolence, that war is peace. In such a world, those who are truly sane are automatically perceived by the world as insane, since their grasp on reality will be seen precisely as a fall from reality and the creation of their own counterworld. The insane then imprison the sane, and, if imprisonment fails, consign them to death. Jesus, the only perfectly sane person who has ever lived, was murdered precisely because he bore witness to reality, and this was viewed by the powers and principalities, quite correctly, as a threat to their own authority to deliver the world over to genuine insanity. In a world of cannibals, one either becomes a cannibal or is devoured.

PART TWO

BLESSINGS ON THE VICTIMIZED

Seeing the crowds, he went up on the mountain. When he sat down, his disciples came to him, and he opened his mouth and taught them, saying:

Blessed are the poor in spirit; God's Reign is for them.
Blessed are those who mourn; they shall be comforted.
Blessed are the meek; they shall inherit the earth.
Blessed are those who hunger and thirst for righteousness; they shall be
  satisfied.

(Matthew 5:1-6)

CHAPTER 4

DISCIPLES AS THE AUDIENCE

The crowds typify the world entrapped in the Darkness. Although in Matthew's Gospel occasionally they are Gentiles, usually they are Jews—Israel of the exile, victims of the power of Death, sheep scattered and without a shepherd. As the crowds, however, they are the world. Sometimes Jesus pities them; sometimes, he berates them for their fickleness. He heals them, feeds them, teaches them, moves freely among them, and at times withdraws from them.

The crowds follow Jesus with eagerness, astonishment, fright, and awe. Considering him a prophet, they are so supportive that the officials fear them; eventually, however, the crowds fall away and abandon him.

The disciples are those Jesus specifically calls unto himself, making them his inner circle. They become his students, learning the mysteries of God's Reign, that after Jesus' death and resurrection, they in turn might go out, under his authority, preaching, teaching, and healing as they proclaim the Reign.

The disciples are the beginning of the renewed *assembly,* which is the correct translation of the word usually translated *church.* They are taken from the ancient assembly (Israel) precisely because Jesus' intention is not to bypass or destroy the ancient people of God, but to restore them that they might fulfill their original task of being the means of the world's blessing. Their task, as the renewed Israel, will be to reach out to the Gentiles and, in fulfillment of Isaiah's prophecy that God would make Levites of some of the responding Gentiles (Isa. 66:21), draw them into the community of witness.

The distinction Matthew emphasizes between the disciples and the crowds typifies the difference Jesus consistently makes between disciples and the world. To become a disciple is to break with the world. One cannot serve two masters. The dead must be left with the dead. Salt weakened by the presence of foreign substances is fit only for destruction.

Just as torah was given not to the entire world, but only to Israel, and was not intended as legislation to be imposed on Assyria or Babylon, so the Sermon is not a law to be imposed on the nations, but is instruction for the people of God. God had given torah to Israel as a gift, that Israel might live well in the midst of a chaotic world. When viewed as a burden rather than as a gift, it became an obligation; instruction, wisdom, and guidance (which always required adaptation or interpretation) became Law, Rules and Regulations to be expanded or multiplied.

The Sermon is blessing for those who hear the gospel. It brings examples of what repentance means. It is neither law to be obeyed for salvation nor heroic ethic by which to combat the Darkness. It is, rather, explanation of how the assembly of God's people is to order its life in order to bear witness to the character of God. Should any city or nation choose to order its life by any of the implications of what it hears in the Sermon, the disciples should not discourage this, for such an adoption might be seen as an effort to glorify God, which would fulfill the ultimate purpose of disciples' actions. Disciples must resist vigorously, however, the inclination of any city or nation to assume that by such legislation it becomes the people of God. That a nation's constitution and laws are rooted to one degree or another in certain ethical teachings of the Old or New Testaments, or are at least parallel to those teachings, does not make that nation Jewish or Christian or Judeo-Christian any more than a nation that forbids murder is thereby communist because communist nations also forbid murder. Just as being a disciple of Jesus is not simply to follow a moral code, so also to be a nation that legislates certain New Testmaent ethical precepts is not to be a Christian nation. Any nation that claims to be the people of God commits blasphemy. Any leader who quotes passages such as, "If my people who are called by my name . . . ," and applies these to his or her nation thereby puts that nation over against the people God has chosen—the synagogue and the church—and usurps the prerogative of God to say who are his people.

Nations that have presumed to be the Holy Nation have always done so as part of a world view that sees their enemies as the enemies of God. The enemy is viewed as the embodiment of Darkness; they, the nation making the presumption, as the embodiment of Light. War, preparations for war, and the stockpiling of weapons as a way of avoiding war are then baptized as holy. Christendom itself began not when Constantine declared Christianity the favored religion of the Roman Empire, but when the church, led by church historians such as Eusebius, embraced that declaration and spoke of Constantine as God's new messiah. Any time a nation pretends to be the people of God, that nation is, relatively speaking, less to be condemned than is the church that acquiesces in the claim or endorses it. The nation is simply manifesting the Darkness of which it is assumed to be a part. The church is denying its baptism, its identity, and its Lord.

CHAPTER 5

BLESSINGS

Blessings are of two primary types. *Empowering* blessings are those intended to effect the well-being they express. "Blessed be" or "Blessings upon"—the formulas for empowering blessings—mean, in effect, "May all things go well for." This is the type of blessing Isaac pronounced on Jacob, thinking him to be Esau, and which could not be called back. The empowering blessing, within bounds, takes effect simply by being spoken.

The other primary blessing is the *instructional* blessing, one that tells what one must do in order to *be* blessed. An example of this is in Psalm 1:1-2: "Blessed is the one who neither walks in the path advised by the wicked, nor persists in the road taken by sinners, nor sits in the seat of those who poke fun at the power of God; but who finds delight in the LORD's instructions, who meditates on *His* instructions both day and night."

The blessed person is the one for whom all things, at least the truly important things, manifest the goodness and generosity of God. To be blessed is to be in such a state that despite any hardships, you are not crushed in despair, but endure, maintain your integrity, and are sustained in hope. The curse, the opposite of the blessing, says "May your life amount to nothing," or "May your life be dammed up like a river that has been stopped in its course."

The well-being effected by the blessing or embraced by obedience to the instruction is not to be equated with material prosperity. Certainly, in the Old Testament, wealth and progeny are marks of blessing. Property, a large number of children, serenity, and respect in the community are manifestations of God's favor. That is why Job's predicament was such a puzzle. God himself had declared Job to be the most righteous man on earth, yet Job suffered immensely. It is also why the book of Job ends with Job once again wealthy and the head of a large family. It is also the reason for the problem created when the rich and wicked prosper while the faithful, whom they oppress, are poor and bereft.

In the New Testament a different situation exists. Wealth, as the French Reformed theologian Jacques Ellul has pointed out, becomes a snare for those possessing it. On numerous occasions in the Gospels, Jesus warns of the dangers of wealth, calls for those who would follow him to give their wealth to the poor, and, in Luke's version of the Sermon, even pronounces a woe, a form of curse, upon the wealthy.

This is not to overlook that some of Jesus' friends were wealthy. They are models, however, of how one's wealth is to be put at Jesus' disposal.

Moreover, the New Testament frequently comes quite close to seeing persecution, not wealth and favored standing, as a sign of blessing. Jesus tells his disciples that when they are persecuted, they are to leap for joy, for their reward from God will be great, and he portrays their situation as one that places them in the company of those ancient messengers of God, the prophets!

Blessings originally did not have any specific content, but were all-inclusive. They meant, "May all things go well with you!" Later, blessings became more specific, but by becoming specific they became more narrow in intent. The story of Noah blessing and cursing his sons and grandson gives us a clear example. A pure blessing would have been, "Blessed be Shem!" Noah's blessing on Shem, however, is, "Blessed by the LORD my God be Shem; and let Canaan be his slave" (Gen. 9:26 RSV). At the heart of the blessing, however, is the relationship between two or more parties brought to voice in the blessing. God's blessings are not to be understood as specific rewards and conditions—although some blessings may be specific—but as descriptions of one's relationship to God and the purposes and intentions of God voiced in the blessing. That is, when God blesses someone, any specific content that might be called forth by the blessing is secondary to the person's relationship with God that the blessing represents.

THE BLESSINGS OF THE SERMON

The Matthean beatitudes are in third person and are neither completely open-ended nor narrowly defined. Some speak to those who are trapped in certain conditions; some are instructional, indicating the response expected of those who, in every generation, embrace God's sovereign reign. All speak of what it means here, in the midst of Death and Darkness, to have seen a great Light and to have become bearers of that Light. They move from showing the wideness of God's love to pronouncing the most radical expectations of those who take up the call to discipleship.

Although the fifth, sixth, and seventh beatitudes speak of the response expected from those who have heard the proclamation of God's sovereignty and have embraced it, the first four speak of those on whose behalf that sovereignty is asserted. These four promise blessing not on the basis of something the hearers must do, but on the basis of God's own determination with regard to those who live under certain conditions. As with the salvation oracles of the Hebrew prophets, hope lies neither in human achievement nor even in human repentance, but in God's mercy.

CHAPTER 6

THE POOR IN SPIRIT

The God of Israel is moved to action by divine compassion for all who are in agony. God blesses those who seem no longer to be sustained even by hope.

There is a tendency for commentaries to interpret Matthew's version of this beatitude as a spiritualization of the original, which is generally agreed to be the version found in Luke. Matthew's blessing, it is said, is upon humility. Such a rendering assumes that *in spirit* is an adjective modifying *the poor,* as in the Qumran Community Rule. In the other beatitude that uses the genitive case *(the pure in heart),* however, the word *heart* indicates the locus of the purity, not its character. It is more probable, therefore, that *spirit* tells us the locus of the poverty, not its character. The blessing is on those who are impoverished in spirit, that is, in life, in energy. They are characterized by what Isaiah calls faintness of spirit (Isa. 61:3), or, in the Greek Old Testament, weariness of spirit.

Matthew has occasionally reworded his sources to bring them into line with the vocabulary of Isaiah. What happens in Jesus is the fulfillment of the promises of Isaiah, promises Isaiah associated with the end of exile. The prophecy of Isaiah finds its fulfillment in the deliverance of the entire world. The poor in spirit are not merely the people of God, lost in the exile of the Roman Empire, although they include these. They are also all those in the Gentile world who find that life and hope elude them because of the Darkness, even those who do not understand their situation in terms of the categories and metaphors of the paradigm. The poor in spirit are *all* people, at *all* times, and in *all* places, who are victims and bondservants of the Darkness in the Old Age. They are those who see no way out, those for whom life has become a dead end, those who have passed over the edge of desperation and no longer have enough energy left even to be desperate. The poor in spirit are those who know only the numbing cold of the Darkness, even those who perceive their condition as solitariness in a

Godless world, not knowing that it is the hollowness of a creation in exile from its Creator.

The poor in spirit are both those who know themselves abandoned by God and those who assume that there is no God to abandon them. These, says Jesus, are the special objects of God's determined, zealous action. The real enemy is not Rome. The real enemy is the entire host of demonic powers and principalities, who serve as heralds of the Darkness. Had Israel been her own master in her own land, that in and of itself would not have indicated that the Old Age was any less real or that Israel was any less under the power of the Darkness. Rome, Israel's master, was as thoroughly captive to the Darkness as was Israel. Israel's liberation through the work of the Messiah would set her free to bring light and life to the entire Gentile world. Matthew has not spiritualized the beatitude; he has universalized it.

THE MISSION INTO THE DARKNESS

Those who have heard the message of God's Reign and who, at least to some extent, have begun to walk in the Light, empowered by the presence of the New Age, must now step back into that Darkness as bearers of God's Light. Gone now must be any self-consciousness of being blessed. Their own blessing they must allow to be not a matter for self-satisfied contemplation, but the source of their movement toward others. So far as their thoughts of who is blessed are concerned, their eyes must be turned to those who have given up, those who no longer hope. The disciples are indeed blessed, but this first beatitude speaks of those to whom the disciples are sent. We who read it in cold print and perceive it as the word of God truly hear God speaking through it only when we hear it addressed to us as a reminder of how God regards those on whom we otherwise easily might look with condescension and contempt. To be a disciple is to follow fully, to follow Jesus' care for the outcast and the despondent, to adhere to Jesus' total lack of concern for his own well-being and his sacrifice of himself that others might find life. It is to follow Jesus' refusal even to save his life at the hands of his enemies, but to view the enemy as those to be rescued from the Darkness. Since God's Reign is on behalf of all those victimized by the Darkness, those consenting to that Reign have no choice but to share in its outreach. The life of discipleship is all-consuming for the one who takes it up.

GOD'S REIGN ON THEIR BEHALF

The blessing on the faint of spirit is intended to strengthen those who hear and to motivate the disciples to reach out to the faint of spirit. The blessing is no pie-in-the-sky expression of good wishes, but is the proclamation that enables the downtrodden to hang on in the face of overwhelming odds.

It is not a way of saying that life is not as bad as the oppressed think it to be; because for them it *is* that bad.

It is not an assertion that, after all, others are worse off than they; because when you are on the ropes, someone else's problems do not comfort you.

It is not a reminder that they have some inner resource on which to draw and that all they need do is look within; because they *have* no inner resource. They are poverty-stricken of the very energy of life. They can look only outside themselves to the God who created them.

It is not some assurance that their future condition will somehow balance the scales and compensate for the horror of their former anguish.

It is simply the assurance that despite appearances to the contrary, God is determined to act on behalf of all those who are victims in this world.

All talk of inner resources that can be tapped if one simply knows the key, all talk of some divine presence within each person, all talk of drawing on the powers of the universe is simply a pseudo-Christian expression of the atheism that parades in our world even in the guise of Christian preaching and teaching, perhaps especially in the guise of Christian preaching and teaching. It is atheism in that it no longer believes in or affirms or obeys the Transcendent God who rules supreme over human history, but urges, instead, that we look to our own resources supposedly placed in us as the image of God. Or it reduces God to the patron god of the West or of the United States, thereby denying his nature as the one who both stands over against all nations (including the Western nations) and stands on the side of all people, including those who, in every nation, consider themselves atheists because they deny the god espoused by the society. Whichever is done, reducing God to a god of the inner life of the individual or to the patron god of the nation, is still to worship a god that does not exist, while ignoring, even denying, the One who is.

Blessing in a world that is both atheistic and insane likely will take forms that are bizarre to those who are enthralled by the god of the Darkness. Blessing as a relationship with the one true God will involve the blessed one in the same rejection and mockery that is expressed toward the God who blesses. It is not a coincidence that the One who proclaims the reign of God calls those who come under that reign to take up the cross.

The transformation of the creation, which is God's ultimate intention, is so radical that no words used to anticipate it can ever be taken as literal descriptions, but are language by which we are borne steadily toward the new order. Truly to trust God is not simply to trust him to accomplish this or that specific stated goal, but it is to trust him for the content of the future, and for the content of the present as well. The promise that God's sovereign rule is inevitable includes the reminder that it is God's sovereign rule and that God, not we, has the say-so about our condition under his rule.

CHAPTER 7

THOSE WHO MOURN

Mourning is the anguish and sorrow evoked by face-to-face encounter with the conditions of the Old Age. The underlying Greek and Hebrew words commonly refer to mourning for the dead or mourning over catastrophe. Whether, as some have suggested, Luke has altered the wording of this beatitude because of an aversion to the word for mourn or, as others contend, Matthew has altered the original in order to show the connection with the oracles of Isaiah 61, the connection with Isaiah is clearly present.

The proclamation of blessedness to those who mourn heralds the turning point in God's relationship to the creation. Just as the entire world is exiled from God—and that exile is typified in Israel's exile—so God's liberation and comfort are for the entire world. To *all* who agonize over the crippling, destroying impact of the Old Age, to *all* who mourn over the rampancy of the Power of Death in the creation, Jesus proclaims God's dependability, compassion, and strength. The disciples, the ones in whom the renewal of Israel begins, find comfort in their mourning and, in turn, are to comfort those inside and outside Israel who also mourn.

THE WORLD IN EXILE

Although not all who are sorrowful recognize it, all human sorrow is rooted in the world's exile from God. Since it is affected by the fall, all mourning partakes of pride, self-interest, and despair over our finitude. It is stained by a desire for omnipotence. All mourning also, however, is in some respects a mourning over the exile and Darkness of the world, manifesting itself as boredom, depression, fear, anxiety, sorrow over some personal tragedy, despair over the decline of Western civilization or over the decay of national prominence, or as any of a multitude of pains, agonies, or neuroses and psychoses. This is not to say that the mourning to which the beatitude points is to be simply equated with any of these or with a guilty conscience, masochism, enervation, or moral catatonia, although these are surface expressions of that brokenness which exile from God entails. Even the mundane frustrations of life are unenlightened expressions of that Darkness and Death in which God does not will that even the most unsuspecting remain. Self-centered sorrow of the fallen creature, therefore—although incomplete as long as the mourner is oblivious to the reality of the Old Age and does not perceive his or her mourning as a symptom of separation and alienation from the Source of all life—is to be neither ridiculed nor belittled, for frequently it is the expression of a wounded spirit and a broken heart.

This fallen sorrow can give way to genuine mourning when, by the freedom bestowed by the gospel, it becomes purified mourning over the world's exile from God.

Consider the one whose entire life has been a kaleidoscopic mixture of happiness and sorrow, but for whom each day is now filled only with terror and deep depression. The moments of sparkle come less and less frequently. Headaches, depression, those horrible moments when the problem is completely unidentifiable, but which evoke outbursts of tears and drive the anguish into the very marrow of the bone—all these come mysteriously, engulfing mind and body like an impenetrable fog.

We continue to keep up appearances, but the appearances are a mask hiding us even from those who love us most—especially from those who love us most! We *must* not let anyone see what is happening to us.

On those few occasions when we *do* let the mask slip for a moment, giving only a hint of our agony, the husband or wife—trying to be supportive, but really not knowing what to say—pats our hand and says, "Oh, honey, you're just tired. You worry about things too much. You know there's nothing you can't handle." Or on another occasion, when we let the mask slip again, our husband or wife snaps, "I wish you would quit worrying so much! You're just being silly!" Thus, both encouragement and rebuke are but different guises of basic rejection.

Or perhaps we have lost a loved one to death or divorce. Now, life is empty. Some days are like long, dark tunnels leading nowhere—or leading only to tomorrow's tunnel. Suicide seems an attractive option—if only we had the courage.

So we turn to the church. Perhaps God is the answer. Perhaps we can find sympathy and understanding in the pastor. But the pastor's response is that we have to be born again, or that we need (in some vague way) to put God first, or that we need to lose ourselves in some project, or that it is just a stage through which we are going—a thousand and one responses that become not even noise, but the silence of God.

And then we discover that we are not alone on our perch on the edge of oblivion. Around us are many others, some of them our best friends, who day by day also put on their masks, living in secret desperation and hiding it behind the smiles, the loud voices, and the pretenses of piety. We have not been able to help one another because we have been hiding from one another. When one of our number committed suicide, we never guessed that it was over the same fears, the same heartache, the same agonies that we too endure—that our friend simply could not hang on so well as we have.

What none of us has realized is that these common agonies are not merely personal; they are the reflections of the sickness and desperation of the larger society. Our frantic activity has been primarily an effort to overcome our collective boredom, a futile attempt to heal our broken spirits. But all we can hear is the echo of our own desolate cry, the beating of our own broken wings.

This is the exile, even for those who do not believe in a God to whom they can cry out. It is the habitation of Darkness, utter thralldom to the Power of Death. It is the mourning of those over whom the God who is absent keeps watch within the shadows, and whom he girds himself to deliver.

The enlightened mourning toward which the beatitude points, that mourning which recognizes the agony and pain of exile as the separation from God it truly is, is not automatic. It can neither be commanded, invented, nor created at will. It can even be hampered by paralysis of the will, that hardening of heart which, by the judgment of God, makes true repentance humanly impossible.

Genuine mourning, that mourning which laments the absence of God, is born of grace, out of the agony of the Old Age. Thus, true mourning is the manifestation of a certain freedom, not the full freedom of the completed reign of God, but freedom from complete cynicism and imperviousness, a freedom God alone can create. Those who endure exile by making idols—idols such as civilization, cultural "ways of life," or self-satisfying parodies of the gospel, under the guise of "relevant Christianity," idols that are substituted for the face of God—are not truly free to mourn. They are bondservants of the Darkness.

MOURNING AND THE ABSENCE OF JESUS

The deeper mourning toward which the beatitude points is a mourning not only over the exile of the world from God, but also over the absence of Jesus. The transformed Christ, though with us till the end of the age, is also absent. He is present wherever two or three are gathered in his name, and he is with his assembly as it makes disciples of the nations, but he is also the absent bridegroom (Matt. 9:15). Thus it will be until the full presence of the New Age. We are, therefore, at the same time, both reconciled to and separated from the resurrected Jesus. As a people perennially afflicted with disobedience, moral paralysis, and self-aggrandizement, we too bear the burden of separation. Our reconciliation is also our vocation as his Body.

Fasting is a ceremonial means of mourning over Jesus' absence. By rejecting food and drink, followers of Jesus enact ceremonially the recognition that the one who is true bread has been taken away, that he is not yet with us in the fullness of his glory. By fasting we outwardly emulate that loss of appetite which subjective sorrow over the loss of a loved one can create.

In relation to Jesus, however, there is also a mourning yet to come. It is a mourning evoked not by his continuing absence, but by his return.

> Immediately after the tribulation of those days the sun will be darkened, the moon will not give its light, the stars will fall from heaven, and the powers of the heavens will be shaken. Then will appear in heaven the sign of the Son of Man, and all the tribes of the earth will mourn. And they will see the Son of Man coming on the clouds of heaven, with power and great glory.
>
> (Matt. 24:29-30 RSV)

Those who mourn over the shock of his return and those who mourn his absence are not completely different groups. Some who mourn at his return will be those who have mourned his absence, but who have assumed their method of waiting to be a superior way of life, one in special favor with the absent Lord.

COMFORT TO THE MOURNERS

Those who mourn will be strengthened. The Greek root for "they shall be comforted" is widely used in the Bible. In John's Gospel a noun made from it (*paraclete:* one who aids) refers to the Holy Spirit. In 2 Corinthians, Paul speaks at length of God as the God of all *comfort* who comforts us in our afflictions so that we, in turn, can comfort others. That is, we are aided in the midst of life's difficulties so that we may aid others.

Comfort is not mere helpful thoughts. It is not, in fact, basically cognitive at all, but is the strength which comes as a revitalizing *nevertheless* in face of the cognitive aspects of mourning. Until the New Age arrives in all its fullness, comfort does not necessarily remove the difficulty over which we agonize, but strengthens us to endure that difficulty. In the book of Job, Job's three friends comforted him as long as they sat in silence. Powerless to bring back Job's children or his possessions, they lent strength merely by their presence. When Job cried out at the end of seven days, the friends forsook their role as comforters and began to analyze his problems. From that point onward, whatever strength Job had came from somewhere other than the friends. Even the gift of twice as many children as he originally had did not wipe away the loss of Job's first children. Surely, in the years that followed, Job must have lain awake in the middle of the night, smiling over the pleasure given him by his second family. But from time to time, in the darkness of the night, must he not also have awakened from a dream in which one or the other of his children still tugged at his skirt or still laughed in a way that only she or he could laugh? Job's comfort was not a restoration of his family, but the gift of a second family to enable him to endure the memories of his own holocaust.

CYNICISM: AN IMPOSTOR OF COMFORT

Mourning, we grope for even the flimsiest means of comfort, and, in our groping, we lay hold of comfort's substitutes. Vague motions of the Darkness give the momentary illusion of Light, and we accept this pretense of comfort because it eases, for a moment, the pain.

Cynicism satisfies, for a while, enabling us to laugh at the Darkness and to ridicule its power. Cynicism also beguiles us, however, and encourages us to ridicule hope.

Cynicism is one of the most effective disguises of the Darkness, for it encourages attacks even upon itself—attacks which, paradoxically, do not weaken or threaten it, but strengthen it. In cynicism, Death's masochistic drive is nourished and satisfied.

Cynicism is attractive because it offers laughter in the face of sorrow and despair. Because its root is the Darkness, however, it has no strength to resist that Darkness. It can only undercut the promise of blessing as it ridicules the threat of the Darkness.

A major element of the attractiveness of cynicism is that it recognizes the full scope and power of our drive for efficiency-producing techniques. Thus, it poses as enlightenment, as sophistication, as superior intelligence.

Cynicism further recognizes that most efforts to actively combat technique are merely other forms of technique. For example, cynicism observes that the only way to actively combat false propaganda is to use factual propaganda. Both, however, are techniques! Consequently, cynicism either attempts to escape the Darkness by ignoring it (refusing to use any technique at all) or by adopting a pragmatic approach to life (believing that bondage to the Darkness negates personal responsibility and guilt). Posing as the wisdom of the serpent, cynicism is actually the most blind of all to the deceptions of the serpent.

Cynicism, then, is another unfulfilled expression of mourning. Since it is not true mourning, it cannot truly be comforted, but can only continue to suffer and to mistake its own question for an answer. On the other hand, even cynicism, the impostor of comfort, is not completely outside the scope of God's ability to take, in the mystery of his way, the Darkness and use it for purposes of Light. Despite all its natural dynamics, cynicism now and then may be turned, put to use, transcended—perhaps shortcircuited—and made an instrument by which genuine comfort is introduced. The complete rejection of cynicism denies the ultimate power of cynicism, but affirms that even it, by the design of God, may become the means of its own defeat. Even the impostors of comfort, to the extent that they imply that there is a comfort to be imitated, anticipate the true comfort of the New Age, which reaches out to us from the future, enclosing us in its cover, drawing us more fully into the triumph of God's reign.

THE ILLUSORY QUEST FOR MEANING

Some seek comfort by searching for "purpose" or "meaning," especially in suffering. We attempt to understand tragedy or to put it into proper perspective, thereby making it manageable. We hope to reduce its terror through reason. True comfort in a world of Darkness, however, is not a reduction of terror or horror, but is the strength to face, endure, and live steadily despite the terror and the horror. Cynicism trivializes horror; comfort faces it without illusion and undergirds those who must endure it.

Suffering is a condition of the world as a fallen world. It is a condition of the exile, an expression of the Darkness, one of the many faces of Death. It holds no inherent value, but only a threat. Our own suffering, in and of itself, is capable only of crushing us or embittering us—bitterness, of course, being a symptom of a crushed spirit.

This sense of futility, this despair that robs one even of desperation, is the real root of many of those so-called social problems that flit across the headlines, capturing the public attention for a few weeks, and then are lost in the turmoil—problems such as alcoholism, drug abuse, spouse or child abuse, and suicide. All are symptoms of a certain emptiness, a certain hollowness of soul, which comes in the failure of our idols. Analyses of society frequently examine the individual problem areas and then speak of the destruction of society as their effect. Preserving the security of society is then attempted through enacting new laws, new rules and regulations. It is a secular version of the effort to achieve salvation by imposing torah, and it is no more effective in the secular realm than in the realm of the holy.

Drug addiction, suicide, and the like do not lead to the destruction of society. They are the destruction of society actually taking place. The idols we trust can neither move nor speak, can neither give life nor kill. They can only pull us into the power of that Darkness where there is neither meaning nor hope. Then, when the idols do not speak, we mistake this for the silence of God. There are, indeed, times when God is silent, but the idols are always silent. When God is silent, there is the hope that he may one day speak again, and in this hope one can endure the silence, looking to the One who is silent. The silence of the idols, heard when we have ceased our own talking, which we mistook for the voice of the idols and, consequently, for the voice of God, leaves us without hope and without anticipation that they will speak again.

Consequently, we turn for strength to the latest fashion in drugs, to sex, to the arts, to the cults, to the ego-building philosophies and religions of human divinity, to the job, and, when these also fail, to suicide. Indeed, these others may even become the means of suicide. We may obsessively drug ourselves to death, surrender our identity to the cult (in some extreme cases, such as Jim Jones' cult, to the worshiping of Death), or labor ourselves to death.

Ultimately, all human suffering and sorrow are meaningful only in view of the fall and in the context of the agony and death of Jesus Christ. Death, in all its expressions, meets its limits in the crucifixion. Thus, any human suffering is understandable only to the extent that the cross is understandable; and in terms of fallen human wisdom and understanding, the cross is an absurdity. "Meaning" is the pseudo-intellectual substitute for the equally elusive "happiness."

The only purpose or meaning in suffering, in any positive sense, grows out of God's use of suffering. Moreover, that God can and does use suffering for specific purposes does not make suffering any less painful or less evil, but simply bears witness to God's sovereignty over all things, including things that are evil.

COMFORT AS A GIFT REVEALED

The comfort of which the beatitude speaks is not merely an efficient human creation devised by the techniques of the social sciences. It is not a self-sufficiency nurtured through self-help skills or created by positive thinking. Whatever is positive that might be said about all such human creations, the only certain thing is that they are not the ultimate comfort of which the beatitude speaks, even if God chooses to use them as means toward that comfort. The basis for such a dogmatic assertion is the wording of the beatitude itself. Its passive voice is simply a literary means by which piety affirms that God will strengthen the mourners. Genuine comfort—the strength to endure the ravages of the Darkness without bitterness or despair—is solely a gift. It is the expression of God's own presence, the assertion of God's own sovereignty over the Darkness. Consequently, it cannot be perceived as a human achievement. The only things that we, in and of ourselves, can achieve in the face of Death are cynicism, despair, indifference, hardness of heart, and desperation of spirit.

The beatitude on comfort to those who mourn, then, is neither a statement of mere good wishes nor merely a promise. It is, rather, a blessing—a blessing on all who truly mourn and whose agony is a finger pointing toward our true condition. Furthermore, the full revelation of the nature of our mourning is accompanied by the promised comfort, lest the cosmic dimensions of our condition crush us beyond hope.

Because it is truly known only in its being revealed, however, comfort, though sometimes mediated through human words, can never be equated with human words. Indeed, human words often become an affliction for those who mourn. When Job's friends broke their silence and attempted to impose meaning on Job's suffering, they destroyed comfort as well. "Had you remained silent," Job scolded, "that would have been your wisdom!" The ultimate comfort provided by God's Living Word frequently is embodied in the silent human presence. When words *do* mediate comfort, they do so only because they have been absorbed into, affirmed by, and used by the divine Word, the divine Presence, the source of all enduring strength.

DISCIPLES AS MEDIATORS OF COMFORT

Relying on the Transcendent God to weave from the scrawny threads of our comfort a garment of faith and love and hope, we are called, as disciples of the living Christ, into a world that mourns without understanding. We are sent forth into the Darkness from whose dominion we have been set free, and in which our own comfort has come as an unmerited gift. We become bearers of God's Light, making disciples of a world that, at the moment, does not even know the One who calls it and sends us. By our presence—sometimes with words, sometimes without—we are to mediate the comfort we ourselves have received from God.

CHAPTER 8

THE MEEK

The meek are among the poor in spirit. The meek are those afflicted, who, in their affliction, do not take it upon themselves to seek redress or to overthrow the oppressor, but wait upon God's deliverance. So closely related are the Hebrew words designating the poor and the meek that the Greek translation of the Hebrew Bible does not even maintain a consistent translation. One must look to the context to know which connotation is intended.

An enduring model of meekness is the ancient, venerable prophet Moses. Repudiated by his own people, rejected by his own brother and sister, Moses was the meekest person on the face of the earth (Num. 12:3). As the text makes clear, however, Moses made no attempt to defend himself, but relied on God's defense (Num. 12:4-9).

According to the postexilic prophet Zechariah, the king whose reign would signal the dawn of a new era would come

> triumphant and victorious . . .
> afflicted [or meek] and riding on an ass,
> on a colt, the foal of an ass.
>
> (9:9 RSV)

The colliding images of triumph and affliction, victory and ignominious mount reflect anticipation of a ruler who will enter his own city, come into his own rule. He will not choose a lowly status, but, by the inscrutable will of God, reduced to the role of victim, he will come as a victim who rides confident of ultimate vindication from God.

For Matthew, Jesus is the supreme model of meekness. Like the victim-king in Zechariah, Jesus enters Jerusalem as one afflicted, one who must suffer and die (Matt. 21:5), but one who, relying completely on God who has sent him, refuses to take up the sword for self-defense (Matt. 26:51-54).

For Matthew, however, Zechariah's "triumphant and victorious is he," can only refer to the resurrection; therefore, Matthew omits the line. Jesus' triumph can come only after his affliction.

Elsewhere, Matthew reports Jesus' own words concerning his affliction:

> Come to me, all who labor and are loaded down,
>   And I will give you rest.
> Take up *my* yoke, and learn from *me*—
>   For *I* am afflicted and abased in self-will—
> And you will find true rest,
>   For *my* yoke is easy,
>   And *my* burden is light.
>
> (Matt. 11:28-30, emphasis mine)

The disciples are called to share Jesus' affliction and his meekness. As he, in his affliction, is not self-willed, but submits to God's will, so can those who are afflicted, if they come to him, learn from him to rely on God for their eventual deliverance.

Of course, Jesus' supreme moment of meekness is when he hangs on the cross. There, in agony, nearing death, he begins to chant that ancient psalm of meekness, Psalm 22. Whether he completed the chant we can only guess. That he began it is sufficient for our understanding of the scene. With half-dried throat, blood trickling down his face and chest from the thorns and nails, like a hated opponent being tortured to death, he sings:

> My God! My God!
> Why have you abandoned me?
> Yet, you are unlike all the imagined gods!
> Why are you so far from helping me?
> In the midst of the assembly of your people,
>   I will praise you!
> Dominion belongs to the LORD,
>   And *He* rules over the nations!

It is a song of confidence in and submission to the God who, for the moment, has turned away. The cry is, indeed, the terrible cry of one who knows the absence of God; and the confidence and trust of this one who cries in no way overcomes or eases the agony of that moment. It is, however, the agonizing cry of faith. It is the moment of supreme meekness!

THE DISTINCTION BETWEEN AFFLICTION AND MEEKNESS

The beatitude on meekness, unlike the beatitudes on poverty of spirit and mourning, is not universal in scope to the same extent that those are.

Meekness is not related to despair in general or to hope in just any promise of help, relief, or deliverance. It is not hope in an impersonal economic process, in the basic goodness of human beings, in some vague belief in the triumph of good over evil, or in some similar idolatry.

The meek know that there is no help in anyone or anything other than the Living God, the Transcendent Creator of heaven and earth, the God revealed in Jesus Christ. Meekness is confidence maintained in the face of events and factors that might as easily lead to despair or to despair's twin, rebellion.

The meek are not necessarily those unable to defend themselves, although they *may* be unable to do so, but they are those who, whether capable of self-defense or not, know that the outcome of all self-defense is to remain exiled in Darkness held securely by the chains of Death.

Nor, however, do the meek necessarily live in simple obedience to the oppressor. The meekness of discipleship neither requires nor permits obedience to human authorities when that obedience would deny, bear false witness to, or undercut obedience to God. Meekness requires giving in, even to the haughty demand of those in authority over us, such as the Roman soldier who demands that the disciple carry the soldier's load. Meekness requires one even to do more than is demanded, provided such actions do not conflict with or undercut one's obedience to God.

Meekness, consequently, is not to be equated with quietism (although quietism may at times be an appropriate expression of meekness), but is simply the determination to go about one's business as a disciple of Jesus Christ, trusting in God, unafraid, in the very face of Death.

Meekness does not await the rejuvenation of the structures and institutions of the Old Age, but awaits liberation from those structures. While they wait, the meek may use the institutions of society—now out of choice, now out of necessity—in an effort to aid the destitute, to ease the plight of the suffering, or to bring justice to the oppressed. The meek may pursue noble, humane efforts to bring limited relief while they await liberation. Some of this work may even become Christ's own way of working. That is never subject to our determination, however, for from our human standpoint, even when such work is done with confidence in God, it is tampering with the fixtures of the Darkness.

THE MEEK AND THE WARRIORS

Those Hebrew texts that were Jesus' Bible, and which are a part of ours, do not seem at first to call for meekness. The stories of the judges and the early kings recall those times when God led Israel into battle, commanding them to destroy entire cities of men, women, children, and animals. Such stories are primarily responsible for the common error which holds that the

God of the Old Testament is basically a vengeful, wrathful God, an error that can be held only by those who do not consider the Old Testament as a whole.

Quite a different picture emerges when one listens to the Bible as a whole—when the Former Prophets, the Gospels, and the book of Revelation, for example, are heard in the context of God's call to Abraham to be the root of a people who will be God's instrument for the blessing of the nations. The death of the Egyptian army at the Red Sea, for another example, is not properly understood outside the context of Egypt as one of the nations to be blessed. Egypt's army must not be allowed to thwart that blessing by destroying the instrument of blessing.

In the Former Prophets, the accounts of God sending Israel into battle and calling for the annihilation of certain populations cannot be heard properly apart from the fallen condition of all societies, including Israel, and apart from God's determination not to turn his own people into puppets, but to use their warlike nature.

Israel exists to be God's Light in the midst of the Darkness. In the stories of Israel's warfare, Israel is never given automatic license to kill, but, rather, is ordered to kill only in very precise situations. Such warfare is never a secular act, but is always a ceremonially restricted act. For example, sexual intercourse is restricted prior to battle.

The war narratives are never narratives of Israel's wars, but are narratives of God's wars. When Israel goes into battle on her own initiative, she is defeated. The stories do not glorify war, but acknowledge the reality of war and even show the restrictions that God places on warfare.

Moreover, it can be reasonably argued that the Former Prophets are not, as a unified narrative, a collection of war stories at all, but that they are stories about God's sovereignty and Israel's obedience and disobedience, told in a war setting. (An example of a modern book that appears on the surface to be a war novel but is not is *Catch 22* by Joseph Heller. *Catch 22* is about bureaucracy, among other things, in a war setting. That is why readers of *Catch 22* find that it describes their own situation in fields as diverse as business, medicine, education, and religion.)[1]

Those occasions when God calls on Israel to commit violence are violations of God's own character and of Israel's own reason for existing. God has called Israel into a chaotic, violence-laden, Death-oriented world to be the means of Life. Israel is not to use the fallen nature of the world

---

1. I am indebted to my colleague Charles Mayo for this important insight.

as an excuse for her own tendency toward violence. Moreover, whenever things get so far out of hand that God violates his own character by calling forth violence, the reader should not hear this as a portrayal of God's basic character, but should hear the charge: Look at the degree of wickedness! Look at what we, in our heartlessness, finally drove God to do!

Since the war stories from the periods of the judges and the monarchy do not show us leaders who reflect the meekness envisioned in the beatitude, we cannot pretend the absence of conflict in the Bible itself. That warfare of only one kind was permitted however, warfare commanded directly by God and heard by faith, and that the observable odds were not always on the side of Israel, indicate that at heart there is a similarity between the stories and the beatitude on meekness. At the heart of both is concern for solitary trust in the Word of God, without regard to the conditions in which the work of God takes place.

MEEKNESS AND REVOLUTION

An Old Testament example of God's rejection of violence and his call for meekness is the book of Daniel. In the first half of that book, in the Jewish and Protestant editions, the stories about Daniel and his friends in the courts of successive tyrants are stories of promise: God is faithful! Readers are to wait peacefully, therefore, with courage and dignity, for God to deliver them. The visions of the second half of the book reaffirm this message. The kingdoms of all the earthly rulers, no matter how relatively humane they may be when compared with one another, are destined to fall before the might of God. The readers are not to hear this as an encouragement to take up arms in order to hasten the day of God's reign, but are to await, nonviolently, with courage, even if they are killed as they wait.

In the book of Jonah, God is said to have repented of the evil he had planned to do to Nineveh. Given the definition of evil as that which is contrary to God's purposes, this can only mean that God finally decided that he would not go counter to his own nature or purpose. He would spare Nineveh. In this light, those places where we are shown God enacting violence are all the more horrible in that they suggest that in our sin we drive God to go counter to his nature.

All historical revolutions are a part of the Darkness, for all human violence reflects the bondage of the Darkness. Even here, however, we must not be dogmatic in our human assertions, for God may condescend to go counter to his own character and to use some historical revolution or another for purposes unfathomed by us, even granting an anticipation of eschatological freedom in this or that historical revolution. Nevertheless, in no way does this make any revolution, in and of itself, any less a phenomenon of the Darkness.

MEEKNESS AND RIGHTS

Meekness does not even use peaceful means to assert or to achieve one's "rights." The effort to manipulate the social structure and its institutions to achieve political independence in the name of the gospel is actually quite contrary to the gospel. How much more contrary would be a meekness defined by violence! Whenever, by the decision of God, some historical liberation movement becomes an anticipatory expression of the true liberation of which the gospel speaks, that is only because God has chosen to make it so, not because of the use of the words *liberation* and *freedom* in the Bible to describe God's eschatological work.

Just as scripture and sermon are the Word of God *when* God chooses to make them so, and just as the elements are sacraments *by God's action,* so any human actions are the means of God's work (and, thereby, instruments of eschatology) only *when* God chooses and only *if* God chooses to make them so. The exodus of Israel out of Egypt, commonly cited as the paradigm for today's liberation theology,[2] is not a sample of God's ultimate liberation. It is, rather, a step toward that liberation. It is not a pattern for human emulation, but is the unique event in which the people who are to serve as instruments of redemption are brought to life. The Exodus gives us no pattern, or model, for ethical imitation, but reminds us that we are delivered solely by God. The liberation the gospel promises is eschatological liberation. As such, it has no ethic, but creates an ethos radically at odds with the ethos and ethics of all historical liberations.

This does not mean that the liberation the gospel brings is outside history or that those who are liberated are taken out of history. Instead, the truly free community or person is set free in the midst of history, though in a manner not understood by those grounded in history and engulfed in the Darkness. The freedom of transformed, fulfilled history is established in the midst of history and is viewed by those bound to history as a threat. The Darkness can neither comprehend nor overcome that freedom or those empowered by that freedom. Any liberation theology that defines liberation in terms of history's politics and values substitutes the seizure and exploitation of the present world for the inheritance which is to be.

---

2. Liberation theology is a catch-all title for modern theologies that emphasize the gospel as a way of achieving political or social liberation. Most liberation theologians live in Africa or Central and South America. Some support violence and some support nonviolence as means of liberation.

MEEKNESS AND THE JUST WAR

Meekness is also incompatible with the just war[3] as a theoretical construction.

The earliest Christian formulations with regard to just-war theory, of course, were in part efforts to restrain war. With the conversion of soldiers and the growing belief that the now friendly Roman government was a gift from God, how might war be curtailed for a government that still had police responsibility?

In terms of the ethos of a fallen world, it is a noble theory, one with a certain attractiveness for the person going into battle to protect the oppressed and terrorized. In the final analysis, however, just-war theory substitutes ideology for the command of God. It pretends that its participation in the Darkness is not entrapment in the Darkness. It is an effort at self-justification.

Christian situation ethics theory arises from the same quest. Like the just-war theory—the just war being, after all, simply a reaction to a context or concrete situation—situation ethics declares necessity to be freedom, precisely on the basis of its necessity, and baptizes necessity in the name of Christ.

God, however, without regard for our evaluations and pretenses, uses, ignores, or thwarts our warfare for his own purposes—purposes which, more often than not, elude our understanding. The conclusion that a particular war is preferable to the injustice of a particular existing order may or may not be correct. In any case, to participate in any war is to participate in the Old Age. Only if God, for reasons unknown to us, condescends to use that war for purposes related to the eventual triumph of his Reign does it have any connection whatsoever with the liberation of which the gospel speaks. All theologies that seek to justify armed revolution are idolatrous in that they assume that we have the divine right to judge and to justify ourselves, a right which God reserves for himself alone.

Of course, both liberation theology and the just-war theory are correct in their assumption that the Word of God becomes flesh in fallen history and that, consequently, any faithful theology must speak of action in the political realm. That the meek inherit the earth, not heaven, rules out any effort to ignore the agonies of history. We cannot evade the world into which we have been born and in which we have been called. The fatal flaw of the just-war theory and of those forms of liberation theology that sanction violence as a

---

3. The just war refers to a war that certain Christian traditions have said Christians may take part in because the war meets certain criteria such as being waged by one who bears legal authority over the nation, being limited to only as much violence as is necessary to rebuff the enemy, and being likely to produce better conditions than exist prior to the war.

tool (and not all liberation theologies do sanction violence) is their description of *how* disciples are to act in the realm of politics and in other affairs of the world. The call to be holy (different, set apart) is replaced by the ethos of the Darkness, in which disciples are permitted to act (even ordered to act) just like everybody else.

Since this beatitude is not a command, however, it cannot be understood as a law for those who are not disciples. It is not an address to the oppressed people of the world telling them how they are commanded to live in the face of oppression. It is not a law against revolution. In fact, it is not a law at all, but a promise, an assurance of God's faithfulness. The meek, in their trust in God, are not models of pacifism or of any other ideological position, but are models of faith in the midst of Exile, Darkness, and Death. The disciples may warn oppressed "Gentiles" of the folly of retaliatory violence, but they cannot legitimately counsel nonviolence on moral or ethical grounds. Those in places of influence may even urge the oppressor to cease oppressing. On the other hand, to urge the oppressed to be meek and not, at the same time, seek an end to the oppression is to take one's place as a false disciple, a conspirator with the oppressor. The meekness beatitude can never legitimately be used to suppress the efforts of the oppressed to liberate themselves politically, economically, or in any other way. In fact, those who have commonly used such passages in an effort to suppress revolution might have heard, had they listened more carefully, a warning of their own impending doom, for the promise of the renewed earth is a promise from the God who sustains the entire creation. It is by the Creator's subjection of the oppressor that the oppressed are set free.

THE MEEK AND THE EARTH

This beatitude is a word-for-word quotation of a promise in Psalm 37. In that psalm those who have been robbed of their share in the Promised Land are promised that God will give them charge over the land. All they have to do is wait patiently for God's fulfillment of the promise. For Matthew, however, the promise has taken on greater proportions. The earth God will give to the meek is the whole earth—the earth that, with everything in it, belongs to God (Psalm 24).

This promise has nothing at all to do with "going to heaven." The Reign of God, of course, is not confined geographically to some realm above the clouds, but encompasses heaven and earth and all creation. The hope of all earthly life, however, lies precisely in God's transformation of the earth. Contrary to popular belief, the New Testament nowhere speaks of God's people "going to heaven," but speaks of God's descent to a transformed earth, here to dwell with us. The expectation of "going to heaven" is an expectation of loss, but the earth is to be fulfilled, not lost, as God makes all things new. Desertion of an earth that had been or was to be destroyed would indicate that God himself had been defeated. The New Age fulfills the Old Age.

Here, of course, we can speak of the unseen and radically new thing only in terms of what is seen. It would be as erroneous to concentrate on images of the earth as we know it—with humanly conceivable modifications, of course—as it would be to envision human existence in the New Age as merely our present condition with the wrinkles pressed out. The emphasis of the beatitude is that those who are oppressed, but who rely on God for deliverance, will find that reliance justified.

The conditions of the New Age transcend the time and space conditions to which our human thought is limited. The symbols can mediate the reality to us, but they cannot enable us to imagine it as it truly will be. If flesh and blood cannot inherit the kingdom, then rock and soil cannot, as we know them. Whatever fulfills flesh and blood, however, fulfills rock and soil as well.

Since this fulfillment is, by definition, not to be realized in the boundaries of our time and space, it is subject to manipulation both by those dualists[4] who discount the agonies of the flesh and by those antidualists who, despite their antidualism, concentrate on political, economic, or military security. The latter can easily be understood as reacting to the onesidedness of the former, which has been the more traditional point of view. Those who wrote the Old and New Testaments, however, did not fall into either of these distorted ways of thinking. Meekness was not viewed as timidity, stoicism, or servility. To be under the rule of the most despicable of tyrants did not mean that one was not free. On the contrary, relying on God, one was free to act in obedience to or in defiance of the ruler. One was free to give up one's life, if need be, not because one knew that a separate, spiritual world awaited if one died, but because one knew that ultimately there is only one creation and that the resurrection fulfills this present, mortal existence. Consequently, one neither despised this world nor considered living well within it as a test of God's faithfulness. One neither counted suffering a triviality nor feared it as a sign of the failure of the gospel. Driven by the promise that the meek shall inherit the earth, disciples can neither allow oppression to go unnoticed nor pretend that the destruction of the oppressor brings true freedom. The truly meek are free to walk without fear or illusion among their brothers and sisters who are dying and to face the assaults of those who are destroying. They are free to obey God's commands, free to

---

4. Dualism here refers to the belief that the world is a combination of spirit and matter. Usually, spirit is said to be basically good; matter, bothersome or evil. Although most Christian theology has been dualistic, this is a result of the adoption of a Greek world view. The understanding of the world found in the Bible is antidualistic.

refuse to worship the tyrant, free to hide, free to serve in the government or to resist the government (at God's command), free to hold out the chest to the firing squad. In a world of Chaos, Darkness, and Death, salvation and true freedom are measured not by whether one lives or dies, is hungry or well-fed, is tortured or tolerated by the powers, but by one's tenacity and courage in the strength of God's grace.

THE BEATITUDE AND DISCIPLESHIP

By definition, meekness involves confidence in the God of Israel. Such confidence, however, is not found only within the following of Jesus, but among those outside the following, as well, whether descendants of Abraham, proselytes, or God-fearers. There are those outside the commonly recognized structures who are outside not because of any lack of confidence in Jesus Christ or in the God of Jesus Christ, but because of their abhorrence of the institutional church's atheism and blasphemy.

A vivid example of the meek, within our own history, has been those Jews who died in the gas chambers of Europe, singing the songs of Zion as the deadly fumes spewed from the faucets.

The disciples are called to step out into the Darkness to proclaim to the meek, wherever they are, that their confidence has not been misplaced. God is faithful.

CHAPTER 9

THOSE WHO HUNGER AND THIRST FOR RIGHTEOUSNESS

In the beginning was true righteousness. God declared all that he had made good. It was just as he had intended it. All things pulsated and moved with rhythms in perfect accord with God's own purposes and intentions. The righteous God and the creation which God had declared good, or righteous, stood before and alongside each other in perfect harmony.

Then—disruption! Seeking a goodness and righteousness of their own, seeking what they considered freedom from the confines of the divine harmony, our primal ancestors turned away from their Creator. In response, the Creator became the Judge and consigned the world to unrighteousness, to independence, to the Darkness, to Exile, to Death.

The world stood now not before, or alongside, but over against God, asserting its own chaotic rhythms over against the divine design. In the chaos of independence, the earth produced thistles and thorns—economic crises, militarism, hunger for power, thirst for control, personal disorientation, boredom, loneliness, cynicism, jealousy, pettiness, disease, and despair.

Once the world stood over against God, however, so fascinating and beguiling was Death, yet so haunting was the memory of God and God's righteousness, that the world created pliable, imitation gods. Human desire was projected onto the cosmic screen.

VIOLENCE AS IMITATION RIGHTEOUSNESS

Alienated from God, we are automatically alienated from one another, left to mortal combat in the name of our false righteousness. In the world's hunger and thirst to see order restored, it is the world's own view of order, the world's own view of righteousness that is craved. The hunger and thirst of the world in Darkness is expressed in the quest for power, more often than not in the name of our gods, even in the name of God. Every revolutionary manifesto in the modern world has affirmed with confidence that God, nature, nature's god, the flow of history, or some other universal Referent is on its side and that the envisioned coming world order is rooted in the Ultimate Referent.

In a world of chaos, the thirst for righteousness erupts as the thirst for revenge. Harmony will be restored, it is assumed, if enough scores for enough victims can be evened—the ones seeking to even the scores usually viewing themselves as either the severest of the victims or the vigilantes of God. The just war is carefully defined to include the provision that fighting and winning the war will create conditions better than before the war—*better,* in a relative sense, becoming a substitute for *good.* Again and again, we go to war to destroy fellow creatures of God. Rather than confessing that we are trapped, along with the enemy, in a tragedy in which we and they share a common guilt, rather than confessing that we are no more righteous than they, we portray the enemy as beastly, heartless, and inhuman and ourselves as the guardians of truth, goodness, and all other human virtues.

RIGHTEOUSNESS AND INSTITUTIONS

In its hunger and thirst for righteousness, the world establishes institutions. Whether institutions be of the sort that have roots beyond human memory, as in the case of the family, or of the sort that are of recent, known origin, as in the case of modern corporations, all institutions are more than mere networks of human relations. They are, as well, realities with lives of their own—realities that have overpowered, engulfed, and distorted those human relations they pretend to preserve and enhance. Institutions are themselves order-imposing realities whose ordering activity is antithetical to God's ordering, is self-serving, and ultimately enhances, though in less recognizable and more insidious form, the very Chaos it pretends to overcome. Even the family, as an institution, is an imposition of structure upon the originally spontaneous relationship among blood kin. As an institution, it was imposed after the Fall of the human race and creates as many problems as it solves.[1]

Seeking to make things become "the way they ought to be," the world slashes with its scythe against the thistles and thorns, struggling to mold new life from dust, stone, and ashes.

The state imposes its righteousness not only on its own citizens, but on other, weaker states as well, and the ultimate means of ensuring that

---

1. I obviously disagree with the usual view that the family is an institution, or order, of the creation, a designation applied by ethicists. The distinction should be made between family as a relationship and family as an institution.

state-defined righteousness is violence. Either let the righteousness of the state satisfy your hunger and thirst for righteousness or face the violence of the state. Of course, if the state can persuade us that its righteousness is God's righteousness, that the state's good and evil are God's good and evil, that the enemies of the state are, by definition, enemies of God, then we will feast on the manna of the state and presume it to be the messianic banquet. Propaganda will have been heard as the Word of God.

None of this is to deny that human government, in general, is established as God's instrument. Its purpose, in God's scheme of things, is to preserve order and establish justice. The history of East and West displays the rise and fall of untold numbers of empires and states, tyrants and saints, into whose hands God has given the awesome responsibility of governing. They have, without exception however, manifested the essential marks of fallen creaturehood in their drive for self-preservation at the expense of those they have governed. As concrete manifestations of the transcendent Powers and Principalities, all governments have relied on violence and death as their ultimate weapons. Even the most humane and noble authorities, without exception, have had no choice but to rely on violence, which is a part of the very nature of the state. Those in quasidemocratic or quasirepublican countries such as the United States have naively assumed that the solution to the deceit and violence of government is to elect "good" men and women to public office. They are oblivious to the fact that government goes on quite apart from the character, will, or motives of individuals who hold office within it. They fail to realize that the only human future possible for anyone remotely approaching goodness (which could only be as a gift of grace, because—as our Lord has reminded us—God alone is good) is rejection, scorn, and, perhaps, execution at the hands of a fallen world. The goodness imparted through grace is automatically viewed by the Darkness as absurdity, weakness, or even evil.

Whoever thinks to bring "Christian influence" to bear on government soon discovers that the only advice or exhortation to which government listens, unless God intervenes, is that which appeals to the state on the basis of its own self-interest and self-preservation. The only humanly possible way to persuade the state to take the gospel seriously is by voicing an ethic born of an ideology—which by biblical definition is a tool of the Fall and, consequently, is not truly "gospel," but is simply another elixir from the caldron.

Any advice or exhortation that consistently and accurately reflects those characteristics incumbent on disciples—namely, the rejection of violence, acceptance of death rather than imposition of it, and unyielding determination to seek the well-being of the enemy, even at the cost of one's own life—is doomed to rejection, for, as a fallen creature, a nation is not capable of committing suicide for the sake of the enemy. Any leader seeking to lead his or her government into that way of life would be rejected by those he or she was charged to lead, either by ballot, trial, or assassination. The state declares righteousness for its people, as it is expected to do—as, outside Eden, it is condemned to do—but it declares a fallen righteousness, a righteousness of violence, the righteousness of the Darkness, the righteousness of Death.

HUNGERING AND THIRSTING AND MOURNING

Hunger and thirst for righteousness go beyond mourning in that mourning is a response to an absence; hunger and thirst for righteousness are the agonizing, enervating, incapacitating reaction of the whole body to the absence of that upon which life depends. As mourning is a reaction to the accomplished work of Death and catastrophe, hunger and thirst are reactions to the immanence of Death and catastrophe.

All hunger and thirst remind us that we are not self-sufficient, but that we depend on others even for the fallen expressions of well-being. I cannot long feed on my own flesh or drink my own fluids. All human hunger and thirst, then, whether or not we perceive them as such, are paradigms of the condition of the world engulfed in the Darkness of the Old Age. Just as one who is starving may, if given options, choose a rich food that only momentarily holds off Death, but does not provide nourishment, so one who starves and thirsts for the presence of God may not know the true nature of the hunger and may grab the first substitute that appears. Such a person may even create false gods on which to feed. We create false nourishment, just as we create false comfort. As the hart (deer) in the wilderness longs for the flowing stream (Ps. 42:1), however, those who accurately perceive the world's exile long for the return of God. Their own tears are their food and drink. With stone for bread and scorpions for eggs, they wait, sustained only by the promise of God's faithfulness.

FOOD TO THE HUNGRY, DRINK TO THE THIRSTY

Those who hunger and thirst for righteousness shall be filled. The disciples, even as hungering and thirsting people whose appetite has not yet been fully satisfied, are called to be those through whom both the hunger is clarified and the feeding is wrought. Disciples are called to be the instruments of that righteousness, primarily by manifesting in their own lives the restoration of order so that those among whom disciples live and move, in the most ordinary as well as the most extraordinary of circumstances, may sense in them that which will clarify their own hunger and give them cause to glorify God. Disciples of Jesus have received at least an initial taste of that righteousness for which we and others long. By his presence among us, the resurrected and transformed Jesus begins the work of restoring our lives. We still hunger and thirst for the full satisfaction of our craving, but we have tasted that righteousness which, in God's own time, will be poured out in overflowing streams. If we see no restoration at all, it is not because God has not extended himself, but because we have, for whatever reason, failed to see.

The apostle Paul, in 2 Corinthians, remarks that those who are in Christ are God's righteousness. To be in Christ is to become the means of God's vindication of his faithfulness, the instrument of God's dependability—reflecting, in our reliability, God's reliability. Caught up in the same chaos as are those around us, we are at the same time set apart to partially fulfill God's promise that those who hunger and thirst for righteousness will be satisfied. By our active, zealous care for all people, we become God's food for the hungry, his drink for the thirsty, those through whom he chooses to restore order to a disoriented world and health to a dying world.

PART THREE

BLESSINGS ON THE FAITHFUL

Blessed are the merciful, for they shall receive mercy.

Blessed are the pure in heart, for they shall see God.

Blessed are the peacemakers, for they shall be called the children of God.

Blessed are those who are persecuted on account of righteousness, for the Reign of Heaven is for them.

Blessed are you when people revile you and persecute you and speak all kinds of evil against you falsely because of me. Rejoice! Be glad! For great is your reward in heaven. So did people persecute the prophets who were before you.

(Matthew 5:7-12)

CHAPTER 10

THE PROPER RESPONSE TO LIBERATION

The second set of four beatitudes speaks of resistance. These beatitudes hold out promise for those who, though living in exile, refuse to live by the values and with the same assumptions of the alien lords. The first four beatitudes were, from one standpoint, promises to, or about, those who found themselves trapped in particular situations; the second four are promises to those who are liberated into certain conditions. If the second four are not heard as promise, they become command, but even then they are not mere legalisms and not rules leading to salvation, but are what is required of the bearers of God's Light in the midst of the Darkness. They are the fruits by which the good tree can be known—not that people might adore the fruit, but that they might celebrate the glory of the God who is able to produce such fruit.

These four are addressed to the disciples and concern not only them, but also those to whom the disciples are sent. There are those outside the circle of disciples who are merciful, who are devoted to God, who seek to be peacemakers, and who are persecuted because of their devotion to God, and the disciples are to acknowledge them and not be surprised when they too are blessed.

Two passages especially indicate this recognition of God's work and blessing outside the circle of the disciples. One is the incident in Mark about the stranger who is exorcising in Jesus' name (Mark 9:38-41). The disciples are told not to forbid the exorcist, because "[whoever] is not against us is for us" (RSV). In Mark's version this saying is preceded by Jesus' observation that no one who does a mighty work in his name will be able for very long to speak evil of him. It is followed by the promise that whoever gives a cup of water to the disciples because they bear the name of—that is, are recognized as servants of—the Messiah will "by no means lose the appropriate reward."

Matthew has not reported the story of the exorcist, but includes in a different setting a modified version of the closing line: "Whoever gives a cup of water to a disciple because he is a disciple shall not lose the appropriate reward" (Matt. 10:40-42).

The other passage in Matthew that carries hope for those outside the community of disciples is the great judgment scene (Matt. 25:31-46). The nations, lined up for judgment, are judged not on the basis of their confession of Jesus as personal Lord and Savior, but on the basis of how they have treated disciples—Jesus' little ones. Those who have ministered to disciples in their need have, in effect, ministered to Christ incognito and are received into the kingdom.

This is in no way an invitation for disciples to be less diligent in their efforts to make disciples of all nations. It is a recognition, however, that outside the assembly, outside the church, there are those who, by the grace of God, have been freed from the Darkness at least enough to be merciful and who, also by the grace of God, are devoted to the God of Israel. Whether for Matthew this was understood as a reference to God-fearers or Jews, such as Joseph of Arimathea or Nicodemus, is impossible to say. What it says beyond Matthew's own intent and understanding is that out there in the Darkness there are still those, preserved by grace, who do not identify themselves with the community of disciples, the church as a recognizable body, but who have been touched by the Light and live empowered by that Light. The task of disciples is neither to acknowledge them as disciples incognito nor to impugn them because they do not bear the name of Jesus, but rather it is to seek to make disciples of all, without condemning those who do not respond. The disciples are chosen to be God's means of bearing Light to the Darkness, and they are to be as zealous in that rule as if the future of the world depended entirely on them, but they are to maintain that zeal in humbling awareness that God is not thereby bound to them with recourse to no other means.

CHAPTER 11

THE MERCIFUL

Even in exile it is possible to resist the claims of the alien lords, the Powers of the Darkness. In the Old Testament Joseph and Daniel show clearly that, within limits, exiles are permitted to participate freely in the alien culture, even to perform certain governmental tasks. Daniel, however, also shows that exercising this permission leads, sooner or later, to a confrontation in which compromise is no longer possible. At that point, the alien society is suddenly revealed in all its previously hidden fury. No society will long tolerate allegiance to anyone or anything other than itself. Eventually, disciples are faced with the responsibility of resisting.

Even Joseph, who died in power and in favor with the alien lords he served, was maintained in power not by accident, but as a part of God's own hidden plan. By Joseph's presence as a representative of Israel, Egypt prospered; and that prosperity led, in turn, to the safety of Israel. In the same manner, Esther was brought to the throne specifically in order to save her people. Even Daniel and his friends were not mere pawns of chance, but were in Shinar as a part of the plan of God.

For disciples, therefore, there can never be an ideological decision either to participate or to refuse to participate in the structures of government. Ideology is a possibility only for atheism or apostasy. For disciples there can only be the question of whether God has opened a particular door at a particular time; if the answer is perceived as yes, the disciples should enter that door aware that though it is the way of service, it may also be the way of martyrdom. True resistance is never a matter simply of saying yes or no to a particular situation, but is always a way of thinking and of conducting oneself in the context of that yes or no. The way in which one says no can be a surrender to the very Darkness to which the no supposedly is spoken, and the way in which one says yes can be sturdy resistance.

MERCY VERSUS THE DARKNESS

Mercy is an enemy of the Darkness. As a primary expression of Death, the Darkness shows no mercy. That mercy to which we refer when a suffering person dies is only relative mercy. That from which the person is said to have been spared is itself an expression of Death. Consequently, although dying may be seen, from a mere human perspective, as relief, it is in fact the relief of Death—the relief of loss, of absence, of annihilation, and not the relief of healing or restoration to life. Dying is not, in the final analysis, mercy—except in the most distorted sense of that word—but is one of Death's fleeting triumphs.

Mercy is resistance to the Darkness. In some ancient schools of philosophy, mercy was viewed not merely as dangerous—a danger to rational, sound judgment—but even as immoral. Mercy for the one proven guilty in a court of law was, and is, considered an injustice with regard to the victim. To argue, on the grounds of mercy, against capital punishment is to fly in the face of the Darkness' demand for retribution. The ultimate justice of the state and of its courts is not mercy, but Death.

In the book of Isaiah, the word most frequently translated "mercy," "compassion," or "love" *(rechem)* refers to the attachment between members of a family. The Hebrew word most often used is, as Phyllis Trible has pointed out, the word whose root also refers to the womb. To have mercy, from this perspective, is to have the same feelings for and determination on behalf of the other person that a mother has for the fruit of her womb. The word seems to be almost a technical word for the covenant relationship between God and Israel and the relationship on the horizontal level envisioned in the covenant.

The Greek word that appears in Matthew's beatitude *(eleeimones)*—a form of the Greek word most often used in the Greek Old Testament to translate all the Hebrew words related to mercy—refers to faithful relationships within the family. Although not everything is clear with regard to Matthew's selection of this word, it is clear that mercy is the manifestation of a sense of unity and solidarity with, and of responsibility for, those who are in need. It is not simply an emotion. It is determined action, which resists the Darkness by asserting community over against the isolation, separation, and distinction characterizing the Darkness.

JESUS AS THE INCARNATION OF MERCY

Jesus is the supreme expression and example of mercy. He acts to overcome those expressions of the Darkness that he encounters, not only within Israel—blindness (Matt. 9:27) and epilepsy (Matt. 17:15-18)—but also, anticipating the assembly's task, among Gentiles as well (Matt. 15:22-28). His parables make clear that to refuse to forgive others and to demand redress is to deny mercy, thereby placing oneself outside the Reign of God (Matt. 18:23-35, esp. v. 33) and being allowed to fall back into the prison of the Darkness.

God's universal mercy is not a reward for human goodness, but is an expression of God's own compassion for and solidarity with his creatures. Although our mercilessness can cause God to decide to withdraw his mercy, it is a mercy God withdraws—indicating that God's mercy precedes human mercy.

In debates with his opponents, Jesus always places mercy over against those institutions established to serve a human need. Twice he quotes Hosea's familiar assertion that God desires "mercy, not sacrifice" (Hos. 6:6; Matt. 9:13; 12:7). On one of those occasions, he admonishes the Pharisees to learn what Hosea meant. Apparently, their concern for ceremonial purity has led the Pharisees to reject any contact with sinners and tax collectors, lest those contacts render them unable to participate in ritual. As leaders of the community, however, the Pharisees should understand that their role in worship is a role exercised on behalf of the entire community. The sacrificial system—indeed, the entire cultic system—was God's gift for the sustenance and renewal of the whole people. The act of worship by any worshiper is properly understood not individualistically, but as intercession for the corporate body of God's people and, ultimately, for the whole world. The act of worship is genuine only when it reflects this corporateness and mutuality. To allow concern for the system systematically and categorically to exclude certain people from the system and from the fellowship of the community is a contradiction. Such protection of the system undercuts the system. Mercy uses the system to provide the aid for which it was intended. To cut off from aid those who need it is to overthrow mercy. Jesus has come to obtain for "those who are sick" the "physician's aid," which the system was to provide, but which the leaders of the people have withheld. It is as if a hospital were to reject certain patients on the grounds that their illness would contaminate the medical services it had been built to provide.

In another incident, much the same point is made with regard to the sabbath. The sabbath, as was the cult, was established as a gift to meet human need. It was established as an act of mercy. If God rested after six days of labor, then surely human beings must need a day of rest from their week of labor, a day of rejuvenation and restoration of health. Now, however, the gift had become protected by a multitude of restrictions. Assuming both human frailty and human self-deceit, and recognizing that violation of the purpose of the sabbath by some would make observation of it by others more difficult, the leaders of the community had attempted to preserve the sabbath's integrity, thinking thereby to protect its ability to provide that mercy for which it was established.

In this world of Darkness, however, institutions look to their own interests, not to the needs of those for whom they were established. Institutional regulations to protect the human-oriented integrity of the institution quickly begin to operate not for the preservation of the institution's integrity, but for its survival. Such had been the fate of the sabbath. (Of course, the Pharisees in Matthew's Gospel represent neither all Jews of the era nor all Pharisees. Jesus himself acknowledges that the Pharisees' tradition recognized the propriety of suspending certain restrictions of torah when human need is involved.)

Jesus restores the sabbath's identity as a day of mercy, and disciples are to understand proper activity on the sabbath in terms of Jesus' example. He accuses the scribes and Pharisees of deception and pretense. Pretending to be devoted to torah, they have emphasized the wrong areas of torah. The tithing of cummin, mint, and dill is not attacked on the grounds that these are insignificant. As spices, condiments, and medicinal herbs they could have important roles in sacrifices and in the medical needs of the temple. Those areas in which human beings and God are held together, however, are "weightier matters of torah" than are those in which God alone is the one to be considered, and excessive concentration on the latter to the detriment of the former can result in a loss of confidence on the part of the oppressed—loss of confidence in the mercy of God. If God's representatives are not merciful, how can one assume that God is merciful? In this way, the tithes themselves are undercut.

In yet a third place (Matt. 15:21-28), Jesus has mercy on a Canaanite woman and her daughter by healing the daughter. By the standards of the natural world, Jesus should have refused mercy to this member of a blood enemy people. To have mercy on the enemy is an act of madness. For Jesus, however, the desire to hurt, to force one's will on another, to seek one's own well-being at the expense of another—that is true madness.

The full dimensions of the promise of this beatitude are suggested elsewhere in Matthew's Gospel by references to those who are rewarded or blessed on the basis of their mercy to disciples of Jesus. Those who have given a cup of cold water to a disciple because of the disciple's identity "will not lose their reward" (Matt. 10:40-42). On the day of judgment, those who have visited disciples when they were in prison, fed disciples when they were hungry, clothed them when they were naked, or cared for them when they were sick will discover that they have been ministering, unknowingly, to

Jesus and will hear the invitation to enter into the realm of God's Reign (Matt. 25:31-40).

For a church that has come, over the centuries, to think of the definitive goal of its mission as conversion of individuals to a cognitive affirmation of Jesus Christ as personal Lord and Savior, such passages are sharp jolts. Those who are not among the followers of Jesus are blessed and received into God's Reign on the basis of their mercy to Jesus' disciples!

Is this not precisely in keeping, however, with the ancient promise to Abraham—the promise that God would bless those who blessed Abraham and curse those who cursed him, that in Abraham and his descendants the whole world would be blessed?

To acknowledge that disciples are bound in freedom to the Sermon does not enable them thereby to use the Sermon as an instrument to determine who participates in God's Reign and who does not. God refuses to be bound to our judgments, even to those made on the basis of the written witness of his word to us.

MERCY'S UNIVERSALITY

Mercy is not to be confined to action on behalf of only those within the community of faith. As indicated later in the Sermon, mercy is to be universally expressed in unreserved acts of good will for all people. It drives the true disciple out into the Darkness, and there, in the very heart of the Darkness, it is the human means by which those still dominated by the Darkness can be made aware of the Light.

Nor may we assume that mercy is to be shown only toward the oppressed and not toward the oppressor. The beatitude contains no qualifying phrases. The ethos of the Darkness compels the oppressed, when they have opportunity and means, to rise up against their oppressors and to show no mercy; and even disciples may be inclined to cheer when they see the trampled, the bruised, and the bloodied finally turn and plunge the sword into the vitals of the tyrant. This, however, is the ethos of the Darkness. The goal of the Darkness is to consign the enemy to Death.

Disciples are not to be concerned with revenge, with appropriating power, or with worshiping Death, but with mercy. The meek are not merely to await God's deliverance with *no* action toward the oppressor, but, rather are earnestly to seek the oppressor's well-being. The meek and the mourners are not released from their Darkness so that they may become new Lords of the Darkness. Those who have been in the land of Death are not set free in order to send their captors into exile. God does not intend a prisoner exchange with Death, but the defeat of Death and an end once and for all to its right to hold prisoners.

Inevitably, of course, the question of justice is raised. There is no conflict between God's mercy and God's justice, but only between God's mercy and both human mercy and human justice. Justice, in the Bible, is the restoration of equilibrium. The judges of Israel were figures charged with the task of restoring God's order. True justice calls for the well-being of all; anything else is injustice, or is the world's justice of revenge and retaliation.

Mercy is more than mere sympathy. It is the exercise of power on behalf of the one in need. Mercy, then, not only is not incompatible with, or in conflict with, justice, but also is the driving force of justice. Justice is one face of mercy. By the exercise of mercy, the disciples do not undercut justice, but bear witness to God's justice. The assembly, consequently, must neither imitate nor bless either the world's oppression or its counteroppression. The assembly that calls for the oppressed to rise up and throw off the yoke of tyranny is not preaching true liberation but bondage to Death and the Darkness, which are the very nature of the Old Age.

Unfortunately, the alternative to revolution has usually been misunderstood to be sluggish acquiescence. Such is not the alternative envisioned in the gospel. In those New Testament books where acquiescence to cruelty is urged, it is the acquiescence of love, concerned neither with being morally right nor, in a sense, even with success in being obedient. It simply is concerned with glorifying God and bearing witness to him. Biblically sound liberation theology centers on liberation from the alternatives of the Old Age—revolt and sluggish acquiescence, and liberation to the new possibilities of God's reign—the possibilities of mercy and love.

Nor does the gospel call the oppressed to submit to the oppressor in absolute, ultimate obedience. It proclaims that mercy—not revenge, not domination—characterizes God's reign. The oppressed who show mercy on their oppressors do not know what effect their mercy will have. The result may be martyrdom. The Reign of God is still a hidden reign. On the other hand, since God still opens the eyes of the blind, the result may be conversion. Either result holds out the possibility that at least some people, seeing, will recognize the good works and glorify God.

JESUS AND LIBERATION

The interpretations of Jesus' preaching and the New Testament's teaching about liberation as a basis for armed military action overlooks (1) that it did not mean this for Jesus, (2) that in those instances where Jesus opposed Rome or the religious authorities, his actions were precisely the opposite of armed, military action, (3) that the New Testament books consistently exalt martyrdom above militarism, and (4) that the Gospels and Epistles set Jesus forth as the model for his followers. Just as his Reign is not of this world

(John 18:36), the shape and substance of that Reign's liberation are not of this world.

The example of Jesus driving money changers from the temple is frequently cited as an example of his acceptance and use of violence. That action, however, was a prophetic act, one unrepeatable as a pattern of conduct. When Jesus drove out the money changers, he was doing as Ezekiel, Jeremiah, and Isaiah had done before him: He was carrying out a prophetic act that would set in motion dynamics of the Word of God.

To take up arms in military revolt is not to perform a prophetic act, but is to attempt to set up a new regime, which must be perpetuated by force. No matter how sympathetic we may be with a particular rebellion, even if we come to feel it necessary to participate in the rebellion, such actions have no connection with Jesus' actions. To speak of war as peace and of armed rebellion as the way to freedom makes sense in terms of the world's language, but from the standpoint of the Bible, it is Babel, what Orwell called "doublespeak."

Because of the multitudes who suffer oppression from tyrants, it is difficult to write such words today. The hardship of the oppressed ranges from inconvenience to agonizing death. To speak any other way, however, would be to twist the Bible to fit our own desire for release from guilt. On the other hand, any effort to use the gospel to secure our own position and to avoid acknowledging our own corporate guilt in the tyranny of this world is also to twist the gospel. It is no less blasphemous to use the scriptures to defend our actions for liberty than to use them to defend our enslavement of others. To do either is to betray the gospel. "Blessed are the merciful" is applicable equally to oppressor and to oppressed. To use the beatitudes to defend our own position among the oppressors is to stand in the ranks of those who are threatened with no mercy from God. Any follower of Jesus who speaks of such an alternative outside a genuine solidarity with those who are oppressed may speak doctrine, does speak rules and regulations, but does not speak the word of God. Nor does that one proclaim the freedom the word promises. To make of mercy a rule or regulation is not to speak the gospel, but to betray it. Only when the speaker is in such unity with the oppressed that the question becomes, How best can we live out the gospel with its freedom and its mercy? is the beatitude truly spoken as gospel.

The offense of those who have not shown mercy to others is not merely that they either have oppressed others or have ignored the oppressed, but that they also have borne false witness against God. They are subjects of the One whose basic character is manifested in mercy, but they have acted as though that One knows no mercy. They are salt that, having lost its savor, is fit only to be thrown out. Yet, ironically, in that very "throwing-out," in God's refusal to have mercy on them, they become, despite themselves, a sign to the world. By his refusal to have mercy on the merciless he reveals his judgment on oppression and on silent acquiescence in oppression.

MERCY AND POWER

Mercy presupposes power. It may be economic, political, and military means to overcome others turned to the welfare of others. It may be only the power to appeal to God on behalf of others. The genuine restoration of our humanity, however, creates sympathy for and sensitivity to the plight of the opponent and demands that we manifest mercy. Mercy seeks to understand the opposition of others, attempts to place itself in the situation of others. Who can measure the power of the word of forgiveness of the victim whose body is pierced by the sword or torn apart by a bomb as that word is spoken, perhaps unheard by the executioner, at the moment of death? Who can know the power of the prayers of the martyrs beyond this moment in history? Mercy presupposes a power not of this world. It is the power of God as he chooses to use it, but when God does so choose, it is the power of the powerless!

MISUNDERSTANDINGS OF MERCY

Like meekness, mercy is not to be misunderstood as surrender to the wishes and desires of the Darkness. Mercy does not say, "Whatever your goals, no matter how destructive of human life, I will not oppose you." Mercy seeks the well-being of the enemy even at the cost of one's own life, but that does not entail allowing the enemy always to determine what is his or her or their own well-being. Mercy feeds the enemy when the enemy is hungry, clothes the enemy when the enemy is naked, shelters the enemy when the enemy is homeless, and ministers to the enemy when the enemy is sick or imprisoned. Mercy is love at work, love in the New Testament sense of agape: complete, unqualified determination to see the other's well-being accomplished, even if the other is the enemy and it costs you your life.

Mercy for the murderer does not mean handing the murderer the weapon with which to commit the murderous deed. Nor, however, does mercy permit taking the murderer's life. To the cry, "But where is your mercy for the victim?" mercy's reply is, "The victim is dead, and beyond our ability to help. We must look to the well-being of the survivors—both the murderer's and that of the murderer's kin and the victim's kin." The well-being of the murderer does not mean releasing him or her to murder again. Murder, however, more often than not, is not planned or plotted, but is a relatively spontaneous response. To seek the well-being of the murderer, then, means to bear witness by how we deal with the murderer, to the love of God, in the hope that God might take our care and concern and use it as the instrument of divine transformation.

Nor is mercy to be confused with naiveté. Mercy, though reflecting the innocence of the dove, is undergirded by the wisdom of the serpent. Mercy is thoroughly realistic. Indeed, genuine mercy is more realistic than those who accuse it of being simple and naive, for mercy—with the wisdom of the serpent—knows fully well the terrible potential for wickedness that lies in the human breast. Mercy knows fully well that its future likely is martyrdom. Yet, as a lamb among wolves, it refuses to become a wolf, or even to seek disguise in wolf's clothing, in order to survive.

RECEIVING MERCY

Those who resist the Darkness by acts of mercy are blessed. They receive the promise that as they have treated others as though they were family, God will regard *them* as family and will come to *their* aid. No doubt, this refers in part to the day of judgment, but, given the meaning of mercy as coming to one's aid, it also refers to the present. Those who come to the aid of others in need will find that in their time of difficulty God will at least strengthen them to endure. If they die at the hands of the oppressor, God will strengthen them to die with courage and with hope for life in the transformed creation.

We have, then, not a legalistic rule that, in order to be rewarded, one must follow despite any hatred for another person. Mercy is not simply holding back a grudge or suppressing a hostile act, but is extending care and concern. When confronting the enemy, mercy is manifested as forgiveness. Such mercy is possible only in that freedom which God brings as he reasserts his sovereign power. Wherever it is found, it is to be celebrated by disciples as a sign of the universal mercy of God.

CHAPTER 12

THE PURE IN HEART

This beatitude undercuts all idolatries. The heart—which, biblically speaking, refers to the desires, motives, will, and intentions—may be either directed toward one goal or fragmented and directed toward competing and conflicting goals. Whatever one's heart is set upon as the goal to which every act is directed is one's god. The impure heart, then—the heart of conflicting loyalties and competing gods—is a heart divided against itself. Both the cluttered, impure heart and the heart that makes something other than Israel's God the sole center of devotion engage in idolatry. Only the heart that is single-mindedly set on God, in contrast to idols, can truly be called pure. Only to these does God make himself known.

Psalm 24 promises God's self-disclosure to those who have not turned to other gods and who have not committed acts of injustice or violence against others. To these, God will show his face. Although from one standpoint, when the glory of the Lord is revealed, all flesh shall see it (Isa. 40:5), it is specifically revealed—and, consequently, is perceived as glorious—to those who have awaited it with patience and confidence, in acts of mercy toward their oppressors, and without idols of any sort.

Purity of heart is neither a reference to sexual desires, whether those desires be licit or illicit, nor an attack on so-called creature comforts. It is possible, of course, for any sexual desire, licit or illicit, to become the one thing that gives meaning to all of life, or for creature comforts to become the center of our concern and the goal of our striving. The beatitude, however, is concerned not with the content of our thought, but with the direction of our desires. It neither condemns, discourages, approves, nor commends sexual desire. Sexual desire is an element of human nature. As such, it is marred, as are all other elements, by the conditions of the Fall. Sexuality can be used to manifest devotion and affection or to impose violence and pain. Through grace, however, it can be the means of manifesting that determined love for another, which, despite the limitations of sin, bears witness to

God's own love. If those mystics who have attempted to use the eros of sexual attraction to convey the agape of the divine-human relationship have engaged in excess, surely it is equally an error to assume that the relationship manifested in the human sexual encounter is by definition unrelated to the character of God. By the human faithfulness manifested in sexual relationships, we bear witness to the faithfulness of God to the creation.

PURITY OF HEART AND IDOLATRY

This beatitude is concerned, in essence, with the first and second commandments: No gods are to take the place of Israel's God, and no tangible objects are to be assumed to bear the inherent power of God or are to be viewed as having the power of God inevitably resting on them. One of the roots of Israel's rejection of representations of God, no doubt, was that God had provided his own representative in the human race. That is, human beings were created, originally, to be God's representatives in the world. Even if one of the consequences of the Fall was the loss of the image, it is not a prerogative of human beings to establish other representations. To assume that any tangible object is in any sense a representation of God is to regard it as an object to be defended and exalted, even at the expense of human life. Obedience to God is not expressed by the defense and exaltation of objects, however, but by justice and mercy.

IDOLS, PURITY OF HEART, AND THE LIVING GOD

Objects of religious veneration and devotion are especially vulnerable to the idol-making tendencies of the human heart, because we so easily attribute to them an inherent ability to lift us to God. We make a certain identification of the object with God, and the object then is assumed to bear some quality or "nature" that renders it semidivine. The Living God, however, rejects all such attributions of automatic possession of dignity or power. God allows no object to be identified with himself, either as a representation or as a supposed instrument, in any manner that would imply that it partakes automatically of his power.

Any doctrine or creed presumed to be more than a humanly constructed pointer to a mystery that cannot be defined is an idol.

Any theology that pretends to be more than a human formulation seeking to interpret divine revelation, a formulation created in sin and frailty, is idolatry.

Any work of art—such as, for example, the magnificent mural on the ceiling of the Sistine Chapel or Salmon's Head of Christ—that comes to be viewed as more like God than some other work has become an idol.

When sacraments are assumed to have inherent power—power apart from God's active presence—they have ceased to be true sacraments and have instead become amulets and idols.

Any object, liturgy, or thought perceived and treated as though it is capable of lifting us to God, any object, liturgy, or thought that is created as a "handle" to enable us to reach God or as a means of re-creating the encounter with God, is an idol.

Much popular piety—such as that reflected in most revivalism, in insistence on spectacular conversion experiences and speaking in tongues, in efforts toward "spiritual formation," and the like—is idolatry in that it lays down unvarying rules of how God works and of the characteristics of the apprehension of God's revelation, presence, or call. To insist that the apprehension of God's presence will unfailingly be characterized by a particular feeling or "experience" is to identify too closely the human experience with the divine presence. Experience subtly displaces deity. God is displaced by an idol. Faith is displaced by religion.

IDOLS AND HOLINESS

To declare something holy is not automatically to make of it an idol. To be holy is to be set apart, specifically, to be set apart for use by God or by humans in relation to God. The elements of the sacraments, for example, once consecrated, are not to be handled commonly. Wine (or grape juice) and bread not needed for the communion are not to be returned to the bottle or to the box from which they came, for they now belong specifically to God, not to us. They can no more be reconsecrated at a later time than can a person be rebaptized. Nevertheless, they have no power within themselves. They communicate power only when God uses them. Their holiness consists not of what they possess, but of their being possessed by God.

The idol has also been set apart, but its separateness is based on the assumption that in and of itself it can help in the human quest to make contact with the divine. This inherent ability may be of the extreme sort, which requires praying to the idol or avoidance of touching it. It may, on the other hand, be of the more rational sort, in one's protest that the object or symbol simply helps one to concentrate on God. If asked why this particular object or particular symbol is better able to serve this role, one may point to history, experience, or even revelation. In the final analysis, however, either the assertion that *I* am better able to concentrate on God or that the object or symbol is better able to aid my concentration on God attributes a connecting point between the thing and God that is missing in other things. Why should a triangle be any more helpful than a Cheshire Cat in our effort to reach God with our thoughts? The Transcendent God is not more like a triangle than like a Cheshire Cat. The triangle, of course, is said to represent the Trinity, and the Trinity, in turn, is said to be the three-in-one nature of God, which God himself has revealed. In fact, the Trinity is a concept developed by ancient and medieval theologians as a means of interpreting the biblical witness in a new cultural setting. This is not to suggest that those theologians were wrong, but simply to point out the human side of the doctrine.

Theologians developed the doctrine of the Trinity and the many versions of the doctrine not to capture God, but to interpret the biblical witness. As a three-sided figure representing the Trinity, the triangle—as the representation of a representation—actually removes us a step farther from God.

Visible objects such as symbols, therefore, are always in danger of becoming idols because we so easily assume they can help us in some way to reach closer to God with our thoughts. All such supposition presumes that we can reach God of our own accord, that at any time of the day or night, all we have to do is concentrate on the object, for God is there waiting for us to reach up and touch him—that he gives to these objects the indelible ability to serve as ladder, or doorway, or means of the human ascent to God. They are, in brief, assumed to possess a certain divine quality and are, consequently, as certainly idols as were the Asherah and the Temple. Only when an object—including the Bible and the sacramental elements, or an action, prayer, or other components of worship—is embraced by God and used as God's means to reach us, is this able to serve as the means of divine-human communication or contact.

The ordinary idols of modern Western society do not parade themselves as challengers to God, but rather as self-effective means of devotion to God. Serve God by serving the nation; obey God by obeying the state; love God by loving human beings; give to God by giving to the church. Always, the assumption is made that the act brings us into contact with God.

A similar call comes from modern expressions of ancient religions—Hare Krishna, Transcendental Meditation, Zen, Unification, Scientism, Rosicrucianism, and so forth. But it also comes within Christianity from those who seek a new dignity for certain elements of gnosticism, from Pelagian evangelistic movements with slogans such as "I found it!" and from those who impose some further authority over against the canonical testimony—such as Mormons with the writings of Joseph Smith, Christian Science with the writings of Mary Baker Eddy, and even overzealous Methodists and Lutherans with the theology of John Wesley and Martin Luther, respectively. Whether the call is to open oneself to the God who is the source of all religions, to tap the power that pervades the universe, to reach up and take hold of God, or to latch onto some infallible interpretation of the Word of God, it all boils down to the same idolatry, the same denial of the gospel. It is the subtle attempt of the Darkness to persuade us that contact with God is in our own hands. The god with whom contact is made, however, is not the Transcendent God, but is the power of the Darkness, which, ironically, like the Living God, has found us rather than our finding him.

IDOLATRY AND THE BIBLE

Even the Bible can become an idol. The authoritative written tradition, simply as a printed sign, has no inherent life. It lives only when it becomes the bearer of life. As mere writing, the Bible is not something to be heard, but something to be looked at. I can see the words, I can see the style of the script, the color of the ink, the texture of the paper. I can even find a Bible with Jesus' words printed in *red!* But whether the words are in blue, black, red, or purple ink is irrelevant as long as they are only something to look at or something to think about.

To look to the Bible, therefore, is not necessarily to turn to God for direction. To look to the Bible as a printed text is to look to bloodless, inorganic, synthetic human creations. It is to place the Bible between ourselves and God. It is to make of the printed page an idol, an idol to which we really do ascribe power.

When the Living God chooses to speak through the written words, those words remain ink on paper, but at the same time they become the common words through which we are addressed by the divine Word. The rule becomes the means by which God's instruction is spoken to us, here and now. The theory of the future, the apocalyptic vision, becomes a promise to us, here and now, undergirding us with strength and courage.

This is the reason why the movement to return daily reading of the Bible to the public schools should be so objectionable to disciples of Jesus Christ. The public schools do not bear witness to the God of Jesus Christ, but to the god of the Republic. The God of Jesus Christ is no more the god to whom public prayers are addressed, to whom reference is made in the pledge of allegiance and on our currency, who is mentioned in the Declaration of Independence, and who is celebrated by the advocates of civil religion, than were the gods of the Romans.

The god of the Republic—Nature's god, as the Declaration of Independence calls him—is a god who blesses this nation above others, who gave the land to the white man and led in the extermination of native peoples, and who blessed the bombs of numerous wars. This god is, in effect, the god of Canaan, the god of Babylon, the god of the Darkness. This god is, bluntly, the Prince of Darkness—Satan himself.

THE ALIEN GOD OF THE CHURCH

To say that the church now worships not the true God of Israel, but Satan, is simply to say that the church today finds itself in the predicament of the establishment represented by Jesus' opponents in the Gospel of John. They claimed in all sincerity to have Abraham as their father, but Jesus pronounced them the children of the Diabolical One. Claiming to be men of vision, they were, in fact, blind. They did not understand their actual condition, and were so angered by Jesus' description of who they were that they were determined to kill him.

Yet, to say that the church worships Satan does not mean that every Christian, every congregation, or every denomination blindly does so. It is to make a pronouncement about the church as a corporate being—a corporate being whose condition makes an impact upon all within it, but whose condition does not override the ability of God, in his grace, to preserve a faithful remnant in the midst of the apostasy. There are, no doubt, faithful disciples, as well as faithful worshipers of God outside the strict circle of disciples. Indeed, to assert that the church as such is so entrapped neither permits disciples to make judgments on this or that specific individual nor calls for a search for those specific individuals who are trapped. Pulling up the tares risks pulling up wheat as well, and in the present case it is not specific shoots that are the problem, but the field itself. To burn the field would destroy the wheat as well. Above all, it is not given us to decide which shoots are which or to burn the field as an act of judgment.

There is a connection between the apostasy of the church and the silence, or abandonment, of God. Although the silence most often declared is a silence of the idols, who could never speak anyway, there is reason to believe that God also is silent, has abandoned the church and the idols. The cultural—and in some instances countercultural—identity of the church, the absence of any distinctly new element in any of the church's pronouncements, and the varying degrees of identity with the nation in both Eastern and Western wings of the church bear witness to the silence of God so far as the institution goes. Consequently, they also bear witness to God having, at least for the moment, abandoned the institution as his instrument.

This does not automatically mean that those within the idolatrous community should leave the community, as though remaining within will rob them of some imagined purity, or as though leaving will restore or maintain such purity. Only by the call of God is it relevant for the remnant either to leave or to stay, and it is quite possible for God's call to be as diverse as are the people he has preserved. Whether the call to stay or to leave is heard, the reason for either is that the remnant might continue, in the midst of the Darkness, to bear witness to the Light in that place where each is called.

For the pure in heart, no person, no nation, no program, no object, no organization, no institution, no personal goals, nothing other than God, can be or will be the primary focus of the will or of desire. To no one and no thing will be attributed the ability to give meaning, coherence, or value to life and history.

The admonition of Romans, Ephesians, and 1 Peter with regard to being subject to other persons or institutions is always in the context of the command that God alone is to be Master. Earthly overlords are those to whom we are subject in that we acknowledge their role as human maintainers of order. There is no indication that we are unquestioningly to obey, no matter what is commanded.

From this standpoint, the beatitude is related to Satan's test of Jesus in the desert. "All these [kingdoms of the earth] I will give you, if you will fall down and worship me" (Matt. 4:9 RSV). The scope of this test is understood fully only when we realize that Satan is the agent of Death. His suggestion that Jesus worship him means, "Acknowledge that in this world destruction and chaos are so overwhelming in their impact that not even God can bring anything good from them. Acknowledge that Death is stronger than God; worship Death as God."

The alternative to such a challenge is not to view the agonies of the world as trivial or even as answerable and understandable from a human point of view. Nor is it to assume that we will always be able to speak a comforting human word in the face of catastrophe. We may be able to do no more than sit and share the agony. Satan's challenge to Jesus, in effect, is that since we cannot give a human answer or provide human comfort, we should confess that Death is the most powerful thing in the world and that God is powerless, or unconcerned. "Embrace the Darkness. Affirm its insights and values!" Ironically, our efforts to fight Death are also acknowledgments of its power and are, therefore, the worship of Death. Purity of heart, on the other hand, is the determination to trust God even when our experience tells us that it is foolish or futile to do so. Purity of heart trusts God not to do what we think God should do, but in the darkest moment, to accomplish what he wills.

ON SEEING GOD

The pure in heart will see God. In the Old Testament, references to seeing God are of two kinds. One is the vision of God in the last day when he reveals himself as deliverer and judge. The other is that vision which comes to the person who stays overnight in the temple. In both cases, the emphasis is on God revealing himself, not on our seeing because we look.

In fact, in no instance in the Bible does anyone ever see God in and of himself. God is hidden by that which is seen, hidden by that through which he reveals himself. The thunder and fire do not show us God, but are the means by which God reveals himself, even while refusing to show himself.

Although God has cast the world into exile and enshrouded it with Darkness, it is possible, by the power of God, to await God's appearance. It is possible in the midst of chaos to maintain purity of heart.

Purity of heart looks neither to the imaginary gods (which are imaginary only when compared with God, yet very real to those not pure in heart), nor to idols, whether the idol be the written text of the Bible, common sense, statistics, common courtesy, academic freedom, academic integrity, racial kinship, consensus decision-making, process planning, moral or physical purity, national defense, or any of hundreds of other noble or ignoble elements of life, which, by being turned into idols, lose any nobility they might otherwise have had. The call of idolatry is Circe's call. Purity of heart closes its ears to all such calls and listens only for the voice of the Living God.

CHAPTER 13

THE PEACEMAKERS

Just as in the beginning there was true righteousness, so also in the beginning was there peace. Throughout the creation there were harmony, order, and health—true peace. In the Fall, this peace, which was of the basic nature of things, was lost. The order God had established was disrupted, and the creation was allowed to slide back into Chaos. Harmony was displaced by discord. Health was attacked by Death. Everywhere, the Darkness qualified the Light. The history of the world, consequently, has been a history of Darkness. Even those times that have been sufficiently free from tension and disorder to be called times of peace have always been temporary, have contained the seeds of Death, and, eventually, have given way to all the horrors of which we are capable.

PEACE AND CHAOS

For most of the cultures of the ancient Near East, the violence of the present world is rooted in the concept of the very formation of the world. In the myths and metaphors of those cultures, the formation of the world takes place when the chief warrior of the gods defeats the cosmic dragon of chaos and divides her body into two parts, one part forming the earth, the other part forming the heavens. In these stories, violence is perceived to be at the very heart of reality. The universe exists as the result of a primal act of violence.

The biblical narrative about origins is strikingly different from this dominant ancient Near Eastern one. Although the metaphors of the dragon and the dragon slayer appear frequently in the biblical texts, the creation is said to have taken place not by violence and warfare, but by the simple, authoritative, spoken Word of God. In the Genesis narratives, violence is not characteristic of God's way with the world, but is his reaction to the continuing rebellion of his creatures. In Genesis 1–11, the only violence enacted by God is the Flood, and the wording of the story suggests that God decides that the Flood solved nothing. Even when God is portrayed as using violence to achieve his purposes, he is portrayed, usually, as using the violence already present among his creatures and turning it to an eventually peaceful purpose. Certainly, God's ultimate plans are for *shalom*—peace, health, renewal, wholeness—as seen in Isaiah 2:1-5; 9:6-7; 11:1-9; 52:7-8; Jeremiah 31:31-33; and Ezekiel 40–48, to name merely a few passages. God's ruler will be the Prince of Peace, and the whole earth will be a peaceable domain.

PEACE IN GOD

Isaiah 2 portrays the future restoration of peace as a world in which all the nations come to Mount Zion to learn torah. They come to Zion, however, not because of any sacredness of the spot itself, but because that is where the one true God is to be found. Zion is exalted as the place where God establishes his throne, but it is God's presence, not Zion's exaltation, that is crucial. The heart of the passage, then, is that the future healing of the nations is to come as a result of the nations turning to God's torah for their day-to-day governance. Cast aside are natural, human wisdom and the reasoning of power politics, and in their place is the divine instruction.

The New Testament, in its hope for the future, radically alters the status of Zion. Jesus declares that the day is coming when God will be worshiped neither on Gerazim nor on Zion, for God is not a material being and cannot be worshiped in a material place of concentration. Further, the book of the Revelation portrays future Jerusalem in ways that make it impossible to view the New Jerusalem as a spot of time-and-space geography. Jerusalem, as a city in our human categories of time and space, is caught up in an unknown future that transcends time and space.

This poses no serious problem for the Isaiah oracle, however, for, as already pointed out, the key to Isaiah 2 is not the exaltation of Mount Zion, but the presence of God. The nations walk in peace because they follow God's instructions, not because they make pilgrimage to a holy mountain. In response to God's instruction, tools of war are transformed into tools of life. Instruction in warfare ceases. Micah 4 extends this vision by speaking even of the absence of fear as each person relaxes under his or her own vine and fig tree, no longer encamped in the tents of war and death.

Jeremiah 31 speaks of the new covenant in terms of torah so thoroughly ingrained within the human will, so thoroughly serving as the root of all human motivation, that even to have a desire is to manifest the will of God. Torah is carved into the heart as a name is engraved on a brass plate. There is no more turning outward to discover what God teaches, for God's instructions will have become, by an act of God, so internalized that they are instinctive.

JESUS AS THE MODEL FOR PEACEMAKING

Jesus himself, of course, is the supreme model of peacemaking. He has already cast aside the sword and spear. He already lives solely by the Word of God. As the instrument of God, he brings God's peace. Even in the face of death, he refuses to defend himself. He dies rather than call forth the angelic forces to destroy his enemies that he might live. Unable to show objectively that his death will accomplish anything or will have some beneficial effect, he dies, trusting in the God who has, for the moment, abandoned him. His words, from one Gospel to another, include words of personal desolation ("My God, My God, why have you forsaken me?" "I thirst"), words of promise ("Today, you will be with me in Paradise"), words of commitment to God ("Father, into your hands I commit my life's breath"), and words of peacemaking ("Father, forgive them. They don't know what they are doing").

THE NATURE OF HUMAN PEACEMAKING

Because of the thoroughness of the Darkness's impact, apart from God's intervention there can be no true peace. Under the Reign of God, however, peace is inevitable. There shall be peace! The biblical oracles and visions are not intended to stir us to create peace, but to enable us to anticipate peace and, in anticipation, to live even now as people of hope. In the same way, the disciples are to proclaim God's blessing on those who, in the midst of Darkness and exile, respond to God's peacemaking by imitating him. Since God alone creates peace, this imitation can be fully accomplished only as the community or the disciple gives itself, himself, or herself confidently into God's hands to be used as God's instrument of peace. God, however, does not ridicule anyone who with unselfish motives earnestly strives for peace; and whenever those strivings bear momentary, limited fruit, they become, by the grace of God, anticipations of God's true peace.

PEACE AND THE ENEMY

Together, the beatitude on mercy and the nature of true peace (a combination of healing, renewal, and restoration) make it impossible to define peace primarily as the defeat of the enemy. Rather, true peace involves the elimination of enmity. True peacemaking seeks true freedom for all—the liberation of the oppressor from the bondage of oppressing as well as the liberation of the oppressed from the bondage of oppression.

Without freedom there is no peace. In biblical terms, however, freedom is not independence from God or independence from one another, but is release from the Darkness—release from Sin, from Death, and from self-seeking. Freedom is complete alignment with the will of God and devoted service to others. Freedom is release from the assertion of human power and authority over others, for from these come only oppression and subjugation. To seek power over the oppressors is to seek not their peace, but their death. Even in so-called just war, to seek power over the oppressor is to exercise preference for one set of victims over another.

Of course, the Bible is filled with passages concerning God's judgment on and defeat of the wicked, and Luke's version of the beatitudes is complemented by woes said to be laid up for those who are now rich, filled, and merry. The "Magnificat" (Luke 1:46-55) speaks of God turning the tables on both the lowly and the mighty. That, however, is a celebration of God's justice and God's concern for the oppressed. It is not a program for human revolution in which the overturned table becomes a new form of uprightness. In purely secular terms, the standard sequence of events in so-called revolutions manifests not the progress of true peace and true liberation, but the transfer of power and authority from one group to another. The wielders of power and authority are released from that bondage to another more visibly recognized as such. Even when certain sufferings and injustices are alleviated, those who have been under obvious bondage are released to a more subtle and invisible imprisonment. Those who have assumed earthly power find that anxiety becomes their daily companion and that the price of power is eternal vigilance and paranoia.

This is not to contend that wars to ease the yoke of earthly oppression should never be fought or that the social and political conditions that arise from a so-called war of liberation are never any better than those that evoked the combat. The criteria by which the just war has traditionally been defined may be applied, within limits, to specific situations. One must question, however, the legitimacy of such exalted terms as *justice, liberty,* and *peace,* no matter how much more desirable the new situation may be. When social conditions make war desirable or inevitable, those who follow Jesus must not seek, by manipulating language, to make of war anything other than what it is: an expression of our fallen condition. If Christians decide that matters have become so unbearable that they must kill, let no one who has not shared their lot condemn them for that course of action. Only those without sin are in a position to cast the first or the last stone. At the same time, to defend such action as an expression of love or justice is to turn the cross of Jesus on its head.

FRIENDSHIP AND ENMITY: A DOUBLE-SIDED COIN

A basic reality of any state of oppression or warfare is that it imposes on both sides bonds that threaten to destroy both. The wall of separation between them grows out of that which, paradoxically, binds them even more closely together in their mutual plunge—the power of Darkness and Death. A basic characteristic of the fallen world is that opponents need one another. We were created to live in society, not in isolation. God has made us not only for himself so that, in Augustine's words, we are restless till we find our rest in him, but also for one another, so that we are equally restless without other human beings. Friendship and hostility, comradeship and oppression—all are ways of expressing our sociality. In friendship, we trust the other and see no need to manipulate the other to preserve our lives or those things we count valuable. In hostility, the social aspect of our nature is twisted, expressing our fallenness, and we seek to bind ourselves to the other in domination and exploitation.

PEACEMAKING AND THE CREATION

Peacemaking is not merely a work on behalf of nations and individuals, but is a work on behalf of the entire creation. Genesis 3 depicts the hostility that has set in between human beings and animals, between human beings and the earth, and between male and female. The struggle between the descendants of the woman and those of the serpent typifies the continuing separation between human beings and the other animals, a separation extended in the wake of the Flood when humans are given permission to eat animals for food. The desire of woman for man and the domination of woman by man (Gen. 3:16*b*) are not sexual desire and sexual mastery, but are the mutual effort of one sex to control the other.[1] Such mutual efforts at exploitation were not a part of the original condition of the creation, but reflect the character of the Darkness. The earth for which the man and woman are to care—the Hebrew speaks of them servicing it—now becomes a stubborn antagonist against which human beings must struggle in order to eke out a living.

Isaiah, however, looks forward to a restoration of the original peace of Eden. Wild beasts and domesticated beasts shall live so peacefully together, and peace between humans and other animals shall be so fully restored, that even a small child can rule. The serpent shall have been so restored to

---

1. The conjunctions *yet* and *and,* found in the rsv and the kjv, respectively, have led English readers to connect the reference to desire with the reference to child-bearing and to interpret it as sexual desire. In fact, there is no conjunction at all in the Hebrew. The two parts of verse 16 refer to different matters.

peaceful pursuits that children can play over their nests without fear (Isa. 11:6-9).

Several of the prophets envision a world in which the land once again is fruitful, overflowing with such abundance that no one ever again need fear hunger and starvation.

The apostle Paul declares that already, in Christ, there is neither male nor female. All the dividing elements of hostility have been overcome in the cross.

PEACEMAKING AS TESTIMONY

To be peacemakers is to bear witness by word and deed to the hope and the reality. To be peacemakers is to make one's deeds consistent with one's words, lest the words of promise be undercut and made a lie by deeds of hostility and war-making.

To be a peacemaker is to intervene into the Death-oriented spiral of the world. It is to act in openness to that peace which God brings, an act bearing witness to the Light.

In a world God has consigned to Death, however, we cannot create peace except as God wills to use our actions as his means of peace. Sometimes, God can and does use even the worst people or worst nations for purposes of peace. On occasion, Israel and the church have been used for God's good purposes even when they were themselves of ragged repute with him. God's freedom and his determination to use us despite our condition, however, are precisely *his* freedom and are in no way an excuse for a lack of urgency on our part.

Obviously, such a concern for peace entails rejecting all forms of violence. The consequences of violence, unless God intervenes, are always violence. This does not mean that nonviolence will necessarily bring peace, justice, and equity. Nonviolence can and may become a technique, a human method, just as is violence. All human techniques partake of the fallen nature of the world and, as such, living in Death's shadow, have no power in and of themselves to accomplish anything other than the purposes of Death. Nonviolence as a human technique may even be said to be a spiritual form of violence. The nonviolence of freedom envisioned in the Sermon on the Mount is not an ideology or a self-imposed mode of coping with the world. It is not a technique having a moral superiority to other techniques or possessing greater efficiency in achieving a desired goal. Rather, the nonviolence of the Sermon on the Mount is a way of living that grows out of and manifests the Reign of God. It is not a gospel ethic, but is one dimension of the ethos of the Reign of God in the New Age. As such, it is not adopted, but is given.

PEACEMAKERS AS THE CHILDREN OF GOD

In the Old Testament Israel is called God's son (Hos. 11:1). The entire nation, including male and female members, stands in a relationship to God most adequately described by the intimate language of family. Elsewhere in the Old Testament (Ps. 2, for example) the king is called God's son, a designation of the special role the king has as God's representative, ruling Israel not in his own right but on behalf of God. In the New Testament, Jesus is called the Son of God, indicating both his identity as Israel's true king and the intimacy he shares with God. Although there certainly are great differences between the temporary rulers of Israel and Jesus as the true king, there is one important similarity: The character of the king should reflect the character of God. The intimacy of the relationship is established for God's own purposes. The title is both a gift and a responsibility.

In the New Testament, the church is the "children of God," which indicates its role in the continuing work of Israel and of Jesus Christ. A popular assertion in some circles is the brotherhood of man under the Fatherhood of God, an affirmation that assumes that all people are the children of God. From a biblical perspective, this misuses language. The biblical writers assume that all people are creatures of God and that God loves his entire creation. It is precisely because he loves the entire world that he called Israel to be his instrument in rescuing the world from the Darkness. Israel is to be the means by which the world's Death plunge is broken, life is restored, and harmony with God is reestablished.

The New Testament writers, in various ways, view the church as an enlargement of original Israel, an enlargement resulting from the influx of Gentiles. From this standpoint, it is incorrect to speak of the world as God's "children" or to say that God is the "Father" of all people, for such family terms speak of both an intimacy and a responsibility not shared by the world. When Israel's task has been completed, all people will be God's children and all may call him Father, for all will have been brought into the intimacy those words imply. There is an intimacy of relationship and responsibility between God and his assembly, however, not now shared by the entire world.

The assembly, however, is assembled by the call of God and, consequently, is known absolutely only by God. The assembly cannot be simply equated with the institutional church. Those who do the will of God are members of Jesus' family (Matt. 12:46-50). Although the boundaries of the family of God do not at present surround the human race, neither are those boundaries confined to those who bear the institutional birthmark.

PEACE AND THE GOSPEL'S DISRUPTION

The family identity of disciples of Jesus is of greater significance than are ties of blood or law, for it is born of the mysterious ties of God's Word. Its purpose is the manifestation, by a human community, of God's character in the world. Although apart from God's work there is no enduring peace, the Reign of God frees those who embrace that Reign to reflect the character of the Father. The proper response to this gift is to follow its impulse, praying that the Father will take those actions and appropriate them as his own for the healing of all nations and all nature.

The work of God that creates new family ties, however, disrupts natural families (Matt. 10:34-38). This warning was remembered and transmitted by a Christian movement that knew that many of its members had come to be regarded by their families as dead for having become followers of Jesus.

Surprisingly, the passage about dividing families contains one of Jesus' few references to peace in all the Gospels—and here it is a negative reference. "I did not come," he says, "to bring peace, but a sword." In the eyes of the world, the gospel, when truly proclaimed, has been a divisive force. This is not to say that the divisiveness the church has brought has always been rooted in the gospel. Unfortunately, it has also divided where it should have united. The divisiveness of hatred, fear, and bigotry in the name of Jesus Christ, however, is not a genuine expression of the division Jesus speaks of, but is the work of the powers of Darkness. Nevertheless, divisions in response to the preaching of the gospel do not, in and of themselves, indicate that the gospel has failed or that it is not authentically proclaimed. Peacemaking in the name of the gospel is not peace as the world understands peace, and even may be scandal in the eyes of the world. Paul and John saw divisions as necessary so that the true followers of Jesus might be recognized. The peace Jesus denies is the peace of the Darkness, and Jesus' sword is the two-edged sword of the Word of God, which pierces the Darkness in the name of true peace.

Since the quest for peace is resistance to the Darkness, it automatically puts one into opposition with the world. It creates opposition to the use of force as the means of ordering society, whether in the cannibalism of institutions, including the church, or in the national obsession with military security, whether in the use of overt physical terror in some countries or in the subtle use of propaganda to brainwash in others. No institution and no nation or government now on the face of the earth is completely free from some use of violence, to one degree or another, to secure its survival. Thus, the peacemaker's role is a lonely one and is the object of much misunderstanding. In the blinded eyes of the world, the peacemaker, by laying bare the violence that must be overcome, frequently appears to be the fomenter of the very violence being opposed. But this violence otherwise remains hidden or denied. Jesus himself is the prime example of this fate of peacemaking. The Prince of Peace was executed by the world as a troublemaker and fomenter of violence.

As John Chrysostom pointed out, centuries ago, the beatitude concerning peacemaking is followed immediately by one concerning those who are persecuted for righteousness' sake. The work of peace is a threat to those whose anxiety-riddled security is based on violence and Death. To such, the gospel message of peace will not be heard as a liberation but as the threat of destruction. This is seen nowhere more clearly than in the story of Herod's massacre of the children in order to save his ill-gotten throne from God.

Peacemaking is not the result of manipulation by either the scrupulous or the unscrupulous. Hence, international diplomats will never produce true peace by pursuing mutual "enlightened self-interest." Self-interest, inherently, is an expression of the Darkness, and as such, can never produce peace, but only an extension of Death. Enlightened self-interest is a contradiction of terms in any meaningful sense of enlightenment, for such enlightenment can only be the enlightenment of the serpent. Although this craftiness is commended to the disciples as a part of their wisdom, their demeanor is to be determined by a quite different possession—the innocence of the dove, the symbol of peace and of the Holy Spirit.

As in the case of the other beatitudes, so here, Jesus' words are not a command or a rule, but a promise. Those who, in the midst of Darkness, have placed their lives in jeopardy by offering themselves as God's instruments in bringing renewal and healing to the world will hear God's declaration, "These are my children."

CHAPTER 14

THOSE WHO HAVE BEEN PERSECUTED FOR RIGHTEOUSNESS' SAKE

Those who have been persecuted for righteousness' sake are those who have deliberately injected their witness to God's righteousness into the Death-oriented world in which they have found themselves. They are those whose lives have been ordered by purity of heart and devotion to peacemaking. They are those whose complete devotion to God and genuine care for those around them have made them so different from the world and so threatening to the society's values and way of life that the society has sought to eliminate them or, at least, to suppress their witness.

Truly to hunger and thirst for righteousness leads to the attempt to live even now in anticipation of the promised eventual triumph of righteousness. The biblical writers were very aware that we live in a world not characterized by righteousness, one that is opposed to God. That recognition, however, did not lead them to advise disciples to forgo witness to the Reign of God until a more appropriate time. It led them to admonish disciples to live here and now as though the future were already present.

The Old Testament prophets called Israel to live here and now not only according to the covenant, but according to the promise of the one who had established the covenant with them. We hear this call, for example, in Isaiah 2:5:

> O house of Jacob,
> come, let *us* walk
> in the light of the LORD!
> (RSV, emphasis mine)

Isaiah knew that the world is not yet at peace, that the world does not now live according to God's will. He knew that nations and individuals, alike, follow their own courses, each seeking its own welfare and advantage, each living off the weakness of the other.

But Isaiah calls his hearers to live even now as though the entire world already did live by God's will.

The common criticism of those who seek to live by the values reflected in the Sermon on the Mount is that such people are unrealistic. One must be realistic, it is asserted. It is said to be irresponsible to try to live as though the world were not the way it is. To be merciful to the killer who seeks to destroy is unreasonable. To forgive is to destroy the social fabric. People must pay for their crimes. So it is said.

But the gospel calls disciples to insert themselves into the Darkness as bearers of the Light. In Jesus, the New Order has drawn near in the midst of the Old. To ignore the call to bear witness in the midst of the Darkness is to allow the Darkness to go unchallenged, unresisted. To say that we cannot do this or that because the world is the way it is is to ignore or disbelieve the assertion that within the Old Order there is a New Order coming into being. Despite the dominant scheme of the world, now is the time to embrace the New Order.

Such intrusion of mercy into the midst of mercilessness, purity of heart into the midst of atheism, and peacemaking into the midst of violence inevitably results in hostility and anger from those who are dominated by the Old Order. Truly to embrace the New Order and to seek to allow God to use one for peacemaking and the establishment of his righteousness is to make oneself vulnerable to prosecution and persecution from the state, the various movements and agencies of the society, and the institutions, including the church, by which the society seeks to order its life. The Old Age cannot tolerate the infusion of the New. The Darkness will seek to expel or to destroy the Light as the defense devices of the body seek to expel or destroy an invading viral agent. In a world where revenge is the norm, those who seek to spread mercy will find the full vengeance of the society hurled against them. When, by God's grace, some exceptional person does capture the imagination of the larger society by an act of mercy or life of devotion, as in the case of say Albert Schweitzer or Mother Teresa, eventually critics will arise who will seek to mar the reputation and question the motives of that person. Schweitzer was attacked for his supposed patronizing approach; Mother Teresa, for her supposed grandstanding. Moreover, those who exalt the exceptional person do so as long as no demand is made on them, no direct sacrifice required. The world praises the martyr from afar, celebrates the servant as a means of avoiding guilt.

IDEOLOGY AND HARASSMENT

A common, milder form of persecution is harassment. This beatitude might easily be paraphrased, "Blessed are those who are harassed because of their single-minded devotion to God, their determination to live mercifully with the enemy, and their dedication to peacemaking.''

Harassment can come from any quarter—the state, the institution by which one is employed, the church, or even the family. This is especially true when a group's actions and views are rooted in ideology and one member acts contrary to the ideology. Harassment is thus an effort to maintain and enhance the group's version of righteousness.

The person truly seeking God's righteousness, however, is driven by and seeks that which rejects all efforts to enclose it in an ideology. Ideologies have rules and regulations that can be objectively stated and to which one can be held accountable. Ideology demands consistency, with no room for change and spontaneity. The world of the ideologist is an atheistic world, for it substitutes rules and regulations for the direction and commands of the Living God. Obedience to the command of God, however, occasionally involves us in inconsistent views and actions. Consequently, although he may be consistent with himself, in terms of human logic the God of Israel is sometimes inconsistent. In divine freedom God responds to the deeds of the human race according to the conditions of the situation. But as Thomas Merton once said, the only world that is a consistent world is a world without God.

Originally, the word *harass* referred to setting one's dog on a thief or on a disobedient animal to bring the thief to bay or to bring the animal into submission. Later, it came to be used in a more general sense to refer to worrying the enemy, wearing the enemy down, or driving someone to exhaustion.

Harassment seeks to quiet or to deter by embarrassment, inconvenience, constant irritation, or mild pain. It does not seek to change the harassed one's views but merely to silence the person or eliminate the person's disturbing actions. Harassment seeks not peace but conformity, not fellowship but victory, not conversion but domination.

When the church uses harassment as a weapon, as say in the struggle against pornography or drugs or nuclear arms, it forsakes its role as the bearer of the Light and becomes simply another instrument of the Darkness. The task of the bearers of the Light is not to conquer or to subdue or to suppress, but to be instruments by which God, if God chooses to do so, brings the renewing, converting, transforming power of his grace to bear in the lives of all.

WHO ARE THE PERSECUTED?

As in the case of the other beatitudes, this one must not be tied exclusively to those who are closely identified with the institutional church. Not all those who have been touched by the Reign of God are in the disciples' band. In fact, it now not only is possible, but sometimes actually is the case, that church members, church organizations, and entire denominations become the persecutors of those who more accurately bear witness to the will of God. Disciples, therefore, must exercise the discernment that is given as a gift of the Spirit. Disciples must beware the tendency of the church to be enthralled by the society, to equate its values with the values of the society and of the state, and to baptize and seek to propagate, in the name of Christ, those values of the Darkness. Those who are persecuted for righteousness' sake are sometimes persecuted by the very church that professes the righteousness it persecutes.

Do not be misled. Persecution does not make one a disciple of Jesus Christ. Nor does being a follower of Jesus mean that one will never be at peace with anyone. Because the world is still engulfed in the Darkness, however—caught up in violence, warfare, racism, nationalism, sexism, and so forth—the person who has gone through life and never been harassed, should at least ask himself or herself whether he or she is as devoted to Christ as he or she has assumed.

There can be no doubt that, sooner or later, disciples of Jesus will be persecuted—whether by the government, the church, their family, their friends, or any number of others. Persecution will come!

CHAPTER 15

THE REVILED DISCIPLES

Heretofore the disciples have been included, implicitly, in the more general blessings that portray the world for them. Now, they alone are addressed. As they step into the Darkness as the bearers of God's Light, they will be reviled.

To *revile* is to scold, to accuse, or to taunt because of some failure or offense. The devout are frequently the objects of such attacks in the psalms, ridiculed and taunted because they place their confidence in God, and God seems, to the accusers, to have turned a deaf ear.

In Matthew and Mark, Jesus himself is reviled as he hangs on the cross. The crowds who pass by taunt him by asking why, if he is the Son of God, God does not come to his rescue. The two criminals executed along with Jesus also revile him, meaning apparently that they ridiculed his confidence in God, a confidence that seems absurd in the face of their impending death.

The crowds revile by saying, "Come down and save yourself, and we will believe in you!"

Disciples must expect that when they move into the world of the Darkness, trusting not in their own strategies, but in the will and power of God, they will appear naive, foolish, and irresponsible by the movers and the doers of the world. The disciples who left their boats, forsaking their family responsibilities and having no apparent means of income, turned aside from all those things by which the world measures maturity and responsibility.

At the heart of that reviling, which disciples must face—assuming they are faithful disciples—is the atheism of the revilers. Those who reviled Jesus, like those who revile the pious ones in the psalms, were no doubt religious persons. They believed in a god of sorts, a god they even assumed to be the God of ancient Israel and of the prophets. Their god, however, was a god of their own invention—a god who, they assumed, acted as responsible, rational human beings such as themselves should act—reasonably and predictably. They worshiped a god of power, one whose way is violence and conquest of the enemy. Jesus hanging on the cross as a victim of the very empire he should have overthrown was proof, to the crowd, that Jesus did not represent their god. And, indeed, he did not. He was not the anointed one of the god they had substituted for the Transcendent God of Abraham. Their taunting cry to Jesus to come down and save himself betrays their own assumption that God is a god who vindicates himself with objective displays of power.

Disciples who truly proclaim the gospel will be reviled in the same manner as their Lord. "God helps those who help themselves!" is the cry. To the worshipers of the god of power and violence, the call to have mercy, to turn the other cheek, to trust God rather than our own schemes to bring about what God wants threatens national security. It endangers the economy. It undercuts the unity of a nation committed to the defeat of the enemy.

Disciples must face the probability that their witness will be most viciously attacked and they will be most severely reviled from within the very church that was the instrument of their call to discipleship. It was not a fluke of history that Jesus was opposed by and handed over to the state by the hierarchy of the very religious establishment in which he had grown up and which he had come to transform. Religious structures, as institutions, are integral to society, and society comes to rely on them to support and promote the goals of society. Because of their integral relationship to the society, they adopt the values and criteria of the society, for their continuing survival as influential institutions requires this. To be in the ballgame, you must abide by the rules of the game. Put more biblically, to be a part of the world, you must be of the world.

Therein lies the problem. The disciples are called to be in the world. In Matthew's Gospel, however, disciples—as an assembly in the world—are to be guided in their organizational decisions by the resurrected Jesus himself. He will continue among his assembly until the end of the Old Age.

Very quickly, however, in the face of the threat of ridiculous interpretations of the gospel and in the face of superstition, the church lost its nerve and began to grant more and more objective authority to the growing hierarchy. The charismatic movement became an ideological organization. The authority of the Spirit gave way to the power of the bishops. The history of the church, ever since, has been a history of the struggle between ideology and Truth, order and the Spirit, the human word and the Word of God. The church, partaking of the Darkness, made a prisoner of the assembly; and in every era, those who have been most attuned to the call to assembly have been reviled by the church itself.

THE PERSECUTED DISCIPLES

The beatitude speaks, however, not simply of being reviled, but of being persecuted and of being the objects of untrue evil utterances. The Darkness can seldom afford simply to ridicule the bearers of the Light, but must destroy them, seeking thereby to destroy the Light itself. Only when ridicule causes the one who is ridiculed to withdraw, to cease the witness, does the Darkness settle for the ridicule—only, that is, when the Darkness has won. The faithfulness of the disciple, however, propels the disciple onward, the grace of God upholding him or her in the tenacity of the witness, and the Darkness then must take sterner measures. The Darkness will seek to destroy. The state will threaten with imprisonment and death, not knowing that the disciple, upheld by the One who liberates the prisoners and restores life to the dead, fears neither of these penalties.

It is not that the disciple will necessarily become a determined lawbreaker, though the breaking of this or that law will be inevitable, but rather that by his or her very bearing in the world, the disciple threatens the structure of the law by threatening the value system, the social structure, and the ideology the law represents and defends. Disciples are never punished by the state simply for violating this or that law, although for purposes of legality an indictment will be based on one or another specific law. They are punished because they threaten the entire system. The true offense is the disciple's very existence. When Jesus' enemies sought to kill him, they first decided to kill him; then they sought a basis for charges on which to do it. Disciples are killed because they are perceived as enemies of humankind.

Disciples of Jesus Christ can serve as instruments of the state only to the extent that they are willing to live by the rules of the state and to forgo the teachings of Jesus. Those in or aspiring to public office will patronize and publicly employ disciples of Jesus only as long as those disciples are willing to substitute those public officials' political agendas for the commands of the Living Christ, only as long as they are willing to substitute ideology for the word of the Living God. Disciples need never fear the heretical religious leader gaining political power. What disciples should beware is the state granting political power to the religious leader. Any disciple of Jesus Christ who aspires to public office and wins either will do the will of the state in opposition to the will of God or will be crushed by the state and seen by the public as a failure—a perception that, though correct, will be understood as weakness rather than strength.

DISCIPLES AS OBJECTS OF EVIL UTTERANCES

It is only to be expected that disciples who seek to be faithful witnesses will be the objects of utterances of evil—that is, of accusations that their work and words are in opposition to God. The Darkness seeks to discredit those who are faithful by accusing them of being servants of Satan, fellow travelers of communists, reactionaries, radicals, fascists, Uncle Toms, black militants, and so on. The Darkness does not favor one ideology or another, but incorporates all ideologies into its own storehouse of weapons, attempting to set person against person, group against group, nation against nation by accusing each of whichever ideology is most feared by the one being duped. Above all, the Darkness must prevent open, respectful dialogue; for if such dialogue takes place, the partners in the dialogue may come to reconciliation despite their differences. In open conversation, the Holy Spirit may bring new perspectives to all the participants, leading to new approaches to issues and problems. This the Darkness cannot permit, for the Darkness thrives on alienation, hostility, ignorance, and chaos.

None of this is to imply that those who utter evil against disciples are insincere or wicked. Some are; some are not. The Darkness, in fact, is at its most effective when it can seduce the honest, sincere, religious person or movement into attacking those who bear witness to the Light, when it blinds them to its true identity and deceives them as to the Light bearers' true identity.

REJOICE

To rejoice is to know the relief, as a whole person, not just with the mind or the feelings, which comes when an anticipated event takes place. The family that rejoices at the birth of a child is celebrating the culmination of the pregnancy and the long months of waiting. The prisoners who rejoice at their release are celebrating the end of imprisonment.

"Rejoice," in the beatitude, is an exhortation to act in a way opposite the way reviling, persecution, and slander normally would lead one to act. Do not be made to doubt or to be ashamed by the reviling; do not respond with violence or revenge to those who persecute you; do not spend a lot of effort and time attempting to correct the lies laid out by the slanderers. The exhortation not to react as children of the Darkness would react is not based on any practical considerations such as, "I won't respond to the lie, because to fight a lie is to give credence to it." Nor is it based on any naive notion that if the disciple ignores the situation, it will go away. Rather, it is rooted simply in the assumption that the Way of the Light and the Way of the Darkness are radically different. For the disciple to respond in kind to the onslaughts of the Darkness would be to abandon the Light, to disbelieve God, and, consequently, to affirm the charges of the revilers. It would be to exchange the God of Israel for the god of the Darkness.

To rejoice is to respond in the midst of the Darkness as though the whole world already lives in the Light. To rejoice is to live in anticipation of deliverance as though deliverance already had taken place, as though the events toward whose culmination we look were already present. This is confirmed in the accompanying word, translated "be glad," which has deep roots in the ceremonial act that anticipates the coming glory of God in the present celebration. In the ceremony, the congregation acts as though the future were already present.

THE REWARD FROM GOD

We should not be misled by the promise of reward. The reward in heaven is reward from God. As a reward, however, it is not a wage. Wages are earned; rewards are given. Wages are given in obligation for a job accomplished according to an agreement. Rewards are given in gratitude for an act preceded neither by contract nor oral agreement.

To say that God will reward the disciples, then, does not bind God to a specific payment. The precise nature of the reward is not even mentioned. The promise is simply that God will give whatever he chooses to those who endure. Those who have sacrificed will find their life with God far exceeds the life of the persecution.

The basis for rejoicing is also the identity bestowed on the disciples. When they suffer reviling and persecution and lies, they are one with those messengers from God who preceded them. As those who give themselves completely into God's hands to serve as instruments of God's peacemaking, they are promised membership in God's own family. As those who are persecuted, they share in the family of the prophets.

The disciple must face the world fully aware of the desire of the Darkness to pervert and to destroy the witness to the Light. The disciple of Jesus Christ must be prepared to die a painful, ignominious death and to be crushed and ground into powder leaving no headstone, no memory in the world's recollection. The disciple must be prepared to be known only in the mind of God, who knows each of his own by name, and who comes in all his sovereign power to deliver the prisoners from the realm of the devil.

PART FOUR

JESUS, THE DISCIPLES, AND TORAH

You are the salt of the earth; but if salt has lost its taste, how shall its saltiness be restored? It is no longer good for anything except to be thrown out and [trampled by human foot].

You are the light of the world. A city set on a hill cannot be hid. Nor do [people] light a lamp and put it under a [basket], but on a stand, and it gives light to [everyone] in the house. Let your light so shine. . . that [people] may see your good works and give glory to your Father . . . in heaven.

[Do not think] that I have come to abolish [torah] and the prophets; I have come not to abolish them but to fulfill them. For truly, I say to you, till heaven and earth pass away, not an iota, not a dot, will pass from [torah] until all is accomplished.

Whoever then relaxes one of the least of these commandments and teaches [others] so, [therefore,] shall be called least [under God's Reign]; but [whoever] does them and teaches them shall be called great [under God's Reign]. For I tell you, unless your righteousness exceeds that of the scribes and [the] Pharisees, you will never [become a subject under God's Reign].

(Matthew 5:13-20 RSV)

CHAPTER 16

THE TASK OF DISCIPLES AND OF THE ASSEMBLY

Jesus' words on salt and light are not commands, exhortations, or requests, but declarations. Disciples *are* the salt of the earth. They *are* the light of the world.

Already called to be fishers for the Reign of God—a task they will carry out by proclaiming that Reign, overpowering the demons, baptizing, and teaching—they are now told that, as fishers, they serve as salt and light. The warnings that follow the declarations, therefore, are warnings not of the consequences of rejecting the call, but of the consequences of ignoring their task as those who have been set apart.

SALT

In biblical texts salt is a preservative, a component of certain sacrifices, and even an instrument of destruction. Sown into good soil, it destroys (Judg. 9:45); into a dunghill, it purifies (Luke 14:35).

It is no coincidence that these sayings are connected to the beatitude on persecution, for the New Testament frequently indicates those occasions where persecution causes some followers to turn aside from the gospel in fear for their lives. Those who are persecuted for righteousness' sake are promised that God's Reign is on their behalf. Those who are reviled and slandered and otherwise persecuted are promised that God will reward them. Now, however, the disciples are warned that if they neglect their task, they will be destroyed.

The word Matthew uses to refer to the salt losing its taste *(moranthé)* basically means to become foolish. One of its connotations is "to become weak and insipid." Numerous explanations for the loss of saltiness have been given, including its mixture with various things such as gypsum, dirt, and water. Some writers have even contended that the original use of the saying was to show the impossibility of true disciples losing their identity.

The use of the verb denoting foolishness, however, suggests that already in the tradition, Matthew's source had engaged in double entendre and that the specific way salt loses its saltiness is irrelevant. What matters is the dilution itself.

That Matthew is engaging in wordplay is further indicated in that the Greek word translated "fit" means both "having power or ability" and "valid" (or "legitimate") in a legal sense. Salt that has lost its strength only has the power to be cast out, only has the power to be destroyed. That is the only legitimate thing to do with it! Disciples who forsake the teachings of Jesus become mere fools. They become not like children, but merely childish.

Disciples are hereby warned that they must not confuse their witness to the gospel with witness to the way of the Darkness. The purity of their hearts must be maintained as the purity of salt must be maintained. They must not adopt, or adapt themselves to, the values and standards of that Darkness by which the society around them lives. This is the same demand for separation that is ordered in John's Gospel when the disciples are charged to be in the world, but not of the world—the same call that Paul gives when he admonishes his readers (in Phillips' brilliant translation), "Don't let the world around you squeeze you into its own mould" (Rom. 12:2).

LIGHT

The disciples are to be the light the prophet Isaiah promised. Jesus' appearance is the occasion for the Light to Israel (Matt. 3:16), beginning in the Gentile-dominated regions of Zebulun and Naphtali. Jesus himself is also that Light, and through those from historic Israel whom he calls as his disciples, as well as through those of whom the disciples make disciples, his Light will spread throughout the world. Thus, both the geographic reference to the city on a hill (which echoes Isaiah 2) and the domestic reference to the lamp indicate that the ancient promise of Isaiah 2 and the call through Isaiah that Israel be the light to the nations will be fulfilled. This will bring from the nations those who will not merely acknowledge the sovereignty of God, but who will be bound into the community of disciples. Thus, for Matthew, as for Paul, the ultimate goal of the Reign of God is to restore the intimacy which existed in the beginning between God and the world and among the nations of the world. This intimacy will come through baptism into the assembly, in whose midst Jesus continues until the end of the age, and through life lived in the unity of torah (as Isaiah anticipated), as torah is fulfilled in Jesus.

As the star of Bethlehem shone in the darkness of the sky, declaring to the Gentile astrologers that a new heir to the Jewish throne had been born, so the disciples are to be the bearers of the divine Light in the Darkness of the world. They are not to perform that task by building a city, as Cain did, but by proclaiming, baptizing, and teaching. They are not to build a church, but to enlarge an assembly—and even then it is not they who enlarge it, but Jesus who enlarges it through them. Whenever the assembly, in succeeding years, has sought to turn the assembly into a city by making it the heart of a political party, accepting a role as one of the institutions of society, or serving as the underpinning of society, the result has been the dissipation of the salt, the diminution of the light. The Puritans in America developed a society they intended to be the light set on a hill. Many of them intended to create in the wilderness a new society, which—to some extent anticipating the motives of the sponsors of the Statue of Liberty—would be a light of freedom and Christian civilization to be beheld and imitated in Europe. For all that might be said positively about that effort, it was soon corrupted into an oppressive society, an inevitable outcome for any attempt to create the perfect society.

Disciples must always be aware of the possibility of being destroyed. That Jesus establishes his assembly and does not permit the Power of Death (Hades) to prevail against it can never legitimately be taken to mean that each and every disciple, each and every congregation, or each and every denomination is indestructible or safe from complete defection. The salt that has been dissipated is fit only to be thrown out in the waste. The light that is covered quickly dies from lack of oxygen. The city set on a hill cannot be hidden, but it can stand as a sign of tyranny and blood or as an object of shame and ridicule as easily as it can a sign of hope and fidelity.

Disciples can so confuse the gospel with decent society, with the counterculture in a decadent society, or with that quietism that comes from weakness or withdrawal, that the distinct word the gospel always brings to human society is lost in the clamor of tongues. Because the Darkness inevitably and continually opposes the Light, because the Light by its very nature opposes the Darkness, and because the world of human construction is always corrupted by the Darkness, the gospel can never correctly be understood as compatible either with society or with the human movements that seek to transform or to destroy society. Because the gospel is news about the work of a holy (that is, completely different) God, even when some human values or insights seem to approximate certain elements of the gospel—as, say, in the realm of ethics—the opposition is no less real or complete.

The difference between the Light and the Darkness is one not of ethical injunctions or imperatives, but of domain. A citizen of one nation does not, by obeying a law of his or her own nation, become a semicitizen of another nation that has an identical law, nor does a member of one culture become acculturated to another simply because outwardly there may be similar customs. In the same way, a nation or society does not become a manifestation of the Light simply because it enforces certain laws or lives by certain mores that happen to parallel, on the surface, certain habits by means of which the Light may express itself among disciples. The Gentile who by nature does what torah calls for, does not thereby become worthy of the verdict "justified," but may even discover that doing certain things prescribed in torah simply leaves him or her more greatly condemned for not observing the rest of torah (Rom. 2:14-16).

Because the Light is radically different from the Darkness, the manifestation of the Light always opposes the Darkness. The witness disciples are to bear to the Light, therefore, will—when it is true witness—be something new injected into the situation. The recent pastoral statements of the American Catholic and United Methodist bishops on the nuclear arms race are clear examples of how what is intended as, and received as, a gospel witness to a problem of global significance may, in reality, be essentially nothing more than a repetition of what the wiser voices in society have already said and have said better. This is not to say that disciples should not agree with secular voices at certain points, but is merely to warn that simply seconding the wisdom of the world is not testimony to the Word of God. Neither of the aforementioned pastoral letters truly calls for repentance, but in fact says that we cannot expect one nation to repent unless the other one does. What would be completely unacceptable—and even ludicrous—in evangelism parades as Christian realism in the realm of social ethics. Thus, the salt is dissipated, the lamp snuffed out. Is there any wonder that the church loses all reverence in the eyes of the world? The world recognizes it for the cultural component that it has become. Economists and military strategists can argue with the episcopal statements because they are merely economic and military statements.

This merely repeats that condition of the church of Czarist Russia, of pre-revolution France, and of the so-called avant-garde church of the United States during the 1960s. Because of their identification with narrow, ideological elements of the society, they were hated and despised by the opposing sides. The problem, from the standpoint of the assembly's task, is not that the church, or segments of the church, in the instances named were despised, but that they were despised because of the assumptions on which they were based, rather than because of the gospel. They were persecuted not for righteousness' sake, but for ideology's sake.

Even in analyzing the problems of the institutional church, those enthralled by the Darkness are bereft of true understanding. Self-proclaimed liberals see the problem as the triumph of the archconservatives, the aggressiveness of the fundamentalists, or the power of the radical right. The self-styled conservatives view the liberals and radicals, between which they make no distinction, as destroying the church, plank by plank (or brick by brick), and surrendering the church to the so-called forces of secular humanism. The "moderates," forgetting that the book of Revelation says that it is better to be hot or cold than to be somewhere in between, scorn the "extremists" on both sides.

The problem with all three is that they have sold out to human wisdom as criteria by which to evaluate any supposed word of God. Intellectual respectability, preserving the social order, legal justice, scientific inerrancy of the Scriptures, exploding emotions, heavenly tongues, common sense—all are among the criteria by which we evaluate. None are to be despised; none relate to recognizing the genuine Word of God. All easily become ideologies, which render the salt fit only to be cast out and destroyed by that world from which they arose and whose criteria they are.

LIGHT THAT POINTS TO THE FATHER

The task of the Light is to draw attention not to itself, but to God from whom the Light comes. Here, we find the meaning of works, deeds, or—to use the word now fashionable—*praxis* as far as these are related to the gospel. The way the assembly lives is to be a testimony by the assembly so that those who see may be led to glorify God. The assembly's goal is not to be that of the self-centered, obnoxious little song, "They Will Know We Are Christians by Our Love," but the glorification of God because of our love.

This understanding of the deeds of the disciples is essentially that found throughout the Bible with regard to the actions of the people of God. In Deuteronomy 4:5-8, the nations are anticipated as looking at Israel's way of life and acknowledging Israel's wisdom and understanding. This is joined immediately by Moses' reminder that this way of life is a sign of God's nearness, and it must be heard against the background of Israel's own purpose as the instrument through whom God will bless the nations.

In John 15:8, bearing fruit as Jesus' disciples is for the purpose of glorifying the Father; in Ephesians the assembly is said to have been created in Christ Jesus for good works (2:10) and to have been destined and appointed to live for the praise of God's own glorious grace (1:6); and in Romans 12:1 the readers are reminded that they owe their entire being to God, as a living sacrifice.

In terms of Israel's cult, the disciples are a covenant of salt—the initial step in God's fulfillment of his covenant with the entire world of living things. They are the means by which all may hear the liberating message of the gospel and respond by saying yes!

CHAPTER 17

JESUS AND THE FULFILLMENT OF TORAH

Jesus' words about his relation to torah (the Law) must be heard against the background of the origin, purpose, and historical developments of torah. I do not mean origin and history by way of a naturalistic, tentative reconstruction of what lay behind the present narrative in the Pentateuch. As one who regularly practices the modern scholarly approach, I affirm the modern methods as ways of asking certain questions about the text for those purposes for which they are appropriate and helpful. Even from a critical standpoint, however, neither Jesus, Matthew, nor Paul thought, spoke, or wrote with the assumptions of modern biblical scholarship. That is, it is not responsible scholarship to pretend that Matthew, or Jesus, knew the history of the legal code tradition. The history in light of which Jesus' words are to be understood then, is that history portrayed primarily in the Pentateuch and the prophets. It is to this that I turn as prelude to the Matthew text.

THE HISTORY OF GOD'S SPEAKING

Torah is God's instruction, God's wisdom. It is God's will. In the Garden, Adam and Eve—living before torah—were instructed directly by God's own voice. They were not in a state of "dreaming innocence," for God instructed them in good and evil; that is, God told them what he expected from them and of them and what was forbidden.

By eating from the tree of the knowledge of good and evil, Adam and Eve attempted to gain the ability to declare good and evil on their own. In other words, they sought to flee from God, to escape his direct speech and to live on their own terms. When they heard God's voice in the Garden, later, they attempted to hide from God.

God's words to Adam and Eve, in the wake of Adam and Eve's rebellion, were words of indictment and judgment, rather than words of loving instruction; Adam and Eve were cast out of God's presence, to die.

No longer with access to God's direct address, to the tree of life, or to the tree of the knowledge of good and evil, they were to be subject to the chaotic conditions of life outside Eden.

When God began the world anew with Noah and Noah's family, he also spoke new instructions to them. Because even after the cleansing by the Flood the world still was not as it had been before Adam and Eve's rebellion, God's instructions did not merely repeat the instructions given to Adam and Eve. God spoke to Noah and to Noah's family with regard to God's will in the new situation. The new instructions were for those outside Eden. As such, those instructions were no more able to prevent the continuation of human rebellion than had been those spoken to Adam and Eve. From Ararat to Shinar, the rebellion continued.

Then God decided on a new approach. Accepting that the world was now dominated by the Chaos into which he had caused it to plunge, God decided to establish a new human community, a community through which he might bless the world and reclaim it from the Chaos.

The person selected to be the head and origin of this new community was Abraham. With Abraham, God began once more to speak directly with his representatives. He gave Abraham no set of instructions, but sent him forth from Chaldea, from the land of the dumb idols, into a new land, to which God promised to lead the way. After Abraham, however, the voice of God was again heard less and less. God worked in the background, influencing and using human deeds and events, but his presence was known only through visions, dreams, and an occasional messenger.

For the Pentateuch, this long series of events culminates in the establishment of Israel as a distinct people, the gift of the land as a means of maintaining their identity as God's holy nation, and the gift of torah as God's instruction for the nation to enable them to survive in the midst of Chaos. On Mount Sinai, God's declaration that Israel is to be God's priestly nation—the nation to be the mediator between God and the world and between the world and God—reaffirmed the covenant with Abraham, and God spoke to Moses the torah (instructions) by which Israel was to be guided.

Quite apart from any naturalistic description of origins and of the earlier forms of the legal codes, the Pentateuch now describes the instructions and their delivery to Israel as God's address to Moses, Moses being instructed to give them, in turn, to the people. The Ten Commandments are given to Moses, and then, out of fear, the people plead with Moses to serve as God's spokesman for them. The priestly community must have its own priest. Moses, therefore, returns to the mountain and receives the more explicit instructions of how Israel's daily life is to be lived. These instructions elaborate on the Ten Commandments so that the people can realize them in their daily life.

127

After finishing the instructions, God engraves a testimony to the instructions on two tablets of stone and Moses returns with the tablets to the camp. Discovering the people engaged in idolatry, Moses angrily shatters the tablets of the testimony, but later, he returns to the mountain, where God says that he will write again for Moses the words that were on the first tablets.

Now, a strange thing happens. The words on the second set of tablets, which God has said would be the words that had been on the first set, are not the Ten Commandments God had spoken earlier. Anyone can see the radical difference between the two by comparing Exodus 20:1-7 and 34:1-28. Furthermore, when Moses, in Deuteronomy, reminds the people of their history during the desert years, the instructions he supposedly reminds them God spoke include a form of the Ten Commandments obviously parallel to that in Exodus 20, but also different at a few points.

The various scholarly methods that have been used to explain these contradictions have enabled us to suspect a diverse background for the sources and traditions that have been drawn into the present form of the text, but they have not satisfactorily answered the theological implications of the present form of the text.[1]

It should first be noted that there are several steps in the movement from God's address to Moses to the present text of the Pentateuch and that each step removes us farther from the direct address. The first tablets Moses brought down from the mountain held words written by the finger of God (Exod. 24:12; Deut. 9:10). The words are specifically called a *testimony*. They are also said to contain the Ten Words, traditionally translated "the Ten Commandments," or the Decalogue. The written Ten Words, even though written by God's own finger, are no longer God's direct word. They are not revelation. They are *witness,* or *testimony,* to God's word. They are not automatically or inherently the living Word of God, but are subject to human manipulation, interpretation, and distortion.

The words God is said to have spoken to Moses in addition to the Ten Words are, essentially, instructions for specific situations, instructions that tell how the Ten Words are to be obeyed in a specific social setting. They are also even farther removed from God, for they are not words engraved in stone for all to see, but are Moses' testimony to God's words. Once the present text has enclosed them in the narrative as words spoken by Moses to Israel, they are the author's report of Moses' report of God's interpretation of the Ten Words. They have come to be understood commonly as rules and regulations in the Bible. As such, they can only come between the

---

1. By "present form of the text" I do not mean primarily the author's intent. The latter, though important, is a question of ancient history. A theological interpretation of the text must take seriously the history portrayed in the text.

community and God, for whenever God's word is equated simply with the written text, there is no longer any need to listen for the voice of the Living God.

The second set of tablets with which Moses returned contain a strikingly different list of instructions. Ironically, they are the ones which, according to the narrative's own account, would have to have been in the ark of the covenant during all the time the ark was carried in the desert, was used by the Israelites during the conquest, was held hostage by the Philistines, and sat between the cherubim in the temple. I say ironic, because although God tells Moses that he will write for Moses the words that were on the first tablets (Exod. 34:1), they are not those words, but are quite different. Moreover, at the end of the account we are told that God ordered Moses to write the words and Moses obeyed (Exod. 34:27-28). Regardless of any dependable theories on why God said he would write but then orders Moses to write, the surface contradiction in the text as it now stands must be taken seriously. The tablets in the ark were tablets not on which God had engraved a testimony with his own finger of fire, but on which Moses wrote his own testimony to the word God spoke to him. The words on the second tablets were farther removed from God's immediate address than were those on the first.

Moses' recitation of torah in Deuteronomy is different from that in Exodus, because torah is now being given for a new situation. The word of the past becomes a new word in the present. Strikingly, even modern methods of study indicate that the Pentateuch in its present form actually grew by interpretation and adaptation.

THE PURPOSE OF TORAH

Torah, as already indicated, was given to Israel to enable her to live as God's people in the midst of Chaos. It was given not to be a set of rules and regulations to which Israel could look and avoid God—not, that is, to be a substitute for the voice of God, but to be a testimony to the will of God. Those psalms and other writings that praise God for torah and speak of torah's benefit for those who live by it refer not to situations where torah is read as an objective, rigorous code handed down by a stern, demanding god, but to those situations where torah becomes the means by which the Living God continues to speak an immediate word to the worshiper and the assembly. Similarly, the laws of the Old Testament are dead, and deadly, when they are read as relics of ancient history, either to be rigorously obeyed as rules and regulations or to be dissected by scholars as relics of jurisprudence. When, by the work of the Holy Spirit, they become the means of God's speech anew, then they become the Living Word.

Before their expulsion from the Garden, Adam and Eve were in harmony with the will of God, because they were in unbroken harmony with God himself. They were capable of obeying and submitting, of disobeying and rebelling. This is not to say that God had given them a choice of obeying or disobeying. When Adam and Eve rebelled, they asserted a choice that had not been theirs to assert. In so doing, they forsook the capability of doing good, not because the capability was automatically lost, but because God took it from them.

Adam and Eve were truly free when their actions were in harmony with God's will, when their actions were expressions of good, rather than evil. Then, they obeyed not because they had to, but because, as God's representatives, they simply were created to be in harmony with God. They were a part of the good creation, and their spontaneous obedience was a manifestation of that goodness they shared with all other created things.

The rupture that came with their rebellion split apart torah (instruction) as that which they automatically did, and torah as that which they were commanded to do. When God spoke instructions to Moses on Sinai, the instructions were not like those for Adam and Eve in the Garden, but were instructions by which a fallen people might live as God's people in the midst of the fallen world. As God's address, torah was perfect; as human testimony, it shared the imperfection of the human beings who recorded it. The way it becomes God's Word again, however, is not by removal of the imperfections, for the imperfections are not the source of its inability to be the Word of God. The source of this inability is the mere fact of its separateness from God as testimony. Whether the testimony is written or oral is also irrelevant for that inability. Despite its oral or written nature, despite its imperfections, it becomes the living Word, it becomes instruction, when God himself embraces and uses it as the means of divine speech here and now. When "You will not steal" becomes the personal address "*You* will not steal," then the dead word has become the Living Word. When the Exodus and Deuteronomy passages of specific instruction concerning stealing in ancient Israel become the means by which the assembly today not only hears the living instruction not to steal, but also knows through those ancient words what it means not to steal in a radically different world, then the printed word has become God's Living Word.

Written torah binds Israel in that it holds Israel together, keeping her, to the extent that she observes it, from flying apart like the world around her. Torah is to be bound upon the hand and between the eyes, bands that strengthen and protect.

Torah may be perceived, however, as binding and restrictive, as that which prohibits the satisfaction of our desires. When it is no longer the means by which God speaks, it becomes Law! Objective Rule! Regulation!

It either replaces God and becomes an idol or becomes a quaint relic from the unenlightened past.

The fulfillment of history will bring the end of a need for written torah. Chaos will have been overcome. The sea will be no more. The gift will have served its purpose. The life toward which torah, in a chaotic world, could merely point, will have come, and the ordering of life reflected in a provisional way will have been fulfilled in the perfection of the new age. Until then, the bands of torah are not to be loosened. They must continue to hold together or to restrict—depending on whether through the written words God speaks his Living Word.

DIMENSIONS OF TORAH IN THE NEW TESTAMENT

Recognizing the distinction between torah as the written tradition and torah as the present instruction of God has important implications for our understanding of the apostle Paul in the New Testament. In 2 Corinthians 3:6, for example, Paul does not say that torah kills, but that what is written kills. Unfortunately, the RSV translates *gramma* as "written code," and encourages an emphasis on code, which is not the point of the sentence. Paul does not distinguish between torah and the Spirit, but between that which is written (and thereby vulnerable to manipulation and tending to separate us from God) and Spirit. As that which is written, it is a code. As that which God speaks, it is instruction.

Paul's letters were dispatched to the churches under his care with the intention that they would be read aloud in the assembly and with hope that God would use the oral reading of the letters as the means of communicating the divine grace and peace of which Paul wrote. The salutations and benedictions in Paul's letters were Paul's way of extending his apostolic authority when absent, an authority Paul knew to be given him by the Spirit which empowered him. They were also an extension of the prophetic assumption that God, if he so chooses, can take the human word and make it the instrument of divine action. This is clearly seen in Paul's assertion, in 1 Corinthians 5, that although he is absent from the Corinthian assembly in body, he is present by the power of the Holy Spirit and that by the power of the Spirit, his own decree in the matter at hand is made effective.

The difference between the written and the living words is the presence of the Living God in the speaking of the latter.

It is in this context that we are to hear the formula Jesus uses in the so-called antitheses of Matthew 5:21-47: "You have heard that it was said . . . but I say to you . . . ." Jesus cut through the human testimony to torah and made the ancient torah live again because he, as Messiah, spoke it.

Jesus never blatantly rejects all validity of the interpretations, or testimonies, that have grown up around torah. He even occasionally encourages his followers to do what the Pharisees tell them to do. Any changes he makes are rejections of any current validity of the specific interpretation in question. It has become a dead letter. He does not say that it was in error at the outset, but simply that it is no longer the word of God.

In 1 John 2:7-8, the same basic perspective is at work. The old commandment is seen to be, paradoxically, both old and new. It is not a new commandment, but the old one heard from the beginning; at the same time, it is new because the Light now comes into the Darkness and makes it new!

JESUS, TORAH, AND THE PROPHETS

Jesus fulfills torah and the prophets. Already in Matthew there have been indications of the way in which he fulfills the prophets. From the moment alienation set in between God and the creation, God had been at work to bring reconciliation. Specific events in Israel's history were proclaimed by the prophets as events in which God was at work for Israel, frequently in opposing Israel's own will. These events had their meaning as episodes in God's continuing plan for the renewal of the creation, and Jesus is the focal point of that plan. Israel's life takes its meaning from that task for which she was created and to which she was called; therefore, Jesus, as the one in whom God's work focuses, is also the Israelite in whom all Israel finds its fulfillment. Through the Messiah, Israel's task will be fulfilled. Consequently, all the specific events that have been determinative in Israel's life also find their ultimate meaning—not a naturalistic definition, but their cosmic significance—in Jesus the Messiah. Hosea's prophecy concerning God calling his son out of Egypt, formerly full of meaning as a sign of God's providential care, takes on a new dimension in that the exodus is a major step on the road toward the cosmic renewal that comes in Jesus Christ. As for exegesis, God accommodates himself to the interpretive methods of those who serve as his instruments, just as he accommodated himself to the warring tendencies of the judges. Through human insight and through human error, alike, the gracious God works for the fulfillment of his people's purpose.

Jesus, therefore, does not destroy the prophetic oracles, but fulfills them. He is the one in whom that history of which they have been the interpreters finds its purpose and meaning. The oracles are fulfilled by being absorbed into his story. Disciples may analyze those oracles for purposes of historical research and hear them in view of their meaning for ancient history, but disciples can never read them again as *only* ancient history. Nor are they properly read as texts in which the "eye of faith" detects a deeper, truer meaning. Rather, disciples are to read the oracles as elements of the family history, elements whose historical meaning is transcended in their fulfillment in the goal of that history.

Jesus also fulfills torah. He is the one in whom the written testimony finds its fulfillment, in that the New Age, which draws near in him, is that toward which the testimony, as caretaker, has pointed. The rabbis of the first century debated at length the proper interpretation of Jeremiah's "torah written on the heart." Will it be the old torah internalized? a new torah for a new age? a new interpretation of old torah? For Jeremiah, however, it was not the testimony to torah, but torah itself that would be written on the heart, that is, engraved in the very desires and motives of the people. No one any longer will have to ask someone else or urge someone else with regard to God's instructions, for God's instructions will become inward. There will be such harmony between God and God's people that the people will not have to be commanded by God, nor will they be left to their isolated desires to declare good and evil on their own. The intimacy with God and the transformation of their own character, which will have been wrought by God, will result in a spontaneous expression of God's will in their very desires. In the New Age there will be not simply the order and justice torah was written to help provide; there will be that comprehensive renewal and transformation of human character, of the whole community and of the whole person, that torah has been unable to bring about, but on which true order and justice depend.

Although analogies are always limited, a helpful analogy for the future transformation and the heart engraved with torah is the act of breathing. We cannot live without breathing. The breathless body is a body, but it is a dead body. If our breath is cut off we are no longer able to think, to see, or to hear, because we are dead. (The analogy is limited here specifically to the human being as a living, organic body and does not take into account—to accept or to reject—such things as out-of-the-body experiences.) When we are going about our daily activities, we do not concentrate on breathing. We do not exert our will to breathe. We simply breathe. Breathing is an activity of the involuntary muscles. The transformed heart will result in a life that expresses the will of God to which written torah testifies as involuntarily as we now breathe. The fully transformed life will be one in which we do not ask or decide about the will of God, but simply act out of the will of God.

Jesus fulfills torah as the one in whom that transformed heart already appears. His desire is a manifestation of God's will. He does not have to seek God's will, nor does he have to struggle with himself in deciding whether to do God's will, but his very will and desire are expressions of God's will and desire. No longer must God's will be expressed as a command, even a direct command, for the intimacy with God and harmony with God are such that God's will for human life is ingrained in the human character. This is what leads the Fourth Evangelist to speak of Jesus as the incarnation of the *logos,* which for that Evangelist is a term referring to God's wisdom and to God's torah. Jesus, for John's Gospel, is the incarnation of torah—not incarnation of the testimony to torah, but of torah itself.

In this context, written torah, as written testimony, comes to an end as the central point of reference to God's instruction, but it comes to an end in the sense that the one on whose behalf it stood as a witness and a guardian now has come. To the extent that the people of God receive the new character, with torah written on the heart, written torah is useless. To the extent that the people of God still live in the world rendered imperfect by the Old Age, the written torah still has a role to play. Even then, however, Jesus as the one who is the incarnation of God's wisdom, God's torah, sweeps aside past testimonies and speaks a new testimony to the proper hearing of God's torah. Once, we heard one testimony; now Jesus delivers a new testimony. As the full expression of the Light, he does not destroy torah, because torah also is Light. He comes, rather, as the one in whose Light all other testimonies to the Light must find their center and meaning.

TIGHTENING AND LOOSENING

Jesus fulfills torah by bringing it to life again as God's living word. He does not destroy torah by "untying" it (the root of the Greek word translated "destroy" or "abolish"), for to loosen torah would be to loosen the testimony to God's word. The torah to which Jesus refers here, however, is that torah which had come to be regarded as a set-apart tradition. It does not include the later efforts at testimony and interpretation which, by some, were regarded also as torah. That which Jesus fulfills is torah as it is transmitted in the Pentateuch. Jesus comes to give that torah new life as God's living word.

Jesus does not unloosen or destroy written torah, for the New Age is not fully here. It is anticipated in his work. It has drawn near in his work. It is manifested in him, for he is the New Creation among us—but the New Creation invading the Old.

Jesus' opponents have loosened torah by providing loopholes—qualifications and exceptions. They have borne witness to the Darkness by assuming the conditions of the Old Age to be so overpowering that even God's torah must give way before them. Certainly, those who are baptized into the assembly of the New Age are not thereby removed from the temporal confines in the Old Age. They do share Jesus' invasion into the Old Age, however, and through temporally conditioned lives in the midst of the Old Age are to point to the righteousness of the New Age.

In Jesus' day, the possibility that two or more requirements of torah might come into conflict, thus making observance of the whole torah impossible, led to designating the components of torah as heavier or lighter. Jesus attacked certain officials on the grounds that they had disregarded components they themselves had declared weighty and had stressed lighter components instead. The question, Which is the greatest commandment? is the question, Which is the "weightiest of the weighty?"

From our limited, human perspective, the two commandments Jesus cited in response to the question are equally weighty. Neither can displace or take precedence over the other. Because God wills what promotes the well-being of his creatures, it is inconceivable that what promotes genuine human well-being could ever conflict with love for God. On the other hand, whoever claims to love God, but hates his or her brother or sister, is a liar (1 John 4:20).

All other commandments, whether viewed as heavier or lighter, rest on these two supreme commandments. These two undergird, or are expressed by means of, the others.

Torah itself will not pass away until the Old Age has passed away, until the old heavens and the old earth have been fulfilled in the new. Faithful disciples, having cast aside the qualifications and exceptions that have accumulated around torah, will reflect in their lives the true meaning of torah. They will manifest an adherence to God's will that is different from the surface legalism and the exceptions that characterize Jesus' opponents. Disciples of Jesus have been set free from the Darkness that they might obey in perfect freedom. Those who treat torah as Jesus' opponents have treated it will perish in the Darkness as though they had never seen the Light.

Jesus does not teach an "interim ethic" in the sense of a set of laws with which heroically to await the New Age, but he brings the living command of God, providing a new ordering for his followers' lives. By that new ordering they are to reflect the life of the New Age amid the structural realities of the Old Age. By the faithfulness of their temporal lives they are to bear testimony to God's own faithfulness—not by adhering to a lifeless law on parchment, but by following the instruction of their master, who is with them until the end of the Age.

Nor will faithful disciples obey the commands of God in order to earn their salvation (for salvation is not a payment for obedience) nor in order to make themselves good (for only God is good). They will obey the instruction of the Living God for one reason and one reason only, that others, seeing their lives, might glorify God the Transcendent Father. Only *that* righteousness is the righteousness which exceeds all other righteousness— only the righteousness that is disinterested from the standpoint of the self and is an outward expression of that devotion to and trust in God that undergirds one's entire being.

In effect, the Sermon is concerned, from beginning to end, with the nature of true freedom. Freedom, for disciples of Jesus Christ, is that relationship to God in which disciples become by restored nature what human beings have been destined to become by the will of God. True freedom is spontaneous harmony with the will of God, a harmony in which one neither is coerced from without nor must coerce oneself from within, but in which there is spontaneous compliance.

PART FIVE

TORAH FOR THE NEW AGE

You have heard that it was said to people of old: "You shall not kill;" and: "Whoever kills shall be liable to judgment." But I say to you: Everyone who is angry with his brother shall be liable to judgment; whoever hurls "raca!" at his brother shall be liable to the council; and whoever says "fool!" shall be liable to fiery Gehenna.

So if you are offering your gift at the altar, and there you remember that your brother has something against you, leave your gift there before the altar and, first, go be reconciled to your brother. Then come and offer your gift.

Make friends quickly with your accuser, while you are going with him to court, lest your accuser hand you over to the judge, and the judge to the guard, and you be put in prison. Truly, I say to you: You will never get out until you have paid the last penny.

You have heard that it was said: "You shall not commit adultery." But I say to you: Everyone who looks at a woman lustfully has already committed adultery with her in will and motive.

If your right eye causes you to stumble, pluck it out and throw it away. It is better that you lose one of your members than that your whole body go into Gehenna.

It was also said, "Whoever divorces his wife, let him give her a certificate of divorce." But I say to you: Everyone who divorces his wife, except on the ground of *porneia,* makes her an adulteress; and whoever marries a divorced woman commits adultery.

Again, you have heard that it was said to the ancients: "You shall not swear falsely, but you shall perform to the Lord what you have sworn." But I say to you: Do not swear at all—either by heaven, for it is the throne of God; or by the earth, for it is his footstool; or by Jerusalem, for it is the city of the great king. And do not swear by your head, for you cannot make one hair white or black. Let what you say be simply *Yes, yes* or *No, no.* Anything more than this comes from the evil one.

You have heard that it was said: "An eye for an eye, and a tooth for a tooth." But I say to you: Do not resist one who is evil. If anyone strikes you on the right cheek, turn the other to him, as well. And if anyone threatens to sue you and take your coat, give that person your cloak, as well. And if anyone forces you to go *one* mile, go with that person *two* miles. Give to the one who begs from you, and do not refuse the one who seeks to borrow from you.

You have heard that it was said: "You shall love your neighbor and hate your enemy." But I say to you: Love your enemies and pray for those who persecute you, so that you may be children of your Father who is in heaven. For he makes his sun rise on the evil and on the good, and sends his rain on the just and on the unjust.

When you love those who love you, what reward have you? Do not even tax collectors do that? And if you speak greetings only to your brethren, what more are you doing than others? Do not even the Gentiles do that? You, therefore, must be perfect as your heavenly Father is perfect.

(Matthew 5:21-48)

CHAPTER 18

THE "ANTITHESES" AS DESCRIPTIONS
OF THE NEW LIFE

The traditional designation of these passages as *antitheses* is correct only if we mean that Jesus' new spoken word is set over against the interpretations of torah that were given in the Old Age as a concession to the frailty of human nature in the midst of the Old Age. Jesus does not contradict God's torah, but speaks it anew in the realm of the nearness of the New Age. He does not give new rules and regulations for mechanical, self-assertive righteousness, but speaks the Living Word of God to the disciples, commanding them in authority from God. He describes for them the way of life the New Age makes possible. He sets them free to cast aside the values, standards, and practices of the Old Age and binds them in freedom to the way of life that characterizes the Reign of God. Since there can be no contradiction between the character of the Reign of God and the character of God himself, the torah Jesus speaks is rooted in God's own character. Disciples, then, are freely to abide by that torah that others, seeing the manifestation of torah in the disciples lives, might be led to glorify God. Living according to Jesus' testimony to torah is the way in which disciples are salt of value and light of benefit to the world on whose behalf they have been called.

The antitheses are Matthew's testimony to the word Jesus spoke, testimony through which the Living Word may once again be heard when the Living Jesus, who is with his assembly until the end of the Age, chooses to make himself known through them. For those who embrace them freely as wisdom from the Living Christ, they are not rules and regulations, but light in the Darkness. For those whose lives are being renewed in the Light, the antitheses contain descriptions of the life we have a right to expect God to enable us to live spontaneously. For those who are bound by the Darkness and who seek them as means of self-help, they are rigid demands creating stress and anxiety and leading to Death.

The Greek word *arkaiois* is a dignified designation of the earliest generations. Other words could have been used to refer to them as "the old-timers" or "the earliest folk," but the discussion is about matters of weight, about a sacred tradition, about those who first received God's torah through Moses. One must distinguish, however, between the instruction that was given and the testimony which sought to bring that instruction to bear upon specific situations. The living instruction has been mediated through testimony that will no longer hold up. That testimony made concessions to the Old Age. Now, the New has drawn near, and the Word of God, torah for our guidance, must be spoken anew.

Sufficient importance has usually not been given to the tenses of the Ten "Commandments" or to Jesus' words in this part of the Sermon. In both passages, the tense is future, not imperative. (Technically, in Hebrew there are no tenses, only voices; the point is that the Hebrew verb is imperfect, implying continuing action, rather than imperative, which would be a command.) This is perfectly consistent with the nature of torah as instruction rather than legalism. The oral and written testimony first given to the ancient ones who were with Moses at Sinai reports God as having described a way of life, which he set before them and assumed they would live. It is not an imperative, for an imperative is a command; and a command anticipates implicitly that the one who is commanded will either obey or disobey. When one speaks a command, it is not out of the question that the response may be disobedience.

To give a matter-of-fact description of what will take place in the future, however—to set forth a vision of the future, so to speak—implies no such possibility. To disobey a command is to usurp a choice not given, but to violate a vision of the future is to threaten that future itself. To disobey God is to risk judgment; to violate God's plan is to risk the destruction of the world.

Perhaps the best analogy for the way the Ten Words and Jesus' instruction are to be heard is the parent who, before a vacation trip, says to the children, "Now, we are going to Grandmother's house. And when we get to Grandmother's house, we will not be too noisy, we will be polite, and we will not squabble among ourselves."

This is not a command, but a description. "Here is the way things are done at Grandmother's house." If the child doesn't accept the description as just that—a description—but is determined to act another way, then the description becomes *pre*scription. The instruction for the sabbath, for another example, is, in effect, "You don't have to work on the Sabbath." When the gift is rejected, however, the gift becomes a demand: "You *shall not* work on the Sabbath!"

Torah is a description of the good life. Jesus' instruction is a description of the life of the New Age, a life which manifests the character of God. When either is rejected, it becomes command—or, in the worst case—Law!

THE ANTITHESES AND THE CHARACTER OF GOD

The antitheses are not, then, law—in the usual sense of the word—or rules or regulations; they are instruction. They are descriptions of facets of the life of the assembly that lives under the Reign of God in the midst of the Darkness. They are set forth as examples of what the assembly is *expected* to be, not primarily rules for what it *must* be.

At the same time, the antitheses are examples of those works by which the nations, upon seeing, may be led to glorify God. The antitheses are reflections of God's own character. The assembly is to be a community of reconciliation and nonviolence, because God is conciliatory in his work. The entire history of Israel and of the first community of disciples is a history of God reaching out through his people to reconcile the world—indeed, the entire creation—to himself and to bring healing and well-being to it. God's anger and violence are always aimed at those forces which threaten to corrupt and destroy that creation which God brought into existence and which he loves as a parent loves child.

The assembly, by its life, is to bear witness to this conciliatory, essentially nonviolent character of God. To be peacemakers is to be the children of God—those who are like God. To act violently and with contempt toward others is to bear false witness, as the people of God, to the character of God.

From this standpoint, then, the antitheses are not rules and regulations, even for those who embrace them as the gracious promise of God. They become rules and regulations only when the assembly or those in the assembly do not hear them as wisdom for a free people or as the Living Word. In other words, since they are the means by which the assembly is to bear witness to the character of God, for those who do not hear them as Jesus intended them, they do become rule, regulation, even law—not because obeying them leads to salvation, because it does not; not because we thereby make ourselves good, for we do not; but simply and only because the community was called in the first place not to save its soul or to be good, but to bear witness to the character of God.

CHAPTER 19

MURDER, ANGER, AND RECONCILIATION

The ideal life of the people of God described in the Ten Words of Exodus 20 will have no place for violence.

"You will not kill" is a description of Israel's continuing life as God envisioned it. In the midst of a world of violence, Israel was to be free from violence. God promised Israel such a life. The vision was spoken to Moses, and God then testified to having said this to Moses by writing, with his own finger, on the tablets of stone.

When God spoke to Moses, the people were terrified of the possibility of standing before God. Moses, therefore, was urged to stand as their mediator, and God accommodated them by accepting Moses in this role. Taking into account their imperfections, however, God also accommodated his people by speaking to Moses in a body of *mishpatim*. The RSV calls them *ordinances;* the Authorized Version (King James) *judgments.* Neither of these words, however, carries the essence of the Hebrew word, for the Hebrew refers to decisions that restore order, or equilibrium, to the situation at hand. It is as though God recognized in the error of the people a condition that would make his vision of Israel's life at least highly unlikely. He decided, therefore, to accommodate their frailty by further instruction in how they might restore a semblance of the vision when they had violated it. For example, the Ten "Commandments" in Exodus 20 are introduced by a reminder that God set the Israelites free by bringing them out of Egypt. Israel was not to be a society with slavery. Knowing that their conditioning by the Chaos would lead to including slavery, however, God placed restrictions on slavery. Slavery was not to be perpetual, but was subject to the year of release.

In the same manner, although Israel's life is not to be characterized by the violence and blood revenge of the world around them, God recognizes that there will be occasions when his people do kill. The "commandment" as Jesus quotes it in Matthew's Gospel concerns an act expressing blood thirst.

It is the act of killing born of anger or desire for revenge. God's intent for Israel was that she be a society in which blood thirst does not arise. When someone does kill another person, therefore, the killer must be tried. Whoever kills is liable—that is, answerable to—the established body bearing responsibility for establishing equilibrium, for restoring order. The Greek word translated "judgment" *(kriné)* is from a root which has to do with parting and sifting. The one who kills must stand before those who will sift out the facts of the case.

In the various instructions in Exodus and Deuteronomy, a hedge is put around killing; only when God calls for it is it permissible. Rather than naturalistic rules and mores, such as those by which the world around Israel lives, God's instructions will determine who is to be executed. God works toward the vision not by eliminating killing, which could be accomplished only by God establishing a perfection he was not yet ready to establish, but by restricting it. Capital punishment is not prohibited, but is restricted to only those specific conditions God sets down. Even the killing of animals for food is the result of God's permission in wake of the flood, and it reflects the decay of the good creation.

For Israel to take a life in compliance with the instructions, therefore, is a religious act, not a mere national or state act. To execute a member of the assembly on the basis of revenge or political expediency or in order to deter crime is to act on naturalistic grounds born of the Darkness. It is to be a pawn of Death, which entices us to wield death as an instrument. Only when the testimony becomes God's command is capital punishment truly an act in keeping with the will of God. All other occasions, even if the strict letter of written torah is followed, are done outside the relationship of instruction and obedience, which is the true goal of torah.

The state or nation that exacts the death penalty is acting not as the holy assembly, but as one of the nations—one of those creatures of the Darkness who have been brought, along with the rest of the Creation, under the dominion of Christ, but who still have not surrendered and who struggle against that dominion. That the powers bear the sword by the authority of God does not mean that they are any the less motivated by the drives of the Darkness, but simply that even in their work as Darkness-driven powers they are the instruments of God, who takes their evil deeds and uses them for his own purposes, or at least brings his purpose from them.

The civil official who defends capital punishment on the grounds that the Old Testament calls for it is not an example of the state obeying the Living Word of God, but, rather, is an example of the Devil quoting scripture for his own purposes. At the same time, Christians who oppose capital punishment on grounds that it is contrary to the Bible are not necessarily bearing witness to the Word of God; they may be doing nothing more than engaging in legalism. I do not say this in any effort to undercut the efforts of those who oppose capital punishment. Capital punishment should be opposed, and it can be opposed on the basis of obedience to the Word of God; but that opposition must not grow either out of a mistaken idea that the state is the people of God and is therefore obligated to order its life accordingly or out of a legalism that assumes that an absent God has left us with rules and regulations. Nor is it legitimate for those who oppose capital punishment to lead us to assume that this stand places us on some higher moral ground than those who affirm capital punishment. To assume that the state is the people of God is idolatry; to quote scripture at the state is to be irrelevant; to assume a higher moral status is Pharisaism.

The prophet Isaiah promised a day when the whole world will stream to Mount Zion to hear instruction from the God of Jacob. It is not impossible that here or there some nation or another might be attracted to torah by the light of witness borne by the assembly. If so, the assembly should celebrate. This is not what has happened when a "Christian" majority enacts legislation and imposes it, by numerical strength, on the society. That is legalism. A genuine consensus (as opposed to a simple majority) is not out of the question, but we should not hold our breath while awaiting it. Isaiah's vision will be realized only after the Old Age has run its course. Until then, the assembly must bear witness by the character of its life. Obviously, such a view of the relationship of the Bible to human government rules out all efforts toward theocracy—whether that of John Calvin or that of today's Christian Reconstruction Movement.

Authentic witness to the Word of God begins within the assembly by eliminating violence as a means of solving problems. This should spill over into the world outside as a refusal to engage in violence as the assembly in the world. When the assembly speaks to the state, a creature already brought under the dominion of Christ, and cries out after having been addressed, the proper cry is, "In the name of the Living God, No More Killing."

If this seems puny and unconvincing, try to recall how many state or Federal laws have been changed or how many executions have been stopped because someone quoted scripture at the officials or marshaled a convincing rational argument. The prophetic testimony to the Word of God has never rested on the world's wisdom nor on the lifeless legal letter, but on the call of the Living God. If capital punishment is ever discontinued, it will be not because of human arguments, but because of the transformation of the human heart or the increased wisdom of the state, and neither of these is subject to human manipulation.

Jesus returns to the basic testimony itself—the simple prohibition—and moves in a new direction, giving new testimony to the instruction, restoring the vision. The former testimony was correct, as far as it went; but God's vision for Israel, which is now respoken for those who embrace the New

Age, does not permit the earlier narrow definition of violence. In the Old Age, anger was accepted as part of a fallen world. Jesus, however, elevates the violence of the spoken word to the same level as the violent action, which kills. It will not do to say that since God displays wrath, it is permissible for God's people to act in wrath, for whereas God's wrath always is in defense of his creation, human wrath is usually self-centered. Whoever displays wrath, therefore, will be judged. The reason for the anger must be discovered. The motives must be sifted out. Only in this manner can equilibrium be restored.

It is important only up to a point to give a precise translation of *raca* and *moray,* for they are not the only words that endanger the speaker. They are, rather, examples of the spoken violence that endangers the assembly and the disciple. *Raca* is found nowhere else in Greek, and is usually assumed to be a loan word from Aramaic. There is general agreement that it is a word meaning "blockhead" or "empty-head." At any rate, it is a term of insult, and usually the sentence in Matthew is translated, "Whoever insults his brother . . ."

Moray, usually translated "fool," is the word from which the English word *moron* comes. It is also a form of the word used earlier to refer to salt that has been rendered useless. That salt has become insipid or watered down. The word can even be used to refer to those animals that, in winter, become sluggish and less alert. Frequently, it is used to describe someone who is unable to make proper decisions. In light of this, it is surprising that in the Greek Old Testament, this word is not the one usually used to refer to the foolish person of the wisdom tradition, but is used usually to refer to the person who deliberately breaks away from God and also leads others astray. Since the thrust of Jesus' warning has to do with the anger and insult expressed in the words, the full range of meanings—insipid to Godless one—should be included in the meaning that applies here. To accuse a brother or sister in the assembly of being Godless will be grounds for trial.

Raca! and *Moray!* are examples of the violence of language. Whenever they are spoken to express anger, they are verbal insults of the one to whom they are addressed. It would be the height of legalism either to argue that *only* these words make one liable to judgment or to contend that the mere use of them under any circumstances places the speaker in jeopardy. The thing against which Jesus warns is not words in and of themselves, but anger that manifests itself in words that are intended to demean or to destroy. All verbal insults that express anger and a desire to hurt are covered: Raca! Moron! Fool! Scum! Meathead! Idiot! Stupid! Nigger! Redneck! Bitch! Bastard! Communist! Conservative! Liberal! Secular Humanist! Atheist! Right Winger! Bureaucrat! Spik! Jew! All these and all others that are hurled as invectives make up that verbal arsenal from which we are to be, and must be, set free. We must be linguistically disarmed. The anger that expresses itself in the verbal insult is the anger of wounded desire, of frustrated self-interest. It is the anger that counts the other as an obstacle to one's own goals, as an enemy, as less than human. Insult tramples the other person's humanity. It is an attack on one who shares the human race's original role as God's image, and, as such, it is an offense against God himself. The insult hurled at a brother or sister in the assembly, or at one outside the assembly, reveals *us* for what *we* are: those who seek to hurt and destroy! The person I insult may prefer angry words to a gunshot to the head, but, as for what *I* am revealed to be, there is no significant difference. The insult expresses violence as truly as does killing: Both lead to trial before God.

ANGER AND POLITE DISCOURSE

The diversity and subtlety of the Darkness-rooted violence, which lashes out in verbal insults, is especially evident in modern public discourse. In an earlier time, insults were more obvious. The records of debates between candidates for public office in the nineteenth century in the United States reveal invective beside which those of the late twentieth century pale by comparison. We have, in fact, developed a technique of language, by means of which we use words that traditionally have been less offensive, and more sophisticated, to express the subtle insult. The polite invective by which today's political candidates seek to demean and humiliate one another include: irresponsible, naive, well-intentioned, inexperienced, a nice person, ill-advised, and the like—words that pretend to appreciate the other and to be objective and balanced but whose real purpose is to belittle the opponent, to demean a part of the opponent's character or abilities in the minds of the hearers.

In international affairs, the insult is hurled through adjectives such as brutal, leftist, fundamentalist, godless, atheistic, despotic, tyrannical, capitalistic, Marxist-Leninist, radical, and dictatorial. Always, the goal is to dehumanize the enemy or the opponent, to lead others to consider the other as less than human, as not worthy of life.

Such is the way of the Darkness. Such is the way of a world that has fallen away from the original condition in which God created it and in which God desired it to remain. Such is the Old Age from which disciples are delivered, but into whose midst they are called as witnesses of the Light, that the world might be redeemed from the Darkness and that the world's language might be used to celebrate the glory of God and to bridge the gaps that separate us, as human beings, one from another.

LIABILITY

As *raca* and *moray* are examples of anger manifested in words, the Sanhedrin and fiery Gehenna are examples of the possible consequences of anger. The multitude of efforts to determine some ascending order of the warnings here, and the complications acknowledged in these efforts, lead, ultimately, to a dead end. We need not deny that Matthew may have intended some order for purposes of psychological effect, but a perception of the meaning of the passage does not depend on absolute assurance of what that intent was. The Sanhedrin, quite apart from what Matthew specifically intended, is a council of judgment. Fiery Gehenna is a place of punishment.

From a strictly factual standpoint, *Gehenna* is hardly clearer than *Sanhedrin*. The Sanhedrin was the local council of Jewish officials charged with various responsibilities for the community. They were even allowed to impose the death penalty in certain situations. The word *Sanhedrin* came to be used, however, as a more general word for councils.

Gehenna was the Valley of Hinnom, a valley south of Jerusalem, at one time associated with human sacrifice and later used as a sort of city dump for the trash and waste from Jerusalem. The name came also to be used for the fiery place of punishment that some believed awaited the wicked either after death or at the day of judgment. The prophets of the Old Testament had referred to the trash heap and to fire as images of God's judgment on his people. It is not clear, therefore, whether Jesus is speaking literally or figuratively in this passage.

The warning is that the disciple who angrily hurls a term of insult at another member of the assembly will be tried just as certainly as the one who kills. If one disciple calls another a fool, he or she must be prepared to show that the anger was not an expression of self-interest, but a concern for the will of God, and that the one against whom the charge was made had truly acted as a fool. The warning is not against genuine zeal for the will of God when that zeal leads to an accurate evaluation of the situation at hand, but against self-centered anger that demeans others in an effort to achieve one's own goals and ambitions. The former may be a prophetic declaration of the Word of God. The latter will be a manifestation of thralldom to the Darkness, which endangers one's very life.

WHO IS MY BROTHER OR SISTER?

There is a tendency in the New Testament to reserve family designations for members of the assembly. It is entirely possible, therefore, that Matthew intended this saying to convey the respect that members of the assembly are to have for one another. If so, it was not a self-centered concern. Nor did it mean that members are free to be angry with and to insult those outside the assembly. Nor did it mean that Matthew was entirely unconcerned with those outside the assembly. Other portions of the Sermon itself deal quite effectively with how members of the assembly are to relate to and deal with those who are outside. The question here, quite simply, is how the assembly can live its own life in the midst of the world so that as salt and light it can best draw attention to God himself. The word translated "brother" *(adelphos),* of course, is generic; it reflects the male orientation of the community. Certainly it does not indicate that the assembly was all-male or that it was permissible to treat the female members with contempt. It in no way violates the passage to extend it by reading it as "brother" or "sister."

Comments on the community's relation to the world outside will arise more thoroughly later, but here it should simply be pointed out that since the assembly's role is to bear witness to the Light—to be salt and light for the world—and to reach out to all nations, seeking to draw from those nations disciples of the assembly's Lord, it is wholly inconceivable that the words about murder and anger should be irrelevant to those on whose behalf the assembly exists. This assertion, however, need not rest on what seems conceivable or inconceivable to me as one person. There is, within Jesus' exhortation that immediately precedes the antitheses, a basis for hearing all the antitheses as words bursting with implications for the world outside the assembly. The antitheses concern those works the viewing of which is to lead the nations to glorify God.

RECONCILIATION AND NONVIOLENCE

The essence of the antithesis on murder and anger is that the assembly of God's people in the New Age is to be characterized by reconciliation rather than violence. It is not enough to say simply "nonviolence," for nonviolence is essentially a negative concept.

In a world of violence, when that violence reaches into the holy assembly itself, there must be ways of dealing with it lest the assembly become as racked with violence as is the world outside—thereby becoming insipid salt, a light that dies from suffocation. The liability sayings are for the purpose partially of warning, partially of instructing the assembly in how to respond to the violence that occurs within. The person who acts violently must be tried and warned that such actions place one in jeopardy of destruction. If the assembly sifts the evidence and declares the harsh words to have been inappropriate, inaccurate, and rooted in self-centered anger, then the culprit should be warned that his or her actions reflect not the mercy and peace that is to characterize the community, but the corruption of the Darkness. They are the work of Satan. The assembly is not to execute or to expel the offending member, lest the wheat be ripped out with the tares. The assembly has the assurance of the risen Lord, however, that where two or three are gathered in his name, he is among them and that their decisions are his decisions. They are to treat the offending member as though he were a tax collector (Matt. 18:15-20); that is, he or she is to be seen as one still in need of conversion. That offender should also be warned that to continue on the road of violence within the community places him or her in danger of destruction from God on the Day of Judgment.

The offender does have one avenue of hope: the avenue of reconciliation. Since we are not accustomed to the ceremony, the idea of getting up in the middle of the ceremony of sacrifice, leaving the animal or cereal before the altar, and leaving the temple precincts in order to find someone do not strike us with the jolt that it would have struck Jesus' audience. At least something of the impact may be communicated if we imagine a person being baptized or receiving the Lord's Supper suddenly asking that the ceremony be halted while he or she goes across town to apologize to someone. The logical question for the person in charge to ask would be, Why can't you take care of that later? The ceremony is underway. Apologies can wait. It is a commonplace of Israelite prophecy, however, that the value of the ceremony is affected by the relationship between the worshiper and his or her brother or sister. When there is injustice and alienation, sacrifice is hypocrisy. The very validity of the offering rests on the action Jesus prescribes.

Although reconciliation, which is to characterize the community, is less genuine when one is driven to it from fear, and more genuine when a person takes seriously that he or she has acted violently toward a brother or sister, we are reminded that failure to make peace with those we have offended will cause us to be cast into that prison from which there is only a small chance of escape, that prison earlier described as fiery Gehenna, the bowels of Death itself. We should recall here those psalms in which God himself keeps watch over the oppressed and those who have been mistreated, those psalms in which the suffering righteous one cries out to God for vengeance and in which we are assured that God hears such cries and will, in his own time, respond by bringing destruction on the wicked oppressor.

ANGER AND OPPRESSION

But what of anger in response to the oppression of others? Is violence in response to violence enacted against others permissible? The beatitudes suggest that the proper response to violence is mourning, not actions manifesting anger. The Bible occasionally portrays the response of God himself as mourning when one might have anticipated anger (for example, Jer. 8:22–9:3). Even from the standpoint of worldly wisdom, anger obviously evokes violence. Anger seeks victory over the enemy and seeks to punish the enemy for his or her offense. Mourning, on the other hand, recognizes the offender as a human being whose actions and attitudes shut out God's grace and rob the offender of the joy of the kingdom. Whether to oppose the enemy and to seek to keep him or her from activities that oppress and destroy is not the issue. The issue is whether such opposition is undertaken in anger or in mourning. If undertaken in anger, the primary goal will be to defeat the enemy for the sake of the enemy's victim. If undertaken in mourning, the goal will more likely be to convert the enemy.

In the power struggles of this world, where people are imprisoned, tortured, murdered, and robbed of their human identity, the church that sets out to aid the oppressed on the basis of anger toward the oppressor will not bear witness to the gospel, but to the same humanitarian impulses of which even Caesar is capable. It is quite human, for example, to be incensed over the death of a child. It is much more difficult to mourn for the culprit as well as for the victim. Yet, if the child is in the hands of God and the culprit must stand before the judgment seat of God, there is a sense in which the culprit is in graver danger than the victim.

None of this is in any sense a call to forsake the victims of oppression. Nor is it to suggest that we should not seek to restrain those who harm others by their actions. It is not even to automatically rule out the presence of Christians among guerilla bands who seek to overthrow an inhumane government. It is, however, to raise the question of the role of such a person in the activities in which one can legitimately engage. If the presence of the disciple is merely for the sake of supporting the movement, it can hardly be seen as witness to the Light. Even martyrdom is not to be undertaken as stoic or resentful obedience to a regulation, but as responsible love for the executioner (1 Cor. 13) and with forgiveness in our hearts and on our lips (as Jesus died on the cross).

In all of this, we have to do not with rules and regulations for reaction to oppression or with criteria for just war, but with reminders of the New Testament witness to the Word of God—a witness that may, by the grace of God, as we recall it and celebrate it, become for us the means of a new word in our day.

CHAPTER 20

ADULTERY AND THE NEIGHBOR

The assembly of disciples, by its life of dependability and faithfulness within, bears witness to God's dependability and faithfulness. Dependability and faithfulness, however, are not simply legal arrangements, but are relationships engaging whole persons in a whole community. In the Old Testament the sexual fidelity of husband and wife is a common analogy for God's relationship with Israel, and Paul used it in his New Testament letters. The prophets frequently portrayed God's love for Israel and his faithfulness to Israel in terms of a husband faithful to his wife. Israel's idolatry was viewed by Jeremiah, Ezekiel, Hosea, and others as adultery—Israel, the wife of Yahweh, seeking out other lovers. The author of Ephesians saw the husband-wife relationship as an allegory for the church.

Matthew follows this same tradition. Augustine's instincts led him in the right direction when he interpreted this section of the Sermon allegorically as a concern for the church's faithfulness to Christ, rather than being merely a teaching about human adultery.

Although it would be a mistake to suppose that in this passage Matthew is not concerned with the literal meaning of adultery, it would be equally a mistake to ignore the reason for Matthew's concern. For Matthew, the antitheses are, as already asserted, examples of the way disciples of Jesus are to live in order to bear testimony to the character of God.

ADULTERY IN THE OLD TESTAMENT

Exodus and Deuteronomy had elaborated on the basic instruction with examples of adultery and by describing the proper community response to the adulterous act in order that the equilibrium of the community might be restored. Essentially, adultery, by Old Testament definition, is sexual intercourse between a man and a woman who is married or engaged to another man. Other sexual liaisons might be considered fornication, but they are not adultery in Old Testament terms.

That the narrower offense of adultery, not the wider offense of fornication, is listed in the Ten Commandments and is also the one to which Jesus refers indicates that the basic concern in both sayings is not illicit sex acts as such, but that which is manifested in the specific act under consideration. Adultery snips away at the threads of mutual dependability and faithfulness by which the community's order and stability are maintained. Adultery, therefore, undercuts those elements that partake of the covenant itself.

Outside the arrangements for marriage and engagement, sexual offenses are possible, but they are not considered adultery. They do not threaten the social fabric in the same way that it is threatened by adultery. The occasional observation that the Old Testament prohibition of adultery is essentially a property law is only superficially correct. From a legal standpoint, the act violates the property of the husband or husband-to-be, but that is not simply an individual matter; it is a threat to the covenant community as a whole. That which in another society might be seen simply as a property law becomes in Israel a covenant issue, because all of life is seen as a carefully integrated whole under the inclusive covenant between God and the community.

Moreover, the legal questions involved were not solely a matter of the woman as the property of another man. There was also the consideration of the identity of any children that might be born from the adulterous union. (It is not out of the question that this was at least as much a consideration as that of the property status of the woman.) A male child was legal heir to the family estate. In Israel the land had been apportioned to families according to instructions from God. When an adulterous act resulted in a birth, to what family did the child belong? What was its legal identity? What were its rights? Although from a narrow point of view the offended party was the husband or the intended husband of the woman involved and, legally speaking, the wife of the man involved in the act was not affected, to whom would the widow of an executed adulterer turn for protection? If she had children, she became dependent on them prematurely. If she had no children, she became the responsibility of the nearest of male kin. Adultery, then, set up vibrations in the community much as the trapped insect sets up vibrations in every link of the spider's web. Each individual violation of the society's stability threatened the dissolution of the entire order.

In Matthew 5:27-30, Jesus does not explore the rationale for the ancient commandment, but simply assumes it. The value and authority of the command are rooted not in human perceptions of the nature of life and property, but in the will of God. Consequently, a change in society's understanding of the nature of property does not abrogate the prohibition, nor does a change in the metaphysical view of human nature, despite the quasimetaphysical aspects of the rationale in Genesis 2.

From a human perspective, the origin of the commandment may be explained in numerous ways. To the unbelieving, it may even be explained away. On the other hand, because it comes from God, who knows the true nature of life and property and has spoken to us in accordance with realities beyond our perception, it may be understood and obeyed no matter what the cultural self-understanding of a given generation.

THE PENALTY FOR ADULTERY

In the Old Testament, the penalty for adultery is the execution of both parties. Were this primarily for the permission of individual revenge, the instructions would indicate the husband's or fiancé's right to exact the penalty. The purpose, however, is to maintain the stability of the community in the midst of chaos. Whenever there has been an internal threat to that order, the people are to follow God's instructions for the restoration of order. The offending members are to be removed.

Of course, it would probably sound more humane to us were it the expectation that the offenders be imprisoned, banished, or simply censured. To an extent, however, such an evaluation reflects the differences between modern and ancient understandings of human identity. In ancient Israel, identity was defined by family and community. To be cut off from both was to be a nobody and to be prey to anyone encountered. In the Old Testament, Cain and Hagar are vivid examples of the consequences of banishment. Cain feared death, because without his family he would be what some today would call a nonperson. As such, he would be fair game for desert marauders and slavers. Hagar, for protection, sought to return to Egypt, her former home. Neither Cain nor Hagar would have survived banishment had God not intervened. Viewed from this perspective, execution might be seen as more humane than banishment.

As for imprisonment, toward what end? Prisons as we know them are a modern invention. Until the eighteenth century, prisons were places where people were kept to await either execution or natural death (as political prisoners) or to prevent them from stealing or running up debts. The diversity of sentences available today was not an option at the time. You either were released when there was a new regime, pardoned by the old regime, set free when your debt had been paid, or kept in prison the rest of your life. If you were insane, you never got out. Most crimes were punished not by imprisonment, but by various forms of corporal punishment (flogging, branding, or the like) or by forced servitude. It is not too much to say that imprisonment would have been at least as bad as death. What is more, in light of all the public display of moral indignation toward the horror of prisons today, can it honestly be said that there are no prisons now where precisely the same evaluation might be made? Many prisons are institutional tombs filled with the living dead.

God expected Israel to be a community characterized by faithfulness and mutual dependability. Adultery threatened the stability of the community and thereby threatened the community's ability to fulfill its task as light in the midst of the Darkness. Offenders, therefore, had to be removed in order to eliminate the threat to Israel's task and, consequently, the threat to the world's blessing.

JESUS' TEACHING

Jesus affirms the commandment on adultery. His further statement does not set the commandment aside, but intensifies it. Adultery is unfaithfulness to one's fellow Israelite, for it invades his family and destroys his family relationships. Adultery, in effect, is one manifestation among others of following your desire to own that which belongs to another or to have your own way with that which belongs to another. It is an expression of theft.

Just as Jesus went beyond the physical act of murder, however, speaking of the anger in which murder is rooted—anger that is also expressed in verbal assaults—and warning the individual of the reconciliation that must take place in order for the integrity of the community witness to be preserved, here he goes beyond the physical act of adultery, which can be judged by the community, to the tendency of character out of which the adultery grows. In the final analysis, Jesus is concerned not simply with mechanical or naturalistic activities of the eye or brain, but with the whole person. The assembly's witness is not at its most authentic when rules and regulations are being obeyed as obligations counter to the heart, but when the integrity of the assembly manifests the integrity of those who are members of the assembly. The Greek text refers to looking at a woman (the context makes a married or engaged woman the obvious meaning) with the goal of bringing her under your own power. The word usually translated into the English as "lust" is a form of the same word used in the Greek translation of the Ten Commandments to speak of coveting. It means "to seek ownership of" or "to seek dominion over." Jesus warns that any man who wishes to bring under his own power a woman who is legally bound to another man manifests already a fracture of the relationship of faithfulness and dependability, which are the essence of the New Age. The New Age is characterized by the complete, unqualified determination to seek the well-being of others, a characteristic obviously incompatible with the eye on the prowl to assume authority over the wife or fiancée of another man.

This passage, just as the one concerning anger, is intended for the assembly. It is not a law to be imposed on the world outside the assembly. On the other hand, it reflects the life that is in tune with the way God created the world to be, and the assembly's role includes that of so honoring and manifesting the life described in torah that the entire world might be captivated by the vision.

It is precisely because torah concerns the dynamics of the creation itself, and is not merely concerned with visible, measurable actions, that physical actions do not exhaust the meaning of the commandments. The commandments speak to the whole being. Adultery is an act of the whole person. Consequently, even if it is not fulfilled physically, its beginning is not to be viewed as insignificant.

I may be congratulated if I desire sexual intercourse with another person's marriage partner, but out of love for both parties refuse to take any actions that might accomplish my desire; however, my self-congratulations are misplaced if they lead me to ignore that the desire itself—not the sexual desire particularly, but the desire for that which is forbidden—reflects my participation in the Old Age.

The assembly is not an all-male assembly. The technical definition of adultery assumed thus far is rooted in the testimony to God's Word as that testimony was proclaimed in a male-oriented society, a society in which women were legally property. As will be obvious later, in the teaching on divorce, Matthew takes steps beyond the strict limitations of the original social context and respeaks Jesus' instructions from a different outlook. To listen for God's word in a society in which the status of women is different from that of Jesus' day is not to listen for instruction on how to return to the earlier social arrangement, but is to listen for instruction on how the faithfulness and dependability manifested in observation of the instruction in an earlier arrangement is best manifested in a different arrangement.[1]

Faithfulness and dependability of the assembly are expressed, or manifested, in the faithfulness and dependability of all the assembly members, male and female. Specifically, faithfulness is manifested in not seeking to satisfy your own desires at the expense of others in the community.

By the new setting, I do not in any way refer to the setting dictated by the secular realm and that realm's state. Regardless of any similarities there may have been between ancient Israel's marriage regulations and those of other

---

1. I leave aside discussing the entire question of whether the Bible calls for a male-oriented society, and simply assert that every effort to show that the Bible portrays male domination of the female as a part of the original order of the creation falls apart when confronted with the texts of Genesis 1–3. That kind of male domination disrupts the original order and the Fall. Any effort to understand the Word of God for the assembly of the New Age must recognize the New Age's liberation from the Fall.

Near Eastern cultures, marriage in Israel was regulated according to the testimony to the Word of God. Even if it could be shown that some or all of those regulations in Israel were borrowed from various societies, this would show nothing more than the historical process through which God worked and spoke. Further, even if it could be shown that certain regulations in the early church were borrowed from Hellenistic society, this would not automatically mean that those regulations were not in any way the work of God. The faithful assembly will seek the instruction of God in its own regulations and definitions of marriage, not without regard to the society's practices, but without assuming any natural obligation to them.

It is the task of the assembly to decide what setting and what form the vow is to take in order to give it standing in the eyes of the assembly and make it recognizable in the eyes of the society. These may have to be modified and even completely overhauled from one era to the next, just as the decision whether and in what way to recognize the authority of the state's criteria for marriage will have to be reconsidered from one generation to another.

To say that God recognizes no vows of marriage between members of the assembly unless those vows meet the criteria of the assembly is to go beyond the authority given the assembly. What may seriously be questioned is whether those making such vows, while rejecting the assembly and its criteria, have taken seriously their life together as one of testimony to the character of God. But even here we must take great care not to fall into the trap of judging. The assembly is the setting of the disciple's life. It is the assembly God calls, not the individual. At the same time, the assembly is not God, but is only God's representative. As such, it has both awesome responsibility and unbreachable limitations.

REMOVING THE CAUSE OF STUMBLING

The individual disciple who desires the wife or husband of another as a sexual partner has already violated that relationship assumed in the covenant and assumed for the New Age. To suppress the desire and deny its fulfillment because of the law against adultery is not thereby to squeeze oneself into God's Reign. That Reign consists not of stubborn heads ruling recalcitrant hearts, but of whole persons manifesting in the very depths of their hearts the character of God. Those disciples who harbor the desire to possess the husband or wife of another, then, must take with utmost seriousness the necessity of removing themselves from the situation of desire.

The saying on adultery does not lay down an impersonal regulation, does not provide an ideal toward which to strive, does not provide a heroic ethic, but describes the life of the assembly under the impact of the New Age.

It describes the life that, by the grace of God, is to be embraced as a promise and is more spontaneous for some than for others. It also describes the life that bears witness to the character of God and that, therefore, for those disciples who do not find it so spontaneously manifested, is to be obeyed as the way in which testimony is borne, by the whole community, to the character of God.

It is not simply sexual fidelity and dependability with which Jesus is concerned, but fidelity and dependability in all relationships. Sexual relationships are examples, for purposes of illustration, of the character of the God who is the creator of all things and who intends to make all things new.

Jesus' words about what we are to do in an effort to eliminate sin from our lives are open to distortion in either of two ways: by our following only their surface meaning or by our attempting to follow them through sheer human effort, in other words, by stupidity or by heroism. If we take the words literally, we are in danger of assuming that blind people with no hands would either be incapable of sexual desire as such or would be incapable of desire for another person's marriage partner. This is a ridiculous stereotype of persons with disabling conditions. If we assume that we can follow the prescription by sheer human effort, we are saying, in effect, that there is no need for the New Age, simply a need for greater resistance in the Old. What Jesus calls for, however, is the elimination of the characteristics of the Old Age from our lives. Yet, only by the power of the New Age can the assembly bear witness to the New Age. Only by the presence of God's salt and God's light can the assembly be salt for the earth and light for the world, for it is his salt and his light the assembly is called to share.

Plucking out the offensive eye and cutting off the offensive hand are figurative expressions calling us to freedom from whatever holds us to the Old Age and whatever prevents our full participation in the New Age. These are figurative ways of saying that we must not resist the New Age by our self-interest and our attraction for the Old Age, but must allow the New to overcome us and to eliminate from us the desire to cling to the Old. From this standpoint, the references to plucking out the eye and cutting off the hand are hyperbole. In reference to the degree to which the Old Age must be rooted out of our lives, however, they are not hyperbole at all, but gross understatements. We must be rid not merely of any eye or hand, but of anything and everything by which the Old Age enslaves us.

That Jesus uses hyperbole and gives no clear directions is partially because he is using specific teachings of torah as examples, not as an exhaustive list of cases. Overcoming obstacles in one area of activity would be quite different from removing them in another. He also does not give simple, clear directions, however, because to do so would be to cast us back into legalism. Jesus' word is an invitation away from all such bondage.

Disciples are called to freedom from those things which hold them to the corrupt desires of the Old Age. The call to pluck out the eye or cut off the hand is a call to cast off that which binds one to the Old Age. Jesus does not simply say that offense will lead to fiery Gehenna unless we overcome the offense, but speaks more positively of the better way. Bonhoeffer sensed this when he remarked that no sacrifice is too great if it enables us to conquer a lust that could cut us off from Jesus.

This is not a call to set ourselves free, but an invitation to accept the freedom held forth in the call to discipleship itself. So long as we live in the Old Age under the impact of the New, we are not rid of our sexuality as such, but the freedom and faithfulness of the resurrection are to be manifested in the mortal body in every dimension of the body's existence. To pretend that the New Age is here in all its fullness would be to deny our sexuality. To ignore the implications of the drawing near of the New Age would be to fall back into the Darkness.

CHAPTER 21

DIVORCE AND ADULTERY

The topic of adultery is continued from the standpoint of divorce. Just as the proud assertion "I had the desire, but resisted" is not valid, neither is "I had intercourse with her, but she is no longer married (or I am no longer married)." The reality created by marriage is dissolved only at death.

Jesus, in effect, eliminates the loopholes in torah. Moses allowed divorce by a certificate or writ ending the marriage, but this was a concession in the Old Age, a concession granted because of the hardness of the human heart (Matt. 19:3-9). Moses' testimony to the Word of God in the midst of corruption permitted concessions not in keeping with the original intent of God.

In marriage, the two persons become one (Gen. 2:24). This is no naturalistic unity that can be viewed under a microscope. Nor is it a metaphysical reality that can be proven with logic apart from the presuppositions of faith. It is simply a declaration of how the two stand in God's eyes, a standing no certificate from a law court can change. In fact, only because God regards it so is the marriage dissolved at death. Marriage does more and divorce does less than the natural eye perceives. Anyone who thinks that divorce releases one from a situation in which adultery is possible misunderstands both marriage and divorce. (Mark's parallel to Matthew 19:3-9 is striking in that it envisions a woman's legal ability to divorce her husband—an impossibility in Jewish circles, but a new possibility for the church in the Gentile world. Obviously, with increased legal rights comes a greater liability before God.)

Are there any grounds at all on which members of the assembly may divorce their wives? To the assembly at Corinth, Paul had said that those who were married when they were baptized should not seek to be free of the spouse. The member of the assembly, by his or her incorporation into Christ, might become the means of blessing for the spouse and for the couple's children. For Paul, freedom from torah and having died in Christ does not permit one to act irresponsibly with regard to common human relationships.

On the other hand, Paul advised any member of the assembly whose husband or wife was not a member of the assembly and wished a divorce not to try to hold on to the marriage. It is not inevitable that the assembly member will be a means of blessing to the spouse and children who are outside the assembly, and freedom from torah means that one must not legalistically hold on to a rule for the sake of the rule alone.

In Matthew's Gospel the question of divorce is probably asked of families where both husband and wife are members of the assembly. In the Old Age divorce was permissible on numerous grounds. Are there grounds for it for those in the assembly that is to bear witness to the New Age and to the character of God? Contrary to the almost universal interpretation of this passage, Jesus' answer is solidly no.

Usually, "except on the ground of unchastity" is interpreted in terms of the question of whether divorce is permissible. Jesus, it is said, makes the concession known to have been made in Judaism by the school of the great rabbi Shammai and thereby is portrayed in Matthew as more liberal than in Mark. Such an interpretation, however, mistakenly assumes divorce to be the topic of the passage, misreads the predicate of the sentence, and assumes that Jesus is permitting divorce. The antithesis in 5:32 speaks not of whether divorce is permitted for any reason, but of how divorce affects the woman who is put aside and of the effect of marrying a divorced woman. The topic is adultery, not divorce, and the one exception is not an exception that permits divorce, but is one that concerns how the husband's hardhearted act affects the wife who is put away.

The antithesis is not so obviously hyperbolic as the preceding one, but it does contain hyperbole at the point of the consequences of divorce for the divorced woman. The way in which she would become an adulteress would be marrying another man or practicing prostitution. In Matthew's day these would not be the only options (the woman might live chastely with another family that took pity on her, her children might risk their father's ire by giving her a home, or some other arrangement might be worked out), but they would be the options most often open to the woman. There is some exaggeration here, then, in the assertion that the woman is automatically made an adulteress. Moreover, an exceptionally generous man, in order to protect her, might offer to marry a woman whose husband has, for purely selfish reasons, divorced her. That man's generosity and the husband's selfishness, however, do not change the fact that adultery is the result. The real thrust of this passage, then, is the danger into which the man who divorces his wife casts her and any man who might have compassion for her. He puts even the compassionate man in the situation of having to sin in order to show mercy! The man who divorces his wife is in the position of those to whom Jesus asserted a warning about causing "one of these little ones to sin" (Matt. 18:6). A millstone around the neck and death in the sea are a fate preferable to that laid up for the man.

Although the word *porneia* (RSV: *unchastity*) had a variety of meanings in first-century Judaism and in the early church, the context here indicates that it refers to an act by which the woman has already become an adulteress. *Porneia* is, in fact, sometimes a synonym for the word here translated "adultery." The only time a man does not endanger his wife and others by divorcing her is when she has already become an adulteress on her own.

In this passage, then, it does not say that *porneia* results in divine permission being either granted or withheld, because the point is what divorce does to others!

In Matthew 19:3-9, on the other hand, divorce *is* the topic. The conversation between Jesus and his opponents there should be heard in the context not of narrow restrictions that permitted no divorce, but of great laxity. In many circles divorce could be granted for the most trivial of excuses. Jesus tightens the tradition by leaving only *porneia* as grounds for divorce. Only in that case is it possible to divorce a woman and marry again without becoming an adulterer. At this point, Jesus again clearly becomes the authoritative figure who asserts not a new logic, but the Word of God, declaring God's evaluation, God's analysis of human deeds, in ways that presuppose no self-evident beginning points, but merely proclaim the divine judgment. Moreover, even the exception of *porneia* must be considered in light of the need to protect the assembly from the characteristics of the Old Age, lest the assembly—because of the compromised quality of its life—bear insipid testimony before the world.

Matthew does not want anyone to think that Jesus' words about getting rid of the eye or hand that causes you to sin means that you can divorce your wife if she causes you to run afoul of torah. Only if she has already become an adulteress may you divorce her.

For those who seek an easy answer to the legitimacy of divorce, then, the Sermon holds only disappointment. God himself regards marriage as an act that creates a bond indissoluble except by death. Marriage is neither to be "broken into" nor "broken out of." The Old Age is an era of hardened hearts that resist God and that seek only personal gain, personal desire, personal interest. In the Old Age, God accommodated himself to this reality of human life and made a concession to the indissoluble nature of marriage. When a husband divorced his wife, he had to legalize it so the woman would be safe from execution for adultery. When the New Age is here in all its fullness, there will be no such thing as divorce, for there will be no more marriage. All shall be as the angels. Marriage is an institution of the Old

Age, a means of both human relationships and social preservation.[1] In the in-between time—the time between the New Age's drawing near and its full presence—the assembly is to bear witness by its life to the New Age and to the character of God.

In the past, there have been times when the church was too rigid and there have been other times when the church was too lax with regard to divorce. The perfect situation is when a man and woman are able to live together in complete love for each other, each striving to see that the well-being of the other is ensured above all else; or, where children are concerned, that the well-being of the partner and the children is ensured. If two persons are so thoroughly incompatible that a continued life together seems likely to destroy both of them, then there is nothing virtuous about staying together and destroying each other on the basis of a written regulation. The authentic solution would be for the couple to maintain the marriage by each giving himself and herself over completely and unqualifiedly to the well-being of the other. Only this is true freedom.

The concern of both divisions of this passage—the words on adultery of the heart and those on causing others to become adulterers—is faithfulness and dependability. How does the assembly live in order to bear testimony, by its character, to the character of God? By faithfulness to the marriage vow and by refraining from any simple act of the mind that leads to an inner failure of the testimony. An assembly in which marriage is broken by divorce and threatened by lust says to the world that God is undependable and seeks to overpower others for his own selfish purposes, that the serpent was correct when it told Eve that God's instructions for life in the Garden were self-centered and not for the security of his children.

In these terms, again, the male-oriented categories of the instructions are revealed as mere characteristics of the society in which the Word was spoken and are not essential to the context of the Word itself. In an assembly in which there is no distinction between the status of male and female, just as in that in which there were distinctions, the instruction, spoken anew by God, is a call to faithfulness and dependability in all human relationships. Disciples are not to use the technicalities of the law to excuse or permit self-serving decisions that trample on the lives of others. With regard to divorce, all marriages ideally, should reflect that wholly committed love

---

1. As I have indicated earlier, then, the traditional view of the family as an institution of the Creation is erroneous. In order to guard against the Chaos, marriage imposes external regulations on the family. The family, thus, becomes no longer a relationship of spontaneous trust, faithfulness, and order, but an institutionalized agreement. Like all institutions, the family is fallen and is capable of demonic twists.

which reflects the character of God. When (and in this world the *when* means "usually") the ideal is not a spontaneous reality, we are not excused from the instruction. It is to be obeyed, even if as a rule, because we thereby bear testimony to the faithfulness of God, who puts up with us even when we are difficult and uncaring and turn aside from him to other gods. God holds onto us even when we commit adultery against him by joining ourselves to the various gods of this world. The adultery of the spouse may permit divorce, but as a concession, not as a requirement.

If divorcing the spouse becomes necessary—because of cruelty, concern for the children (too often an excuse in which we unconsciously blame the children and induce in them a life of guilt anxiety, since the divorce was "for" them), or for any other "respectable" reason—it will not do to attribute it to anything other than necessity. It will not have been of grace, of freedom, or of anything other than a sense of sheer unavoidability.

In such a case, should or may one marry again? The community witness is broken already by the divorce. The instructions of Jesus refer to divorce undertaken out of self-interest. The divorce forced on another bears witness to something other than faithfulness and dependability on the part of the one who makes the break. Is it permissible, then, to trust that God will look the other way? that God will make an exception in our case? Here, as in the other division of the passage, we are left without straight answers. Jesus refuses to give us a simple rule that we can follow without reference to his speaking again. He warns and he admonishes. What he commands he will command only in the personal encounter with us in the assembly of his people. He simply reminds us that the proper question is not, "Can I marry again and still have my soul?" but "As one who is divorced, how can I now testify, as a part of the assembly of God's people, to the dependability of God, to which, until now, I have borne poor witness?"

LUST FOR POWER

Although adultery is a vivid manifestation of the desire to impose one's power over another in order to satisfy one's lust, it is simply the manifestation, in the sexual realm, of a habit expressed in every other realm of human life. It is important that the word frequently associated with sexual desire, *lust,* is also used in association with other desires. Furthermore, this is not merely a coincidence of the English language, but tore paralleled in the Greek. We speak of lust for power, lust for gold, and lust for various other things that will enhance our place over others, and this is precisely what is involved in adultery: asserting ourselves over others for the purpose of self-enhancement, always at the expense of others.

That which is violated in the adulterous act or the adulterous desire is the same thing violated in all other actions or desires that regard others as instruments of one's own well-being—the identity of the other person as an object of God's care, as one for whom Christ died, as one for whose well-being I should be prepared to die. Lust of any sort changes the other from an object of my unqualified love into an object for my own pleasure or prestige. Because one of the essential meanings of the Fall is that in this world everyone lives at everyone else's expense, lust is one of the most vivid manifestations of our fallen character.

When the subject is considered from this standpoint, the ultimate implications of the divorce-and-adultery sayings are exemplified by politicians who seek to stay in office for purposes of self-aggrandizement, by parents who impose their will on their children in order vicariously to fulfill their own unrealized career ambitions, by children who set their parents against each other in order to achieve their own desires, by teachers who view their jobs as means of career advancement rather than as a way to meet the needs of their students, by pastors who view their work in the congregation as a profession, according to the criteria of secular professionalism, rather than in terms of the suffering servant model, by bishops who perceive their task to be preserving the institution rather than satisfying human need.

The world in which disciples live out their lives is characterized by pillaging others' lives and belongings for self-enhancement. By its scrupulous attention to the security of the other person in his or her everyday existence, the assembly is to exhibit before the World of Darkness the Light of God's new order. It is to be hoped that the assembly might be so thoroughly overcome by the New Age that Jesus' instructions would reflect a way of life that the assembly lives spontaneously, for the sake of testimony. To the extent that this way is not the spontaneity of true freedom, it must be taken seriously as an objective rule for the assembly, a rule that can bear testimony even when the assembly's spontaneity is undercut by the Darkness. As it struggles with the rule, perhaps the assembly once again can hear the Living Word.

CHAPTER 22

OATHS

In some societies and in some eras, death has been preferable to violating one's solemn vow. Today, Western society exalts the temporary commitment, the limited vow, and the conditional oath. We do not regard history as testing our determination, but as liberating us from responsibility. The mainstream churches of the West will hardly be viewed by future generations as churches of widespread martyrdom. In this respect, we would have been quite at home among Jesus' opponents.

Matthew 23:16-22 makes clear that the oath of which Jesus spoke was a vow with an escape clause—a promise with a loophole. Escape clauses were appended because of life's unpredictability. If one has any integrity at all, one honors the spoken vow. Misfortune, however, has a habit of sneaking up on us when we least expect it, and oaths sworn with the best of intentions not only may seem, but actually may be, impossible to fulfill.

The Pentateuch's testimony to torah points out that swearing to God is not a necessity, but that one is expected to honor the oath or keep the word one has spoken (Lev. 19:12; Num. 30:2; Deut. 23:21). Jesus, in calling for a simple "yes, yes, or no, no" (incorrectly rendered in the RSV as "yes or no"), was referring to a response widely regarded in his day as the equivalent of a binding oath. The oaths and swearing Jesus admonishes his disciples to avoid are the technical oaths and swearing, which by their very nature contained escape clauses. Disciples are not to provide loopholes for themselves, but are to confine themselves to those simple responses that make no qualifications. To seek qualifications beforehand is to be less than wholehearted in taking the oath, and to seek a loophole later, on the basis of the formula used, is to seek an escape from one's obligations.

Moreover, oaths are not mere personal arrangements between human beings, but are arrangements in which God also participates. Consequently, to keep one's oath to the neighbor is to maintain covenant faithfulness with God himself, and, therefore, is to fulfill the oath not only to the neighbor, but to God as well. The disciple's fulfillment of his or her obligation is the light that shines in the Darkness, bearing testimony to God's faithfulness. Disciples are not to seek loopholes, because God, in dealing with us, does not seek loopholes.

Anything other than the binding oath, any effort to escape one's obligations, comes from the Evil One, who is the instigator of all things evil and whose goal is to hold us captive in the bondage of the Old Age. Formal oaths are, by nature, concessions in an evil age, concessions for the purpose of preserving at least a semblance of order. Even torah permitted the oath—and in the name of God!—indicating that God himself had condescended to the legal practices of a fallen world. Formal oaths are prompted, nevertheless, by the rule of the Powers of Darkness, and even those in the community of God's people are not free from all influence of the Evil One. The notation in Deuteronomy that a person is not required to swear recognizes the ultimate nature of the oath. Jesus prohibits oaths so that our works may be done not in order to fulfill a legality, but in order that we might bear proper testimony to the faithfulness of God.

The binding involved in "yes, yes" and "no, no" is not contrary to freedom, but, to the extent that it is spontaneous, is genuine freedom, the freedom of the New Age. In the Old Age, freedom and responsibility are defined as separate realities that must be united. Freedom, according to the Old Age, demands responsibility. Or, if one is to be responsible, it is said, one must be allowed a certain freedom. Even in the most honorable of these assertions, however, it is implied that freedom and responsibility are somehow separate. Freedom is viewed as a condition that must have restraints placed on it—restraints called "responsibility"— instruments for conditioning freedom. Thus, one hears, "My freedom is bound only by the freedom of other persons" or "Freedom is the right to do as one pleases as long as others are not affected." Anything other than this is viewed as anarchy rather than freedom.

The freedom of the New Age, however, is release from the self-interest of the Old Age and, therefore, is freedom to love God and to seek the well-being of others even at the cost of our own property or lives. Freedom, in the New Age, incorporates into itself, as a part of its very nature, that which the Old Age calls responsibility. Being bound in responsibility to God and neighbor does not restrict freedom, it is the very essence of freedom.

DISCIPLES AND THE SECULAR COURTS

This passage from Matthew's Gospel is frequently interpreted to mean that Christians must not take oaths in a court of law. It is interpreted, that is, as a new rule, a new regulation, a new law, which Christians must obey in order to ensure their salvation. The primary concern of this passage, however, is not verbal assent to binding relationships, but irresponsibility, undependability, and untrustworthiness as general characteristics. The admonition not to take oaths is an admonition against any response that leaves you a potential escape from your promise to another person or to God.

Many oaths created by secular society do not have loopholes. In a court of law, for example, there is only the technical loophole "so help me God." The meaning seems to be that if the witness lies, it will be only because God has not enabled the witness to know the truth. Ironically, it is precisely those oaths most frequently refused on the grounds of religious scruples—the oath of testimony and the pledge of allegiance to the national flag—that include few or no loopholes.

The oath, as it was commonly understood in Jesus' day, is not to be a part of the assembly of the New Age, for that assembly is to reflect the character of God, who seeks no loopholes in caring for his world. The assembly has not been snatched out of the world, however, but still lives in the midst of the world—the world dominated by the Old Age. It neither can nor should be isolated from the world. How, then, are disciples to react to the world's demand for oaths? How are disciples to respond to the state's demand for oaths in certain situations? Some groups have refused all oaths—whether the oaths involved in taking public office, those required when testimony is to be given in a court of law, or any number of others.

Martin Luther spoke of two realms: that of Christ and that of Caesar. According to that theory, Christians do some things as citizens of the realm of Christ and others as citizens of the realm of Caesar. This approach, however, though not without certain insight, encourages doing what is necessary and dangerously minimizes the inevitable tension between being, at one and the same time, both a Christian and a citizen.

The separatist approach, on the other hand, ignores the extent to which the Christian remains a part of the world dominated by the Old Age. The Christian who is a citizen can escape being a Christian far more easily than he or she can escape being a citizen, but most of the traditional approaches to the problem have overemphasized one or the other of these or have ignored the difference between them.

Many quote Matthew 22:21: "Render . . . to Caesar the things that are Caesar's, and to God the things that are God's" (RSV), and interpret Jesus to mean that Christians are obligated to obey the secular authorities. The Greek text, however, makes clear that the question put to Jesus is whether or not it is *permissible* to pay taxes to Caesar (Caesar being understood as the head of the empire).

Taxes are a symbol of authority. Taxation takes personal property on behalf of the community or the state, on the assumption that at least a portion, if not all, of a person's belongings ultimately belongs to the community or the state. Taxation reminds us that the secular authorities claim ultimate authority over their subjects.

Jesus, as well as his questioners, assumes that the entire world and all within it belong to God. The question put to Jesus had been put to him in order to trap him. The Herodians were supporters of Caesar. The Pharisees, though anti-Roman in sympathies, tolerated Rome. Both groups opposed Jesus and apparently expected him to say that God's people must not pay Caesar's tax.

Quite apart from the trickery of their question, Jesus' reply is that God's people are permitted to give to those in authority whatever God permits those in authority to call their own. Both groups of questioners would have had grounds for thinking they could trick Jesus into outright subversion, but Jesus' reply destroys that hope. It is permissible for God's people to pay Caesar's tax, not because Caesar is of exalted status, but because God has permitted Caesar to establish an economic system as one of the instruments by which Caesar preserves the relative order of the Old Age. God permits Caesar to have his rule, to hold sway over people and nations. This realm of Caesar, however, has now been penetrated by a new king—Jesus, the Anointed One of God—and as citizens of this new order, those who belong to Christ have been set free from bondage to all Caesars and have become free to be servants of God through Jesus Christ. Disciples are not required to pay Caesar's tax. In our freedom from Caesar, however, we are free to acquiesce in certain demands of Caesar—not as servants of Caesar, but as servants of God—when acquiescence is perceived as a way of bearing testimony to the character of God. A mark of my freedom is that I am *permitted* to give to Caesar certain things that I am not *bound* to give him.

On the other hand, if I do not pay taxes to Caesar, I cannot expect to escape his wrath. It is likely that Caesar, not recognizing my freedom, will prosecute me. But even in prison, I am still free.

With regard to oaths, I am forbidden to seek escape clauses in asserting my intentions. This is not a matter of mere verbal clauses, but is a way of life. To reduce the description of the New Age to a set of rules on how I must act toward the society of the Old Age is to misunderstand the freedom that has come upon me. The admonition against oaths is a freedom from oaths. The very freedom that has come upon me is expressed in truthfulness and reliability, not in taking oaths. Caesar, however, has no more reason to expect a disciple not to lie without the oath and the fear of sanctions the oath entails than Caesar has to expect anyone else not to lie. Indeed, given the track record of Christians in the matter of truthfulness, Caesar could even cite examples of Christian duplicity.

The answer to the question of oath taking for Christians in Caesar's world rests neither on determining which rules Caesar has the right to impose on his own people nor on a view of whether Christians are more trustworthy than anyone else; it rests on the nature of our freedom in Christ and on our call to be witnesses who by our works give the nations cause to glorify God. Our primary responsibility to the world outside the church is not to bear witness to a prohibition, but to bear witness to God's Reign. Since God's Reign is characterized by dependability, faithfulness, and truthfulness, not by equivocation and unreliability, the words of those who bear witness to that reign must reflect those same characteristics. In the same way that I am permitted to pay those taxes Caesar has a right to claim, then, I am also permitted to take the oath that Caesar requires. What I am not free to do is to be a liar, not even to Caesar.

On the other hand, just as I am free to take Caesar's oath, so also am I free not to take Caesar's oath. Again, the responsibility is to be trustworthy and dependable.

But perhaps the state, or even the church, will refuse to acknowledge my freedom. Perhaps it will refuse to grant me something unless I do take the oath? Perhaps I cannot serve in public office. Then I have to decide whether my involvement in the Old Age is important enough to lead me to abide by its rules and deny my freedom in Christ.

Christians have been set free from the oath, but the state is free to exact its toll from those who exercise that freedom. One thing is certain: Caesar will have his pound of flesh one way or another, and if we are found to be in violation of an oath to Caesar, we cannot legitimately ask him to look the other way.

As a child of the New Age, the Christian should recognize that one, though not the only, role of the state is to maintain order in the Old Age. The state may even be perceived as having a certain worldly wisdom in its legal structures—certain wise laws by which both worldly order and worldly justice are maintained. In freedom, the Christian will find it expedient to obey these laws for what they are worth in this limited horizon. Ultimately, however, the Christian's purpose must be to glorify God. If I decide, as a Christian, that I must disregard a law of the state, I do so fully recognizing that the state can and will exact its penalty. Being a Christian does not make my violation of a law or an oath "right" in contrast to it being "wrong" or even "irrelevant" for someone who is not a Christian. Nor is it even thinkable to say that the person who allows people to die rather than violate an oath is "right" or "honorable" or "good." Regarding pure human suffering, it would be preferable to dishonor one's vow in order to save human lives, but this would not be the result of being "good," but of being human.

One of the interesting things about Caesar's oaths is that Caesar has learned to imitate the language of the people of God. Thus, Caesar's oaths may include such expressions as "God being my helper, I will," or "So help me God." The vocal statement seems to leave a loophole. "If God doesn't help me, I will not be able to do what I have promised, but then the guilt will be God's and not my own." One need merely ask, however, how many times the courts have granted release on these grounds. No, Caesar pretends to offer a loophole, but it is a loophole that cannot be used. What Caesar actually demands is absolute obedience. Certainly, there are grounds for defense—insanity, coercion, and so forth—but these are not part of the oath. They do not permit remittance from an oath freely and knowingly taken. Caesar's oaths are as binding on those who are Caesar's subjects as are "yes, yes" and "no, no." Those who participate in the freedom of the gospel, however, are no longer Caesar's subjects, but God's subjects. To be responsible to God means that we must weigh all other responsibilities in light of our responsibility to God. In this way, God permits us to take vows to Caesar when those vows are the means of glorifying God in the midst of the Old Age.

In sum, Jesus' concern is apparently with one thing: the obligation to be faithful to what one agrees to do. The prohibition against using the words *heaven, earth,* and *Jerusalem* and against swearing by one's head is a prohibition against leaving a loophole for future convenience. The instruction to let "yes, yes" or "no, no" be one's sole reply is not a prohibition against binding agreements, but against qualifications that release us from the obligation. The real question, then, is how best to manifest the liberated life of faithfulness and dependability in view of those oaths required today.

The free disciple will neither blindly enter into a legal arrangement on the basis that any oath is permissible nor turn the prohibition against seeking loopholes into a rejection of all legal engagements. Instead, the disciple will seek to determine which agreements are the contemporary expressions of the binding "yes, yes" or "no, no" by which we manifest our freedom in Christ. The opportunity to show the true nature of oaths and to express freedom from oaths may in some instances be as simple as responding to the charge with a matter-of-fact, "Well, of course I do," or "Well, of course I will."

The object is not to reveal a bondage to mere words (although even the prohibition of some verbal formulations is involved in our freedom), but to manifest our freedom in Christ. If I refuse because I hear the prohibition as a rule or regulation out of the past, rather than because I hear God's proclamation of freedom to me here and now, I do not bear witness to freedom, but to my bondage to a new law. The authorities with whom I am confronted and those who observe my actions may or may not know the difference. My witness, however, does not depend on the ability of others to recognize it for what it is, for even the executioners of Jesus did not know what they were witnessing. My witness depends on its own character.

THE OATH AND FREE SPEECH

It would be a mistake to perceive the antithesis on oaths as concerned only with the formal oath. Rather, there are deeper, broader concerns, of which oath taking is a specific manifestation. The antithesis is concerned, specifically, with the corruption of language—with the use of language for self-serving ends, for personal advantage, for power, or simply for self-entertainment. To restrict Jesus' words on oaths to a simple concern with oaths alone is to hear them as new rules and regulations, rather than as instruction in freedom.

The antithesis on oaths has as its deeper, more comprehensive base, the true meaning of freedom of speech. When Adam and Eve walked before and with God in Eden, they enjoyed genuine freedom of speech. That is, they engaged in speaking as a means of harmonious communication with God and with each other. The serpent spoke words of the Darkness, words of bondage, words intended to destroy God's creation, or at least to damage it, and to bring Adam and Eve under his own power. The serpent did not display freedom of speech, but speech bound to self-interest. Moreover, when Eve and Adam succumbed to the serpent's speech of bondage, they lost their own freedom of speech. Although the words of God to the serpent, to Eve, and to Adam indicate the sentence under which the whole world is placed, the condemnations in those words were not the first debilitating consequences of their disobedience. The first was their loss of free speech. They could no longer speak honestly and openly. They now used language to defend themselves, for self-serving purposes. They could not endure God's speech, and they could not speak truthfully to God ("I heard your voice in the garden and I was afraid, because I was naked; so I hid").

Adam and Eve's speech became an instrument of alienation between themselves and between them and the animal world. Adam accused Eve; Eve accused the serpent. Freedom of speech had given way to the speech of bondage and necessity.

The fallen condition of language as portrayed in Genesis 3 reveals one of the characteristics of the Old Age. When speech is no longer free, is no longer the instrument of honest communication, it comes into the bondage of the Darkness and is used for self-enhancement. It becomes not simply an instrument, but a weapon. Freedom of speech gives way to duplicity. Lying becomes a basic characteristic of discourse. In its typical reversal of values, the Darkness perceives the unhampered ability to use language for the purpose of Chaos as the highest expression of freedom of speech. The permission to abuse others in political speeches, to report only a part of the facts in the newspapers and on television, to flood the society with sexually debasing photographs: All, though examples of the fallenness of language, are celebrated as freedom.

Perhaps the most influential expression of language's bondage to the Darkness in Western society today is the all-pervasive Lie. Disciples of Jesus Christ in Western society today live in a society characterized by duplicity. One of the primary characteristics of the Powers of Darkness, lying has been elevated to the rank of heroic morality by the government and to the status of art in ordinary commerce. Governments—all governments—decide when to lie to their citizens, in the name of security or safety or expediency, or even in the name of the greater truth. And all in the pretense of the well-being of the people: "It is for your well-being that we lie to you." If it is important to create optimism during wartime, they lie about mediocre achievements or outright defeats by reporting fictitious statistics. If a spy is caught, especially in peacetime, they lie to the nation as well as to the enemy: "We know not the man!"

There is, of course, the more modern lie of the management experts in business, in government, in education, in medicine, in law, and even in the church. It is the lie of the transformed name:

Censorship is renamed journalistic responsibility.
Manipulating people is called heightening consciousness.
Displacing the poor and defenseless is called urban relocation.
Surrendering people to discrimination is called local control.
Returning to white, wealthy control is called restoring the balance before the law.
Lying by governments is called disinformation, as though a lie can inform, but in a *dis*manner.
Lying in business is called creative advertising as though there were creativity in Death.
Lying in political campaigns is called acceptable exaggeration.
Lying by the preacher in the zeal of the sermon is called hermeneutical license for the purpose of conveying a truth.

People who are astounded that their government or certain government officials would lie to them are simply naive about the culture as a whole, for society depends on lies for much of its dynamism. Where would American business be, for example, without advertising, which—as it is practiced today—is nothing but technique? (In other words, duplicity has become a calculated method.) No one who has grown up in a society in which every brand of toothpaste, every brand of gasoline, and every brand of children's breakfast cereal is said by advertisers to be "the best," no one who has observed the use of sex appeal both in its prim, subtle form (which even the staunchest opponent of pornography fails to understand) and in its blatant forms (such as in contemporary perfume and clothing ads), no one who has observed the surface politeness that hides the struggles for power and influence in churches and church institutions should be surprised when it is revealed that government officials at every level make a regular practice of deciding when and how to lie not only to opposing nations, but to their own people. And the admitted lies of government are compounded with the added lie that the original lie was for the citizens' own welfare.

The extent to which we accept the corruption of language because we consider it inconsequential can be seen in instances as diverse as the misspelling of words in advertising in order to catch one's attention and the creating or appropriating of words to lend an air of importance to that which is ordinary or trivial or to pretend that something is other than what it is. In such instances, that which is central to our human identity—language—that which God created for human beings to use in freedom for purposes of community, isolates, alienates, and destroys community. Speech lies in bondage as both victim and instrument of the Darkness.

The terrible thing is not that we come to expect the government, the corporation, the instruments of journalism, and other secular institutions to lie to us. Since by nature, as creatures of the Fall, they *are* liars, it would be a mistake not to expect all of the worlds' institutions to lie, consistently, for purposes of self-preservation, self-aggrandizement, and self-enhancement and to preserve their control over us. What is terrible, rather, is that the Western church has become so thoroughly acculturated to the lie that at every level of its life it exhibits the same tendency of duplicity. Whether it be in the bureaucratic language with which agencies of the church defend their worldly criteria or appointing bodies explain their manipulation of lives; in the cynical explanations of why church funds are invested in corporations that spread death; or in the pseudotheological and economic language with which discrimination against women, blacks, Indians, Asiatics, Jews, the poor, the disabled, and dozens of others is defended as being for the well-being of the church—all is duplicity. For disciples of Jesus Christ to order their lives by duplicity is to display their enthrallment to the Darkness, their alliance not with Jesus Christ—who is the Truth—but with Satan, the Dark Lord of the Lie. Disciples of Jesus Christ are to be characterized by dependability and faithfulness, not by that power-seeking which is manifested in the public realm by the rape of the mind and in the private realm by the seduction of the body.

The assembly of disciples has heard the liberating voice of Jesus. In his call to them, disciples are set free once again to speak. As in the antithesis on violent language, Jesus instructs his disciples in that use of language that heals and restores because it is free speech, liberated by the call of grace. It is no new regulation, primarily, but a description of a new way of speaking. To those who are still to some degree in the Darkness, however, the gift of instruction becomes the command of obedience.

CHAPTER 23

RETALIATION

The instruction to which Jesus refers appears in three different places in the Pentateuch: Exodus 21:24; Leviticus 24:20; and Deuteronomy 19:21. The context of each is quite different. The Deuteronomy passage is concerned with rooting evil out of Israel. The community is not to tolerate violence from individuals, but is to maintain justice and order. Those who perpetrate violence, therefore, are to be judged, and certain offenses are deemed sufficiently destructive of the social fabric to require eliminating the offender. This must be heard, of course, in the context of the Pentateuch's emphasis on Israel as the means of the world's blessing. Anything that threatens Israel's life threatens the blessing of the nations and must be rooted out.

The Leviticus citation is found amid laws of various sorts, all of which describe a life different from the life of Israel's neighbors. Israel's God is different from all the so-called gods of the nations, and he demands a people that is different from the nations. Torah is a means by which Israel preserves its identity. If Israel becomes like the nations, the nations themselves are endangered.

The Exodus passage is found in the midst of a series of instructions for which the primary concern is the protection of the community and its individual members. If a woman miscarries as a consequence of having been struck by one of two struggling men, but suffers no ill effects, the woman's husband is permitted to declare the price the man who struck the woman must pay. If the woman is hurt beyond miscarriage, the man is to receive a similar injury.

This teaching, as are those around it, is meant to protect human beings. In the larger setting, it is meant to protect the community. It sets a limit on the death penalty, but it also describes the way that violence is to be redressed and removed from the community.

All three of the passages containing the teaching Jesus cites, then, are meant to protect those within the community and to preserve Israel as an orderly community in a disordered world. The common interpretation of the instruction found in all three is that it marked an advance in humane jurisprudence in Israel. It prohibited blood revenge, thereby restricting bloodshed. From the standpoint of Israel's prehistory, this observation may be correct. The story of Lamech (Gen. 4:19-24) reflects the Pentateuch's view that at least prior to the patriarchs, blood revenge was a major problem in human society. On the other hand, in the narrative, Lamech is not one of the ancestors of Israel, but is of Cain's line, and in the post-flood narratives leading up to the story of Moses there is no indication that blood revenge was ever approved in Hebrew society. Before the gift of torah, Israel had not been a nation with a national government, but had been among the peoples and had lived according to tribal laws or according to the laws of those peoples among whom Israel sojourned. Even if the instruction "an eye for an eye and a tooth for a tooth" could be heard as an advance over the laws of the nations (which it was not, since it appeared in other ancient codes, as well), its meaning for the Pentateuch would not lie in this advance, but in its role of preserving Israel's purity.

To put this text further into proper perspective, in the place in the Pentateuch where instruction for capital punishment is first found (Gen. 9:5-7), that instruction is set in the positive context of God's gift of life. Human beings are to be fruitful, to multiply, and to fill the earth. An ambiguous note is found in the relationship between humans and the other animals, in that, on the one hand, the animals become food for human beings, but on the other hand, this marks a further break in the harmony of the creation (9:2-3). Human beings were created to be God's representatives on the earth. They were to live in harmony with the other animals. Now that harmony has been replaced by terror. Whether the image has been lost or merely damaged (Seth was created not in God's image, but in Adam's image, Genesis 5:3), the original creation in that image is the basis for capital punishment. An attack on another human being is an attack on God himself. The argument that since God gives life, God alone has the right to take life does not enter the picture here. To murder another human being is to destroy one to whom God at least once gave responsibility to rule on his behalf. Whether the prohibition is because the image remains, though in crippled form, or because of God's nostalgia for the lost image, or because God plans to restore the image, capital punishment is envisioned here as continuing the cleansing the flood began.

Jesus, in effect, removes another permission of the Old Age. He teaches that disciples are not to take a stand over against one who has done them a wickedness. As it is usually pointed out, in its strictest form, this teaching calls for disciples not to take legal steps to take revenge on those who have offended them in some way. In this respect, it is close to that portion of 1 Corinthians in which Paul admonishes his followers not to take one another to court before the secular, government officials, but simply to endure unjustified wrong.

Jesus removes all permission for retaliation. The word translated "resist" means "to take up a stand over against." It was commonly used to refer to taking someone to court in order to exact justice. The assembly is to be characterized by a love for others that seeks their well-being, not their undoing for purposes of vengeance or human justice. Ancient Israel, living in the Old Age, confronted by a fallen world, took the violent nature of human beings in stride and permitted a limited retaliation in that world. The followers of Jesus have been set free from the domination of the Old Age and its thirst for revenge. The assembly is set free to testify to the glory of God and to manifest the life in community that God establishes. That life is not to be based on revenge, but on mercy—on Life, not Death.

Verses 39b-42 give examples of what Jesus means by not standing up against an evil one. The precise Greek wording of the text indicates that Jesus' reference to one who strikes the right cheek is specifically referring to that act which in Jewish circles was considered a supreme insult and, among some rabbis, was deemed sufficient grounds for the death penalty. Those who cite this background as support for their view that Jesus does not here rule out self-defense as such are partially correct, in that Jesus' wish that his disciples not exact the death of another member of the assembly over an insult does not necessarily mean that Jesus would have said we are not to defend our lives from someone inside or outside the assembly. That Jesus would have approved self-defense, however, is not as easily supported in light of the full passage as some would think. For one thing, although the situations described in the previous antitheses seem to be within the assembly, those of the present passage are not so easily restricted. The insult of the hand slap to the face is in no way restricted to another assembly member. Nor are lawsuits from others or those who impose on you. (Indeed, the latter seems almost certainly to refer to Roman soldiers.) Although the reference to begging may have referred at one time to the assembly, nothing in the present context confines it there.

Moreover, in all four examples, what Jesus calls forth is not merely the refusal to retaliate, but the positive act of offering more than is demanded. The "do not stand up against" is interpreted not simply in terms of not hauling the offender into court, but in terms of offering yourself to the offender as a vulnerable victim. In response to those who make demands on or take advantage of or harm them, disciples are to offer them even more than they demand.

Such actions, again, are not correctly understood when described as nonretaliation. Nonretaliation easily becomes legalism. The disciples are to step forth in ways that manifest God's concern for those who are violent and abusive.

Some contend that Jesus is not ruling out self-defense here, but this is far from clear. The eye-for-an-eye, tooth-for-a-tooth tradition included the permission of the death penalty as a means of balancing the social equilibrium. The restrictions that it placed on revenge kept the society from reverting to chaos. Here that tradition is set aside. If capital punishment is now no longer permissible as revenge for the death of a family member, how can I possibly be permitted to take the life of someone to preserve my own life?

On the other hand, this is no rejection of capital punishment or of killing in self-defense on ideological grounds. Nor is it a heroic ethic or super piety. It is, rather, a description of the spontaneous refusal to avenge oneself on another; if it also envisions a rejection of self-defense, that too is to be spontaneous. Only then is it a free embodiment of the instruction. Free people do not live at the expense of the lives of others. Free people do not thrive on revenge, but on mercy.

Torah permitted limited retaliation as a way of protecting the community from the chaos of unbridled revenge. The Old Age was such that limited retaliation was sometimes necessary, but torah provided a margin of protection. Jesus, therefore, gets to the heart of torah by removing the permission of even limited revenge. Thus, he fulfills torah by taking it to its ultimate goal. The offer to the opponent of a further opportunity to insult, giving more than is claimed by one who brings suit, the offer to assist to a greater extent than a claimant requires, to give more than the beggar asks: All are generosities that transcend torah's protection. The free disciple forgoes that protection. Since in terms of the standards of the Old Age the permission for limited redress is a means of equalization, to forgo redress is to sacrifice equality. To carry a load farther than is requested is to place oneself at a disadvantage. The free disciple willfully makes himself or herself vulnerable to the assaults and impositions of others.

This in no way implies that disciples are to comply with demands that would require disobedience to God, for obedience to God is everywhere assumed to be an absolute requirement. With regard to persons that attack or make impositions that do not involve such disobedience, however, disciples are to respond to evil with good, to assault with goodwill, and to unfair demands with generosity.

For disciples to take others—disciples or those not disciples—into a law court for redress of a wrong is to act just like everybody else. To do so is to reveal that they are not among the meek, who are blessed because they await God's vindication. To seek revenge is to hunger and thirst not for God's righteousness, but for the justice of the Darkness. To seek redress is to abandon the blessing of the merciful, who treat others with concern and compassion, at their own expense. To seek the justice of Caesar's court is to seek human redress rather than God's blessing as those who are persecuted. To haul an offender into court is to take advantage of a channel available to one as a subject of the Darkness and, thereby, to become insipid salt and a light that is being suffocated by the Darkness. It is, in effect, to bear witness to the dominion of Death, to assert that the illusory victory of the Darkness is of supreme value, and thereby to become a worshiper of Death and an acolyte of the Dark Lord, Satan.

CHAPTER 24

LOVE OF THE ENEMY

This final antithesis extends the preceding ones. In the five that have come before, Jesus has described a life for the assembly rooted in reconciliation rather than hostility and alienation, respect for the security of the other members of the community rather than invasion of their families, dependability of one's word rather than deception and undependability, and the acceptance of vulnerability in relating to others, inside and outside the community, rather than retaliation and assertion of rights. Now he speaks of that which elsewhere he has called one of the two great commandments: love for others.

The love and hate of which Jesus speaks here are not emotions, but orientations of the will. They refer, that is, not to liking or disliking someone, but to the devotion to or refusal of devotion to someone. In these terms, it is possible to love someone you dislike and to hate someone you like.

The torah passage to which Jesus' first quote refers is Leviticus 19:18, a verse at the end of a passage setting forth instructions on how Israelites are to treat one another. The corners of the field are to be left untouched at harvest time so that the poor from among the Israelites and those foreigners who have taken up residence in Israel will have food (Lev. 19:9-10); stealing and lying are forbidden (19:11-12); dealings with the laborer and the disabled are to be honest and dependable (19:13-14); slander and legal injustice are forbidden (19:15-16); and disputes with other members of the community are to be handled by reason rather than by efforts to undermine those members (19:17). Loving the neighbor as yourself is then contrasted with revenge and grudge-bearing (19:18).

The instruction to love the neighbor both covers the entire list of instructions, as a summary, and is set over against revenge as love's opposite. Hatred and revenge are synonyms. The connection between loving and forgoing revenge—a connection made in the Sermon by the linking of the last two antitheses—goes back to torah itself. When offenses arise, God's people are not required to like or to be chummy with the offender, but they are required to be as concerned with the well-being of the offender as with their own.

Deuteronomy 10:12-19 goes further in reference to the sojourner, the resident alien, than does Leviticus. Leviticus calls for leaving food at harvest time; it roots this in God's holiness. Deuteronomy calls for Israel to love the sojourner and to express this love by feeding and clothing the sojourner, and it, too, roots the call in the character of God. God loves the sojourner; therefore, Israel is to love the sojourner.

From a purely economic standpoint, it might be argued that feeding and clothing the sojourner was strategically wise. Since only Israelites could own the land, resident aliens would starve without some legal provision. Before they starved, however, they would likely have joined forces as Israel's enemy from within and been a constant source of unrest and violence. Valid as such reasoning may be—and sociological and other such analyses are usually legitimate in what they seek to understand—from the perspective of the Pentateuch all such analyses are irrelevant, even if they are accurate in their own sphere of interest. For the Pentateuch, the love of the sojourner is rooted in the character of God and the task of Israel. God, the Creator of all that is, loves what he has created. That is, God is determined to work toward the well-being of his creation. Even God's most fierce judgments must be understood in light of that love. God's wrath is expressed against only that which in some way threatens his efforts to redeem and restore the creation to a condition of integrity. By loving the sojourner, Israel shows that God's election of Israel does not mean that God does not love other peoples and nations, but precisely that God's love for all peoples and all nations is the reason that Israel was elected. Israel was elected to be the instrument of God's unqualified love for all!

Torah, therefore, though essentially instruction in how Israel is to conduct its life within as a showcase for the world outside, does include instruction on how Israel is to live with and act toward those outside Israel and those resident aliens who come inside Israel's borders.

Jesus quotes the Leviticus passage, which is concerned with life within the community, and he joins with it a saying that is not found in the scriptures: "You will hate your enemy." The correct translation of the clause includes the repetition of the pronoun subject and *will* rather than *shall,* because, as argued earlier, the sayings are essentially descriptive. In other words, Jesus is saying, "You have heard that the ancient ones were set forth in a community in which the normal way of living would be to seek the well-being of the others in the community as thoroughly as you seek your own. The community was not expected, however, to place the well-being of its opponents on the same level as its own."

The enemy envisioned in the specific vocabulary of the Greek text of

Matthew is one who opposes you. This opposition can be as specific as a direct, personal attack or as general as a competitive way of life. The fallen human race is viewed as God's enemy in that it sets itself over against God and sets its will against God's will. This is what it means to say that the world hates God; the world sets itself in opposition to God, rather than seeking to align itself with God. Similarly, for God to hate someone, some people, or some nation does not mean that God necessarily has a burning anger against them, but that God sets himself over against their plans and ambitions.

To set hatred of the enemy over against love of the neighbor, then, is to contrast the bonds of unity and common purpose—the efforts for the well-being of the neighbor—with the lack of concern for the well-being of those whose way opposes the way of the community, even the effort to undermine that way and the plans of those who follow it. Such was permissible in the Old Age. Although the scripture does not specifically call for this opposition to the opponent, there are a sufficient number of references there to God's hatred for his enemies and to Israel's responsibility to align itself with God that we need not doubt the existence of the interpretation of scripture in Jesus' second quotation. In fact, the Dead Sea Scrolls contain passages that are quite close to being calls for hatred of the enemy.

Given the more flexible meaning of *hate* and *enemy,* the expectation that Israel, while loving the sojourner, will hate the enemy is not as strange as it may at first appear. It is rooted in the role of Israel as a holy nation—a nation that is to be unlike the other nations—made holy and expected to maintain that holiness because of its task as the instrument of God and witness to God's character. In the Old Age, maintaining Israel's purity required opposition to all who sought to impose an alien way on Israel. Even warfare—when ordered by God, but only when ordered by God—was a means of maintaining Israel's life and task. In the Old Age the enemy had to be overcome, lest the enemy destroy Israel. The enemy within, those among Israel's own makeup who opposed God, also had to be opposed. The most stringent expression of this was capital punishment. Again, hatred does not automatically entail anger. It is possible to follow torah's call for execution and to mourn profoundly the death of the one executed. (This is not at all to say that the state ever does mourn when someone is executed, but is simply to say that it is not out of the question that individuals carrying out the directives of the state might do so.)

Jesus extends the instruction beyond the neighbor and the resident alien to the opponent and does away with the permissiveness of the Old Age. Although action against the opponent may even have been necessary at times in the Old Age, in the New Age disciples of Jesus are to practice active concern for the well-being of the opponent himself, herself, or itself. The victory over the Powers of the Darkness has already been won in the cross and resurrection of Jesus; and now, while refusing to adopt the values, standards, and ways of living of the opponent, disciples are to seek the well-being of that opponent. Any opposition to the opponent must now be from God, just as was true in the Old Age, when Israel was permitted only that opposition called for by God himself. The purity of the assembly is now not to be defended by separation, although separation will be essential, but by unflagging, determined outreach on behalf of the enemy. The vulnerability already indicated in the antithesis on retaliation is extended into an initiative hinted at in the instruction to carry the load of one who requires it of you farther than that person demands. The meek, who are blessed as they patiently and trustingly await God's vindication, are not to wait with bitterness and hostility toward the opponent, but are to wait by actively seeking the opponent's well-being. They are to wait by performing acts of mercy. They are to wait by giving themselves into God's hands as instruments of healing and renewal.

Disciples are to approach God on behalf of the enemy. While the enemy seeks to harass and to vex them, disciples are to pray to God on behalf of the enemy. The response to the state is to be not bitterness and hatred, but prayer for those who are the agents of the state—prayer that they might be liberated from their bondage to the state's blood-thirstiness, prayer that they might turn their allegiance from the state to God, prayer that God might see fit to overcome their hardness of heart and turn them to himself as his faithful servants. Disciples are to wait by praying that their own response to the enemy might be so in keeping with God's own character that even as they die, their deaths might become the means of converting their executioners. They are to wait, in brief, with the prayers of the peacemaker—prayers for the healing of all and the transformation of all. Waiting thus, they will know the approval of God, who will regard them as his true children, bearers of his Light in the midst of the Darkness.

For disciples to wait in any other way is to betray their identity as salt and light. To seek the well-being only of those who seek the disciples' well-being is to act as those in the Darkness act. The inhabitants of the Darkness practice, as a matter of course, that love the Greeks called *phileia,* that mutual aid which says, "I'll meet you half way," or "You scratch my back and I'll scratch yours," or "Any good relationship involves give and take," or "We'll go fifty-fifty." *Phileia* is the love of the Old Age. It is the love most often recommended by Christian counselors and preachers as the way to a successful marriage, or to a successful business partnership, or to a happy parent-child relationship, and consequently, simply reveals the extent to which the institutional church is engulfed in the Darkness. It is the same love that informs those pastoral letters from church leaders who say "We must stop the arms race, but we can't disarm unless everyone else does," which, being translated, means, "We ought to stop the arms race, but we are not ready to suffer and risk subjugation to the enemy, to ensure the enemy's life. We would prefer to risk the death of all to the advantage of the enemy in life." And all in the name of the Christ who refused to take life, but considered it preferable to die that others might live.

Love for the enemy must not be confused with tolerance for the enemy. Tolerance gives the enemy space to operate. It says to the enemy, "Well, make it if you can. Feed yourself, clothe yourself, and heal yourself. I won't interfere." Tolerance and hatred are two sides of the same coin. Tolerance is hatred dressed in Sunday clothes. Love, on the other hand, cannot ignore the enemy, but is constrained to collaborate with God for the enemy's well-being. Tolerance backs away; love steps forward. The assumption that one could rest with hatred of the enemy in hatred's mask of tolerance rested on the prior assumption that God hated the enemy; but he does not. God sends the sunshine, which is needed for growth and nourishment, upon the evil (those who oppose God) and also upon the good (those who are in harmony with God). God sends the rain, which also is needed for nourishment, upon both the just (those who seek to remain faithful to God) and the unjust (those who are unfaithful). God makes no distinctions in providing for the health and nourishment of friend or foe, so neither are disciples to make distinctions. Refusing to make distinctions is a means of expressing our identity as God's children.

It is striking that this is the first antithesis in which Jesus' words are specifically imperative. To this point they have been descriptive, with all of the ambiguity that that implies, as we have already seen, but now Jesus commands love of the enemy. This does not change what has been said about the implications of the indicative form of the previous instructions, but simply indicates that what is not forthcoming spontaneously must be done as obedience to a living command. To the extent that devotion to the needs of the enemy is spontaneous, it is an expression of freedom. Even when it is not spontaneous, however, it is expected as a means of bearing testimony to the God whose aim it is to set all his creatures free.

One of the factors that gets in the way of understanding the radical nature of Jesus' instruction at this point is the tendency to equate Christian identity with citizenship in the nation of one's birth or habitation. Thus, Christians may think of the enemy in purely personal terms as someone outside the institutional church in the nation of secular citizenship. Christians in the United States, for example, are likely to think of opponents of the church in the United States, or of the government of Russia or Libya. One need not deny that these are the enemy of the Christian or of the Body of Christ; but our ordinary way of thinking is confined to this and, by being so confined, misses the truly radical nature of the instruction. Disciples truly understand their identity only when they think of themselves not as American Christians, Russian Christians, or the like, but simply as disciples of Jesus Christ. The most deadly enemy of the gospel and of the disciple is the state in which the disciple resides. That is, the United States as a national government is a far greater enemy of disciples in the United States than the Russian government ever can be. This is so because the United States government convinces disciples in the United States that there is an essential harmony, even identity, between their secular citizenship and their membership in Christ. It must hastily be said, however, that the greatest enemy of the disciple in Russia is the Russian government, for it seeks to draw disciples away from Christ to the state. In the final analysis, it is precisely because of the spurious, elaborate claims that the United States government makes for itself in claiming to be God's people, and the frequently open opposition to the church in Russia, that the disciple in the United States is far more vulnerable to apostasy and Satan worship than is the citizen of the Soviet Union. Satan's mask has been far more subtle and effective in the United States because it has been perceived as the face of God. In the Soviet Union it has been the mask of the invincible state. The consequence of this disguise has been United States Christians identifying the enemy primarily as Russia without and ideological foes within. Such is the confusion of the Christian in captivity to the Darkness.

The assembly is not to wallow in self-pity or to react in bitterness when confronted with enmity from the state or from the culture, but is to give its life to seeking the well-being of the state or the culture. To give oneself, even to the point of death, for the well-being of the state does not mean to give oneself for the desires of the state. In seeking the state's well-being, one may have to appear to the state to be seeking its death. The families at home, on hearing of the destruction of the Egyptian army at the Red Sea, can hardly have imagined that this was for their well-being. The decimation of the military was probably viewed as a disaster from which the empire would be fortunate to rise. The judges, police, and various government officials who are confronted with prophetic acts against nuclear armaments usually do not think of those acts as for the well-being of the people of the nation, but that is because those officials confuse well-being with power, need with desire, strength with weaponry.

Disciples, on the other hand, are easily seduced into bitterness, hatred, and acts of murder in the name of love for the people, liberation of the oppressed, and the command of God—and all because the scriptures have become an objective manual for the support of the latest ideology.

Both disciples and the state are susceptible to the gods of the Darkness and to the Death those gods serve. Release can come only through the Living Speech of the Living God.

CHAPTER 25

PERFECTION

The beatitudes on mercy, purity of heart, and peacemaking and the six antitheses have portrayed the life of discipleship as one that manifests the character of God. Now the comparison is carried to its highest expression. Disciples are to be perfect as God is perfect. In the Greek text, *perfect* means to have reached the goal; it means to be a truly integrated person, one whose actions and motives are in complete harmony. The antitheses and the three beatitudes mentioned are not, as has been said repeatedly, essentially rules and regulations to be slavishly observed. The perfect disciple is characterized, then, not by outward manifestations alone, but by outward manifestations of the transformed heart. The words on perfection are descriptive, not prescriptive. John Wesley was partially correct when he called this passage a promise, for the New Age in all its fullness will bring just this sort of integrity. For Matthew the words are a description to which the disciples are expected to give assent.

To put it another way, the perfection of the disciple, like the perfection of God, is not basically a moral perfection, although moral perfection is involved; it is the full transformation of life, which is manifested in acts of love and reconciliation that arise spontaneously from the heart. It is a description of the community as much as of the individual, and it is an assumption that carries elements of both promise and demand.

PART SIX

TRUE PIETY

Beware of practicing your religious obligations before others in order to be seen by them; for then you will have no reward from your Father who is in heaven.

When you give alms, therefore, do not sound a trumpet before yourself, as the hypocrites do in the synagogues and in the streets, that they may be praised by others. I assure you, they have already received their reward. But when you give alms, don't let your left hand know what your right hand is doing, so that your alms may be kept a secret. And your Father, who knows all secrets, will reward you.

And when you pray, you must not be like the hypocrites, for they love to stand and pray in the synagogues and at the street corners, that they may be seen by others. I assure you, they have already received their reward. But when you pray, go into your room and shut the door and pray to your Father who is in secret. And your Father who knows all secrets will reward you.

And in praying, do not pile up empty phrases as the Gentiles do, for they think they will be heard because of their many words. Do not be like them, for your Father knows what you need before you ask him.

And when you fast, do not . . . look dismal, like the hypocrites, for they distort their faces that their fasting may be publicly known. I assure you, they have already received their reward. But when you fast, clean your head and face so that your fasting may not be seen by others, but by your Father who is in secret, and your Father who knows all secrets will reward you.

(Matthew 6:1-8, 16-18)

CHAPTER 26

THE THREE DUTIES

The English word *piety* is derived from the Latin *pius,* which means "duty." Here as in the beatitudes, which use the same word (there translated "righteousness"), and as in the warning that disciples' righteousness must exceed that of the scribes and Pharisees, the center of concern is the faithfulness of the disciples. Those who hunger and thirst to see God manifest his faithfulness by restoring them to faithfulness and those who are persecuted because of their faithfulness are blessed. The faithfulness toward which they look and which they seek to manifest, however, is not an outwardly correct faithfulness of rules and regulations without regard to that from which the actions spring, but is that integrity of devotion of the whole person which manifests itself in spontaneous acts of mercy, reconciliation, and healing. The obligation, the duty, of the disciple is not simply to do something, but to be something. The faithful disciple's acts manifest what the disciple truly is.

The three examples of the proper performance of duty to God—alms, prayer, and fasting—were the three traditional marks of piety in Judaism in Jesus' day and are also central to the traditional piety of Islam. Jesus warns that disciples are to beware doing for the approval of human beings those things which traditionally were to be done as signs of devotion to God. Acts of free men and women are performed for the purpose of attracting the attention of neither God nor other human beings. Acts that are truly performed freely are not self-conscious acts at all, but are spontaneous. Salt best fulfills its purpose when it does not draw attention to itself, but when it enhances the taste of the food. Light performs properly not when it draws attention to itself, but when it reveals that which otherwise would be veiled in darkness. If salt draws attention to itself, we may be inclined to throw out the food. If light draws attention to itself, it may blind us.

Free obedience is unself-conscious obedience. When such obedience does not cause others to glorify God, but results in either ridicule or ignorance, we should not be frustrated or disappointed that our "good works" or "righteousness" did not result in the conversion of sinners, because they were not done for that purpose. They were done because they were either the command of God or the spontaneous manifestation of that which God has made us.

REWARD FOR THE DISCIPLE

For many, Jesus' promise that God will reward us creates a major problem. Traditional interpretations of Paul's writing perceive a conflict between Jesus and Paul at this point, for Paul's insistence on our renewal as creatures and our restored fellowship with God as the result of God's grace, not our merit, seems to conflict with Jesus' words. Paul's words, however, were set in the context of Paul's own interpretation of his opponents as believing that participation in the new creation results from human effort. That insistence in that context should not blind us to Paul's assumption that our acts reveal what we are, that God recognizes faith by examining our works to see whether they are expressions of trust in God or of trust in torah and in ourselves. It is in the latter sense that, for Paul, God will judge us on the basis of our works.

Nor should we rely on English language dictionaries for an understanding of the sense in which the New Testament writers use the word *reward* to describe God's response to us. Of course, the Old Testament contains passages that indicate we have the right to expect reward from God. (See, for example, the commandment concerning honor to father and mother in Exodus 20:12.) It also contains passages that indicate the reward that we think that sometimes we have a right to expect is not forthcoming. (See, for example, Job and Ecclesiastes throughout.) God has the right to withhold, if he sees fit, that which we think we have a right to expect. Humans have rights, but only such as God pleases to give, not any that are inherent. Consequently, we have no inherent, absolute rights and can make no claims on God for rightful rewards.

For the biblical writers, a reward, in the positive sense, is never the payment of a contract, but is God's free and gracious response to human activity. We have a right to expect only those rewards God promises—none other! Moreover, although we have the promise of reward, we do not have a promise of what that reward will be.

The full meaning of reward in the present passage can be perceived only when we hear the passage itself in the context of Jesus' words concerning people seeing our good works and glorifying the Father. Commentators of earlier centuries were greatly bothered by the apparent contradiction between the reference to our works being seen and the secrecy enjoined in the triad. If our true identity is salt and light, however, and if we are to seek God's kingdom before all else (6:33)—in other words, if our true nature is found in service to the Father who has called us—then the greatest reward would be to stand at the great consummation and hear God say, "Well done, good and faithful servant."

No valid definition of reward, however, can leave out of account the scattered warnings of the persecution and death that can easily come on the disciples. It is clearly indicated that to follow Jesus can and easily may lead to death at the hands of the enemy. The call to take up the cross is no melodramatic admonishment. Receiving a reward does not rule out the possibility of martyrdom.

The possibility that the first-century Jewish concept of merit may have influenced either Jesus or Matthew or both, moreover, must not lead us to think of this promise of reward only in relation to the day of judgment. Reward as acceptance before the throne of the Son of Man (Matt. 25:34-36) is undoubtedly a dimension of the envisioned reward, but reward here and now is also involved. Otherwise, we would be dealing with a view of the assembly and the disciple grappling along in a chaotic world, all alone, and forced to endure by sheer heroism. The assembly, however, is the place where the risen and transformed Jesus has promised to be present till the end of the Age—not meaning the institutional church necessarily, nor necessarily any gathering that the world or the gathering itself might call the assembly, but meaning that assembly which God acknowledges and embraces as his own.

The genuine assembly lives under the call and empowering of its risen Lord. When challenged, it speaks under the power of his Word. The call to take up the cross and follow him grants the assembly the privilege of suffering with its Lord. When it suffers, it endures because of his presence. When its members die, they die with courage because of his strength.

The reward of the faithful disciple, then, is not simply the declaration at the throne, "Well done, good and faithful servant," but is also the promise this side of that gathering, "Where two or three are gathered in my name, there am I in the midst of them," and "Lo, I am with you always, to the close of the age" (Matt. 25:21, 18:20; 28:20 RSV).

In the antitheses, Jesus has given a new interpretation of ethics. Now he warns about the proper exercise of cult responsibility. Both are expressions of faithfulness.

The three teachings are introduced with the warning that if religious obligations are performed for human attention, then God will pay no attention to those performing them. Performing holy acts in order to receive public recognition will accomplish precisely that for which the performance is intended—human recognition—but no more than that. With regard to God, we will remain alienated and in exile, victims of the Darkness.

ALMS

The Greek word translated "alms" *(eleeimosunein)* is actually a more inclusive word that means "mercy" or "pity"; and although Matthew seems to have used it to refer to the practice of giving alms as he knew it in his day, that practice was a single expression of a much greater responsibility to the poor of the covenant community. Mention has been made earlier of the instruction in the Pentateuch that the people were to leave a portion of their harvest for the poor and the sojourners. Further provision was made for a year of release, a year in which all debts were to be canceled, and those who had entered servitude in order to work off a debt were not only to be released, but were to be given certain payment as well. The poor were to receive a new lease on life as a reminder that God had given all Israel a new lease by delivering them from slavery in Egypt.

There was precise provision, then, by which mercy was specifically spelled out. Poverty legislation was mercy set forth in guidelines—not as cold, hard rules, but as simple description of what it means to live mercifully with regard to the poor and the economically deprived.

In Leviticus, the teachings regarding how the community is to provide for the poor are descriptions of what it means to be holy, to be unlike the other peoples. Regardless of the extent to which other cultures may in fact have had provisions for the poor similar to those of Israel, the extravagant degree to which Israel is to go in those provisions is among those things that characterize Israel as holy.

At the heart of giving alms is a concern not simply for the economically deprived, but for all those who are society's victims. Giving alms is a specific example of what it means to be merciful, what it means to reach out with aid to those who are in any way afflicted. And since the assembly of disciples is to be a light to the nations, it can hardly be supposed that the primary concern to live life within the community as a sign to the nations implies that disciples are to withhold mercy from those outside until those outside also become disciples. The scope of the assembly's mercy can be no smaller than the circle of the earth.

Jesus does not say *"If* you give alms" but *"When* you give alms," not *"If* you act mercifully," but *"When* you act mercifully." Disciples, then, have no choice but to act mercifully. To deny mercy to friend or enemy is to deny the call of Christ. It is to reject the assembly's task as salt and light. At the same time, the concern of the piety teaching is that this radical sacrifice of oneself for the needs of others be done not because of the desire for public acclaim, but simply as the spontaneous expression of what one or what the assembly has become.

ACTING IN SECRET

Jesus, therefore, does not counter acting so that others can see with acting so that God will see, for that would be another form of legalism. Anything done in order to impress God with our piety is that self-assertion which seeks to obligate God to us. In the familiar story of the Pharisee and the publican (Luke 18:9-14), Jesus lays a trap into which many fall by saying, "Thank God, I am not like the Pharisee!" Being proud of one's humility is a contradiction of terms. With regard to the teaching on alms, it is as hypocritical to sound the trumpet before God while acting secretly before others as to sound it for the public.

The words of Jesus call us to act secretly, even to some extent with regard to ourselves. The words concerning the left and right hands are, on one level, personification. The hands do not have minds with which to know. On another level, however, it is significant that Jesus speaks of the right hand as the actor and the left hand as the hand left in ignorance of the action, for in the ancient world much symbolism was attached to the hands. The right hand was viewed as the positive hand, the hand of authority and power. The symbolism follows us today in expressions such as "right-hand man" and in the use of the right hand for blessing in the service of worship. The left hand, however, was the negative hand, the hand of duplicity and evil. A left-handed person was not to be trusted.

The warning not to let the left hand know what the right hand is doing is a warning not to let our actions done to fulfill our obligation to God be dominated by those self-seeking, self-assertive motives that turn spontaneous expressions of devotion into efforts at self-justification. God knows our secret, and he is able to judge the nature of our acts. Those done in simple spontaneous response to God's mercy and care are seen in secret, and God's response to us—whatever response God chooses to make—is made in accord with the self-abnegation and devotion to God that God perceives those actions to be.

PRAYER

The warning with regard to prayer is the same as that with regard to alms. If the disciples' goal is to have others see them and admire them for their skill with words, they will achieve that goal. They will be acclaimed as very spiritual people. Their religion will be respected. "If that is what you want," says Jesus, "then that is what you will get." So what? Other fallen human beings will respect the disciples, but they will not glorify the Father who is in heaven. Both in the matter of alms and in the matter of prayer, as well as in the matter of fasting, this is the ultimate problem: Actions that are to be done as bearers of the Light, as the salt of the earth (and which are therefore to be done disinterestedly so that God might use them to bring glory to himself) become mere instruments of self-glorification for the disciples.

The instruction Jesus gives concerning prayer has sometimes been understood in a manner that makes people reluctant to pray before others under any circumstances, even in a worship service. Just as the instruction concerning alms does not rule out giving alms in the worship service, however, neither does the instruction concerning prayer rule out prayer in the congregation. Going into the closet is a hyperbolic contrast to the public display made by the hypocrite. The hypocrite at prayer, like the hypocrite in performing acts of mercy, is an actor, a pretender, someone playing a role, pretending to be performing an act out of devotion to God, but actually performing it because of what he or she expects to get out of it. Consequently, it is possible to violate the ultimate intent of this teaching even in one's closet. Prayer vigils, prayer demonstrations, private prayers for self-centered purposes—all must be evaluated by the central concern of the passage.

Social movements, for example, frequently resort to public demonstrations of prayer as a tool in the struggle. Prayers on courthouse steps, before Federal government buildings, in open parks, before trains or highway trucks—these and many other occasions of prayer have become common for movements of both the left and the right, to oppose nuclear arms, abortion, capital punishment, and various other practices performed by the state or protected by the state.

One also hears prayer used as a ceremony or as part of a ceremony for events as diverse as sporting events, political rallies, beauty pageants, public banquets, public building dedications, and dozen of others.

The problem with these is twofold. If they are simply prayers uttered because it seems appropriate or because someone expects it, then they are uttered in order to satisfy custom, tradition, or human definitions of what it means to be religious. If they are uttered in an honest effort to communicate with God, then they are addressed not to the God of Jesus Christ, but to god in general—a god that by definition is an idol and, in the final analysis, Satan. They seek divine blessings on events that are frequently trivial, are always carried out without regard to the true will of God, and in many instances are actually dehumanizing in their outcome. There is nothing blessed—indeed, there is much damning—about praying on behalf of the works of the Darkness, for all such prayer violates torah's instruction that we are not to be a community that speaks God's name over things that are trivial ("You will not take the Name of the LORD your God in vain").

None of this should be taken to imply that Christians, Jews, and Moslems cannot pray together to the same God. Indeed, all three of these religions are centered, through Abraham, in response to the Living God. Allah, the name by which Moslems refer to their God, is not another name for God, but is the Arabic form (with the definite article) of the same word which in the Hebrew Bible is translated "God." There is a peculiar relationship among the assembly, the synagogue, and the mosque—a relationship rooted in those events through which God has acted in definitive ways to restore the health of the creation, a relationship not shared with the other religions of the world. Ecumenical prayer, as well as other acts of worship in an ecumenical context, by members of these three religions, prayer uttered in gatherings specifically for the purpose of assembly worship, will always be uttered with different assumptions about the One to whom the worship is offered, but if the prayer is true to the traditions of the worshipers, these assumptions will not be so great as to be offered to different gods, but will be the unified worship of all the children of Abraham and Sarah to the God of all.

The secular gathering at which representatives from Christianity and Judaism are invited to pray, however—as a gesture, not of true worship, but of political expediency—is a gathering with goals and purposes usually in conflict with the traditions of those invited and calls, not on the God of those invited, but on the generalized god of the nation or on the god of the movement.

THE PROPER CONTENT OF PRAYER

Jesus turns from the question of praying to be seen to the question of the proper content of prayer. Again, there is a contrast. This time, it is between empty phrases, piled up in large quantity to make up for their lack of quality, and the kind of prayer exemplified by the Lord's Prayer. That the concern is content rather than length suggests that we are no more commanded to keep our prayers short than to pray them in a closet. The Gentiles, according to Jesus, assume that the hollowness of their speech will be hidden by their long-winded speaking, but Jesus rejects not long prayers, but dead ones.

At the heart of the rationale is not an ethical, moral, or aesthetic consideration, but a theological one. Although Jesus' words do not rule out long prayers, they put the burden on the one praying to be certain that a lengthy prayer is for God's glory and not for self-justification.

Such a rationale also raises the question, Why pray? If God knows what we need before we ask and he is a loving Father, what possibly can be the need to pray at all? The basic answer to that question is supplied by the context of the exhortations: Although the three teachings on piety describe the way followers of Jesus are to carry out their religious obligations, the fact that the entire sermon does not concern commands, as commands are understood in the fallen world, indicates that we are not commanded to pray. The freedom Jesus brings results in alms, prayer, and fasting being performed freely. Jesus' words assume that the triad of obligations becomes natural activity in the freedom of restored human nature. In the restoration of our lives from exile, prayer becomes the human act by which we respond to the God who releases us and with whom we have been reconciled. There is no question that God needs our prayers, commands our prayers, or wants our prayers. Prayer is simply assumed in the restored relationship. To resist prayer because the Father knows our needs already would be to imply that prayer is essentially a matter of asking God for things. The Lord's Prayer will reveal the inadequacy of such a view.

FASTING

Fasting had been a common practice in Israel as a means of expressing sorrow, repentance, or both. The disciples of John also fasted, as did the church of Matthew's day. In the discussion of the beatitude on mourning, we have already seen that Jesus and his disciples were noted not to have fasted, although Jesus himself did in the wilderness, but the teaching on piety assumes the relevance of Jesus' words on fasting when the bridegroom is gone. Matthew, that is, simply accepts that Christians will fast. Fasting is essential to protection from the Powers and Principalities, to security in face of the Darkness (Matt. 17:21).

Like that of the other two practices in the piety sayings, Matthew's concern is with the motive for fasting. In 9:14-17, he makes clear that Christians are to fast as an expression of mourning over the absence of the Lord.

FASTING, PROTEST, AND TECHNIQUE

Like prayer, fasting can easily be commandeered as a weapon. It is not unusual for a person, a group, or a congregation to fast as a protest over what the person or body considers a matter of injustice or oppression. Thus, not only do we see congregations fasting during a liturgical season such as Lent, but we also see prisoners fasting on behalf of some political goal, anti-war activists fasting to protest government policy, anti–capital punishment activists fasting to protest the execution of persons convicted of crimes, and so on.

It is not always clear in such cases what those fasting hope to accomplish or what dynamics they hope to initiate. Mahatma Gandhi used fasting as a technique in leading the Indian masses against British colonialism, and some

Western activists have used him as a model. Gandhi's understanding of his fasting, however, was quite different from the motives attributed to him by the media and by some of his imitators today. Gandhi's fasting was rooted in the Hindu belief that the entire world is a myriad of expressions, in time and space, of one ultimate Reality. In contrast to the biblical view of God and the world as completely separate from each other, Gandhi believed that God and the world are one, with no separation and no distinction. For Gandhi, all religious activity is, to one degree or another, for the purpose of overcoming the illusion that the world and God are separate, because the illusion that they are separate is the source of all social evil and personal frustration. When Gandhi fasted, he was opening himself to that full Reality of which the world is a manifestation, hoping that Ultimate Reality would so move through him that the illusion might be at least partially overcome. Since, in Gandhi's view, the entire world is an expression of God, all things and all people are one. Whatever happens to one affects all the others. Gandhi believed, therefore, that by a closer awareness of his own oneness with Reality, he could become the means by which that awareness could spread through the world. Overcoming the illusion would reduce social corruption. Peace, justice, and renewal would blossom.

Contrary to what many believed, then, Gandhi was not attempting to shame the judge or other officials. He was not attempting to stir his followers or his opponents to action on the basis of their concern for Gandhi's health. Rather, he was opening himself up as a channel of "Truth-force" (*satyagraha*).

Ironically, Gandhi's intent was to express that very thing, which, in a Western form, he believed to be deadly to Indian culture: technology. The use of religious practices as a means of achieving, creating, or establishing some end is as much technique (which is the basic nature of technology) as is the use of the most sophisticated computer. It is an effort to put God on a leash.

Fasting as Jesus commended it is fasting not as an effort to achieve something, but as a response to what has already been done. In their fasting in response to the preaching of Jonah, the people of Nineveh fast appropriately and correctly. They fast out of sorrow, with no indication that they expect to achieve anything, but simply as the appropriate, even spontaneous, manner in which to await their death as the judgment of God. Even when the king calls on them to repent, it is not in any assurance that repentance will cause God to be merciful, but only in the hope that perhaps God will.

Fasting as Jesus commended it is the expression of disciples who mourn over his absence and long for his return. It does not hasten his return, but serves only as an outward expression of that hunger and thirst for righteousness which gnaws at the heart of the faithful disciple.

The fasting of the disciples is not to be performed for other human beings. Since even the mourning over Jesus' absence is to be expressed secretly, the disciple may have to risk the charge of impiety. The proper object of piety, nevertheless, is not to impress other people, but to express that new life which disciples receive in the midst of the Old Age and in the very presence of Death.

PART SEVEN

THE LORD'S PRAYER

Pray, rather, like this:
Our Father, who are in heaven,
   Your name be hallowed,
   Your Reign appear,
   Your will be done—as in heaven, so on earth.
   Give us this day our daily bread;
   And as we here and now release from obligation any
      who have offended us,
   So release us from the consequences of any
      offenses we have committed against you.
   And do not put us to the test, but deliver us from
      the Evil One.

For if you release others from their trespasses, your heavenly Father will also release you; but if you do not release others from their trespasses, neither will your Father release you from your trespasses.

(Matthew 6:9-15)

199

CHAPTER 27

OUR FATHER

The Bible makes abundantly clear that, although all human beings are God's creatures and the entire world belongs to him as its creator, "children of God" designates a special relationship effected by Christ for those in fellowship with him. To be a *creature* of God is to be one who is loved by God and toward whose good all of God's efforts are aimed. It is to be one for whom Christ endured the agony of the cross, tasted death, and was transformed in his resurrection from the dead. To be a *child* of God, however, is to be one who has entered into a special intimacy with God himself through fellowship and unity with Jesus Christ—Christ being the only one entitled by birth to call God Father. As the only one born bearing that special intimacy with God, Jesus came into this world precisely to draw all people into that same intimacy, and he invites us to address God as our Father when we share his family intimacy as his brothers and sisters.

The designation "God's children" is not exclusive; it is not intended to lead to pride and snobbery before the world. On the contrary, it is one that indicates responsibility to be about the Father's business of drawing all creatures into his family. The task of the children is to be the Father's instruments in increasing the size of the family until it includes the entire world.

Christians have been tempted, across the centuries, to understand the term "Father" in the New Testament in a way sharply different from the way it is used in the Old Testament and to say that although God is the Father of the individual in the New Testament, he is never portrayed as the Father of the individual Israelite in the Old Testament. Such an observation, however, is an interpretation imposed on the texts, an interpretation that assumes too little about the Old Testament texts because of having assumed too much about the New Testament texts. Just as a person cannot correctly make a New Testament use of *Father* in isolation from Jesus, the Old Testament reference to God as Father of the people of God implies that in the covenant relationship God is the Father of each Israelite. This is not to contend that there is no difference whatsoever between the use of the terminology in the two Testaments, but the difference comes primarily at the point of one's relation to Jesus, not at the point of theology. In both Testaments, the Fatherhood of God is a role in relation to a family; in neither is it to isolated individuals. The extent to which any individual member of the family is enabled to address or think of God as Father is the consequence of membership in God's family. In the Old Testament, Israel is God's child by adoption; in the New Testament, Christians are God's children by adoption.

From the standpoint of the New Testament, Jesus Christ is crucial for the parent-child relationship between both Jews and God and Christians and God. He is the one whose death and resurrection both climaxes ancient Israel's role as God's child and is the great mystery in which the present and future of Jewish and Gentile assemblies are inseparably joined. His identity is the source of a bond between Christians and Jews, which historically has been denied by both. It is as much a denial of his identity for disciples to deny that in him we are family with Judaism as it is for Jews to deny that he is the Messiah. Consequently, Christians who cast aspersions on Jews for denying Jesus' messiahship themselves deny him when they reject Jews as our brothers and sisters in the people of God unless those Jews affirm Jesus' messiahship.

One of the difficulties involved here is that we are dealing with metaphors that are both indispensable and drastically limited. They are indispensable, because to cast off the parent-child metaphor would be to deny something essential to our understanding of both God and ourselves. There is something notably different between the terms *creature* and *child,* and that difference involves relationships. (It might well be argued that even the term "relationship" is a metaphor, but to do so simply indicates the inevitability of using metaphors, since, ultimately, all language is metaphor.) To speak of God as Father is to use a metaphor rooted in our ancient heritage, but a heritage that is testimony to revelation.

To speak the address carries with it the implicit acknowledgment that our personal relationship to God is not a private, purely subjective one, but one maintained only in community with the whole family. Anyone who prays "Our Father," but—because of difference of mode of baptism, cultural identity, political affiliation, moral sensitivity, racial identity, or theological affirmation—rejects others who also bear the name of Christ, brings condemnation on himself or herself.

It is precisely because of this identifying aspect of the very address of the Lord's Prayer that disciples must reject any effort to make the prayer a part of secular activities, such as public school classrooms, which, by nature, are not gathering places of the people of God, but are gathering places of the world under the dominion of Caesar. Far from elevating the gospel and those activities by which the gospel is proclaimed and celebrated, the use of the Lord's Prayer in such settings makes it common, makes it the property of the world—an instrument to propagate not the gospel but cultural provincialism and vague anti-gospel moralism.

THE VOCABULARY OF FATHERHOOD

The Aramaic word *abba,* which is carried over into the Greek of the New Testament and simply spelled with Greek letters, is the characteristic word Jesus himself uses in the Gospels in addressing or referring to God. Usually he refers to God as "my Father," indicating the intimacy that he knows to exist between himself and God. Jesus invites his disciples to share that intimacy by inviting them to pray, "Our Father."

It has been common in recent scholarship to consider the word *abba* primarily a small child's word, akin to that early babbling of our own children, *da-da.* It is said that Jesus spoke to God in ways that would have offended most of his hearers, in the same way that it would offend most people today were someone to pray, "Our da-da who art in heaven."

For those constantly seeking ways, for whatever reason, to emphasize the differences between Jesus and Judaism, this assertion on the nature of *abba* has had great appeal. Several things, however, should be said as a caution against the common interpretation. For one, there is some evidence that although the word *abba* did originate in the early babbling of children, by Jesus' time it had already passed over into general usage. We can see (or hear) in the English language today the same origins of the most common words for both male and female parents: *Daddy* from *da-da, father* from *pater* (which is also rooted in children's babbles), *mama* from *ma-ma,* and so on. All our names for our parents are modifications of words from infancy, and they have taken on meaning through the relationship they address. For a personal example, I have always addressed my earthly father as *Daddy.* On those few occasions when I have wondered how it might be to address him as "Father," it has sounded stilted, pretentious, and ridiculous, just as it would seem flippant to consider calling him Daddy had I grown up calling him Father. Undoubtedly, Jesus' use of *abba* indicated his intimacy with God. The key to that intimacy, however, lies not in the precise origin of the word *abba,* but in the simple fact that Jesus reaffirmed the traditional Jewish understanding of the relationship between God and God's people as that of parent and child. As in the case of human relationships, it is not the choice of words but the genuineness of the relationship that is important. Whether in a situation of agony, joy, or despair, the inward cry of the child is conveyed to the parent by means of, but is not identical with, the spoken words in which the cry is manifested.

EFFORTS TO REJECT THE FATHER METAPHOR

The concept of God as Father has been attacked in recent years, of course, by certain feminists and others as part of an attack on the use of masculine language, as such, in the Bible, in liturgy, and in hymns. Some wish merely to establish a balance of male and female language in referring to God. Others wish to substitute female metaphors for the male metaphors. Others wish to replace traditional metaphors with androgynous metaphors. Still others would eliminate anthropomorphic language altogether.

There can be no argument that male domination of the church across the centuries has resulted in the relegation of women to a secondary place in the church and has supported the suppression of women in the larger society. It can also be shown that texts of the Bible have been misinterpreted by a predominantly male power structure and that a less prejudiced reading of those texts lends support to those seeking a sexually inclusive operation of the church.

Having admitted and bemoaned this usurpation of the tradition in order to protect male power and authority, however, one must raise serious objections to both the effort to reject the Father metaphor for God and the effort to substitute the metaphors of Mother or androgyny for that of Father.

At the heart of the issue is the matter of revelation and of testimony to revelation. The gospel is rooted in God's definitive self-revelation in history—in a particular time, in a particular place, and by a particular means. The apostle Paul referred to the time of the crucifixion of Jesus as "the right time" (Rom. 5:6). If God has chosen or intends to choose other self-revelations, these are verified, oriented, culminated, and purified in that revelation. Unless one assumes that this revelation was haphazard or that the time, place, and means of revelation were merely incidental, one must say that God chose sociological conditions that are neither irrelevant to nor ignorable by theology. God chose a Semitic rather than a Greek setting, and the fact that later theologians adopted the metaphors of Greek metaphysics for their discourse has had a devastating effect on efforts to understand the biblical testimony. For example, the effort to combine Aristotle's Unmoved Mover with the dynamic God of the Bible has resulted in sheer absurdities in the so-called doctrine of God. Indeed, even the idea of doctrine is largely the consequence of adopting an essentially Greek agenda.

Although the Bible cannot be equated with revelation, as the definitive testimony to revelation it is the primary instrument by which God has continued to speak as the Holy Spirit across the centuries, and we cannot go behind that testimony for some purer or more objective form of revelation. Even the assertion that God is holy (absolutely different from all else) is grounded in God's self-assertions of holiness (Lev. 19:2; Isa. 55:8-9) and testimonies to God's holiness (Josh. 24:19; Ps. 22:3; Isa. 5:16; Rev. 4:8).

God's self-revelation in those events to which the Bible bears testimony does not disclose a cosmic Person with a specific gender, but establishes a relationship between the Holy One and the Holy One's creation. The testimony to the revelation uses, of necessity, human categories. In human language we say that the revelation establishes human language as the mode of discourse for responding to revelation. God's self-revelation has come to us in experiences that indicate, to our human perception, both those characteristics traditionally associated with males and those traditionally associated with females. To confine God to characteristics of either human male or human female is idolatry, for the revelation is *not* so confining. To rest in the temporal, spatial dimensions of the revelation as though they were the Holy One's ultimate nature is to reduce God to our experience.

To seek to go beyond or behind the definitive testimony to the self-revelation, however, and to assert characteristics apart from the spatial, temporal medium of revelation is gnosticism. No logical, rational argument can overcome gnosticism, of course, because gnosticism, by its very nature, denies the only basis from which human opposition can arise: the authority of time and space revelation. To pay polite respect to the self-enhancing delusions of gnosticism, however, is to pretend that there is no self-revelation. It is to give gnosticism the benefit of the doubt, which simply indicates a loss of nerve on the part of those who should know better.

THE MOTHERLINESS OF THE FATHER

God's self-revelation to us is inescapably by means of the personal mode. This means that it comes to us in terms of gender. It is quite possible that had all history been characterized by matriarchy or had God chosen a matriarchal society as the vehicle of self-revelation, the self-revelation would have come in terms of God as Mother. Had this been the case, it would be illegitimate and destructive of the testimony to revelation to seek to make our language inclusive by referrring to God as Father. Such, however, is not the case. The charge is sometimes made that suppressing the female principle in Israel and in the early church was an expression of male vanity and power, and it would be foolish to deny that sociologically these factors had an impact. It would be equally foolish, however, to argue that theology is simply an ideology devised to support a political situation (although this happens from time to time). Obviously, one can always describe the conditions of revelation sociologically, but one must always be alert to the danger of assuming that to explain sociologically is to explain away.

We must not ignore the theological dimensions of Israel's rejection of goddess worship. In cultures around Israel, the goddess was intimately tied to nature. Nature, viewed as that to which we return for nourishment and vitality, was the undefiled source of human hope. Life itself was viewed as violent, explosive, bursting forth from Nature. In those ancient cultures the worshiper turned to the goddess as a means of alignment with Nature. Nature was not viewed as fallen and captured by the Darkness, but as good, creative, life-giving. The goddess, as the representative of the fertility of Nature, encouraged one not to seek a transformation of one's own self-centered nature, but to find regeneration by uniting with Nature through worship of the goddess herself. Since, from a biblical perspective, Nature has been corrupted by Death, however, the goddess' call was a call to Death. Human sacrifice was a logical part of such worship. Since the goddess, her children, and all Nature were involved in a mutually beneficial system, the pouring of human life into the system was entirely reasonable.

This in no way denies the presentation of the goddess as a motherly, compassionate, loving parent and even wife. It simply is to say that, theologically speaking, those positive claims of the goddess were, and are, a deception. They promise what the goddess is unable to deliver, for, ultimately, the goddess—like all idols, male or female—is the consort not of the Living God, but of Satan, the acolyte of Death.

It is not at all that goddesses are bloodthirsty and violent and that gods are not. Human sacrifices have been demanded by both. There is evidence that at one point some Israelites believed that even their God demanded human sacrifice. Those who assume that reclaiming a female dimension to theology would automatically lead to a more peaceful, compassionate way of life, however, do not take the history of religions seriously enough.

As the Holy One, God is completely different from his creation and is not, in and of himself, either male or female. Revealing "himself" in terms of male identity, however, he does so in ways that approach other possibilities. In the midst of religions for which sexuality was a vital component, God revealed himself as the husband of his chosen people. The language of the relationship is one of fidelity and adultery. At other times the metaphor is that of parent and child.

The self-revelation of the One Who Is (which seems to be the meaning of the name *Yahweh*) in primarily male categories, however, is heavily qualified by the constant attribution of female characteristics to the same One. As mentioned in the comments on mercy earlier, Phyllis Trible has pointed out that mercy, in the Hebrew text, is a reference to the womb. To be merciful is to act as a mother acts toward the child of her womb. The God whose self-revelation has come basically in terms of male categories has also revealed himself as a God who has dimensions best comprehended in categories stereotypically associated with females. This does not mean that God is both male and female in some literal sense, for God is neither male nor female. It means, rather, that in God there are dimensions, in strictly human terms, of both male and female. For the Old and New Testaments, however, this means, again in human language, that God the Father also displays a Mother's affection.

One implication of this for the assembly is that, stereotypically speaking, women have manifested those characteristics that are central in the character of God. Any relegation of women to a secondary status in the assembly is to relegate to a secondary status in the character of God those characteristics stereotypically associated with women. Moreover, men in the assembly must come to understand their own maleness by way of that particular maleness of God, which is most Fatherly by being Motherly.

TRANSCENDING, PERSONALIZING, AND DEHUMANIZING

Whatever God is in any ultimate sense, God is for us what God reveals to us in self-revelation. The Transcendent God invites those who embrace the revelation to address him as Father. To assume that we can transcend that revelation denies our human nature, and such denial always leaves the door open to dehumanization. If God is not perceived in truly human terms, all human categories such as love, justice, and the like become relative and vulnerable. The incarnation is then merely a whim on God's part—a technique, a method—by which God does not truly come into our world, but by which God keeps his distance from us.

It is ironic that in an age of depersonalization and dehumanization, an era when the personal dimensions of society are eroded with every sweep of the clock hands (or with every switch of the digits of the timepiece), there is a mad rush to deny the human dimensions of God's self-revelation. The effort is seen in referring to God as the Ground of Being, as a Force, as an androgynous figure, or in any number of other terms, all of which equally deny the personal categories in which the self-revelation has taken place. On the other hand, such irony should not be surprising, for the effort to reject or to relegate to a secondary role the testimony to revelation found in the Bible is, in our day, a consequence of applying to theology the same technology that has resulted in the dehumanized and depersonalized culture in which the rejection or relegation takes place. That is, technology—the use of knowledge to develop efficient means to gain power over the very source of that knowledge—when applied to revelation, no longer seeks to help in responding to the revelation, but seeks to organize it (thus, theology) in order to control it. It seeks to put the revelation into packages that can be dispensed for personal salvation, for increasing the size of the institution, or for supporting some social movement. The boxes however must always be attractive to the customer; therefore, in a day of feminist revolution, God must first be depersonalized so that God can then be repersonalized as female, or perhaps as hermaphrodite.

HEAVEN

Heaven is completely removed from earth. In the graphic depiction of Near Eastern mythology, heaven is a realm far above and beyond the created universe, where God dwells in all his purity. It is that realm where God's will is perfectly obeyed, where death and corruption do not invade, where moth and rust do not consume. In contrast, earth is the realm of mortality, imperfection, decay, and rebellion. To be a creature is to be of the earth. In the New Testament, to be a creature, even if one is a child of God, is to be characterized by that existence which is over against God. At the same time that we are invited to call him our Father, thus bespeaking our intimacy with him, we are reminded that a great gulf separates us from him as he is in and of himself. We are mortals, finite creatures of time and space. He is that transcendent Reality from whom we come. He is beyond our thoughts, imagination, and comprehension. His hiddenness from us in and of himself is because of his transcendence in comparison with our finitude. His hiddenness despite his abundant self-manifestation in the world is because of our sin.

The present sequence of the two originally separate creation narratives in Genesis 1–2 indicates this immanence and transcendence of God. In Genesis 1, the majestic, transcendent God brings order to Chaos by sheer command. In Genesis 2 this transcendent God creates by coming into his own creation and molding the first creatures from the dust. As creatures of the dust, we are invited into fellowship with the transcendent God who, at the same time, is both as near to us as our breath and as distant as the outer reaches of the cosmos.

CHAPTER 28

THE HALLOWING OF THE NAME

It is widely asserted that in the ancient world the name of a person or thing stood for, or was, the person or thing itself. We are told that God's Name is God's Reality. On the other hand, when God tells Moses "I Am Who (or What) I Choose to Be," or, in abbreviated form, "He Is!" or "The One Who Is," God both reveals and conceals himself. The event reveals that God is, but it also reveals that God is not apprehended by our human thoughts. Yahweh gives Moses a name that does not contain himself. Thus, the ancient concept that the name is the reality, is, at the same time, both affirmed and demolished. It is as though Moses had been given a question mark as a declarative sentence.

God's Name and God's Reality, then, are not the same, contrary to what modern scholarship has asserted on the basis of the ancient cultures. The One Who Is enters into the elements of the culture and explodes them while using them. When God tells Israel that he is to be worshiped at the place where he causes his name to dwell, the place of his habitation (Deut. 12:5), this is not to be understood that God in all his Transcendence is enclosed within that place, but that he mediates his presence in human terms through his Name. The great mystery is that the Name truly mediates the Presence of God, yet is in no way to be equated with God. Again, we are traveling in the territory of language, language that is neither dispensable (since God chooses it as a means of mediation) nor absolute. We can only embrace the language with all its promise and all its limitations.

When God tells Israel that he is to be worshiped at the place where he causes his name to dwell, he is asserting not simply that they must not worship him at any other place, but that they cannot worship him at any other place. Genuine worship is neither a subjective, inner feeling such as one might get while watching a sunset or listening to a great musical work; it is not a series of acts before God (as in "having a good time before the Lord"); nor is it outward acts performed routinely in the hope that God will hear. Subjective, emotional "feelings" may come about during worship; some services may be filled with joy; and some worship may be routine. All these, however, whenever they are present, are incidental and say nothing at all about whether true worship has taken place. They are psychological and physiological accidents. Genuine worship is never a human-initiated activity through which to reach God or catch God's attention; it is human response to the initiative of God. It is genuine not on the basis of our having offered it, but on the basis of God having called for it, our having responded, and our having responded with clean hands and a pure heart. All else is trampling God's courts—noisy clamors, pointless posturing, and floundering.

That God's name might be hallowed—that is, set apart and not treated commonly—then, is not that God himself might be hallowed, for he is hallowed, by definition ("I Am Holy!"). The hallowing of God's name is the hallowing of, the refusal to use commonly, those titles by which we refer to him, those titles he has given us as the means of responding to him. The hallowing of God's name is the refusal to treat our relationship to God as though it were like all other relationships with other people and things. Precisely because the Name, though not identical with God, is in fact a primary means of our relationship to him, to treat the means as though the means were ordinary is to treat God commonly. It is to ignore his holiness.

The opposite of God's name being hallowed is that it be profaned or held up to ridicule. The Ten "Commandments" prohibit lifting up the name of the LORD emptily ("You will not take the name of the LORD your God in vain.").

This instruction has a much more profound meaning than our common interpretation of it as prohibiting unseemingly language. In its present location, it follows the prohibitions of worshiping other gods and of making idols, and it precedes the prohibition of making the sabbath a common day. At the heart of all three of these surrounding teachings is the prohibition of treating as trivial that which is to be set apart. To have other gods alongside Yahweh is to treat him as just another god, even if he be viewed as the king of the gods. To make a graphic or plastic representation of God is to attempt to draw him down to the scale of created things. To treat the sabbath as merely one day among seven is to trivialize the great rest God himself established and is to trivialize his gift as though he has given that which is irrelevant. Prohibiting trivialization is the key to the teaching on speaking God's name in vain.

In its present location the petition that God's name be hallowed is set over against efforts by some to exalt their own names by public, self-oriented prayer. To call out to God in a manner designed to call attention to oneself is to lift it up emptily. It is precisely this effort to use God for personal gain that led to the downfall of Judah and profaned God's name among the nations.

The temple, according to the great prophets, although the place where God had promised he would cause his name to dwell, had become an idol. It had ceased to be perceived as the gracious gift of meeting place where cleansing and renewal might be practiced and had come to be perceived as an assurance that God would protect Israel regardless of Israel's actions.

God's name is profaned and its holiness is obscured when it is used to bless economic structures that oppress the poor, when it is used to justify military conquest of one nation by another (even if that venture be by a nation professing itself to be Christian against another nation professing disdain for or opposition to God), and when it is used to support social structures in which one group suppresses or puts at a disadvantage another group in the name of superior morality. And these are only some of the ways God's name is used to promote self-interest or even self-deluded altruism.

Whenever God's name is spoken in blessing over someone or something, it is implicitly for the purpose of bringing that person or thing within the scope of God's own holiness, but there are some things that should not be hallowed. Some should not be hallowed because they, by nature, oppose the purposes of God; others, because they are mere human creations, stained by our fallen condition, created for purposes of our self-gratification. To attempt to hallow the latter is to ascribe to them a dignity or a significance they not only do not have but can never have. One of the great mischiefs perpetrated in the realm of ideas is the assertion that nothing we do is of too little significance to concern God. It is this distorted view of the nature of the world and of God's holiness that leads to prayer for the blessing of sports events, to assertions by beauty pageant winners that God enabled them to win (one never hears the losers or even the runners-up say that God had anything to do with their place in the outcome), and to solemn invocations at all sorts of events, that are products of the Fall, not orders of creation, and not even candidates for inclusion in the new order of God's Reign.

Of course, in our appropriate explanations that the prohibition against taking God's name in vain concerns many things other than what is commonly called cursing, or swearing, we have occasionally left the impression that cursing and swearing are not covered by the commandment. Is it not an empty use of God's name, however, to ask God to dam up another person's life so that nothing good and creative can come to or from that person?[1] The proper action of disciples is to pray for others, not curse

---

1. To curse, of course, is to damn. The words *dam* and *damn,* however, come from the same original. As often happens, their spellings diverged because of different uses. A curse using "damn" actually calls for a "damming up." At the risk of overextending these remarks, I will add that the expression "not worth a dam" comes from the old expression "not worth a tinker's dam." Tinkers were stereotyped as cursing profusely. Consequently, their curses were said to lose force because they were uttered so carelessly. The later expression "I don't give a dam" was based on the small value of the tinker's curse.

them. If the reply be that the speaker of such an imprecation doesn't really mean that, that he or she is not serious about it, but is simply using a figure of speech, then that means that a thoughtless, careless use of God's name is involved, a use that is covered by the prohibition of trivializing the name.

A more subtle problem lies in the area of humor. Jokes and anecdotes about God, Jesus Christ, and the Holy Spirit are common stock among professional "religious" people, and a psychological study of this phenomenon, no doubt, would be illuminating. One must neither jump to conclusions, however, that all humor in which holy things are the topic is profanation nor conclude that such humor is always to be accepted on the grounds that God himself has a sense of humor. The key to the appropriateness and acceptability of such humor should be its impact on the reputation of God. From this perspective, the humor of Mark Twain is neither an attack on God nor a trivialization of God's character, but is precisely the opposite. Twain's humor is, in fact, a biting attack precisely on that trivialization which some other humor expresses. His numerous writings on religion were, for the most part, sharp assaults on those ridiculous caricatures of God with which church and society are frequently engulfed.

HALLOWING AND CONTEMPORARY PIETY

The hallowing of God's name is frequently most abandoned by those who profess most vigorously their love for God. In popular culture there is a distinct cheapening of the gospel—and, consequently, of God's name—by those who portray the relationship between the individual and God as the source of the community's relationship to God. Contemporary Christian music, for example (mentioned earlier in another context), whether it be crooned or shouted, emphasizes the one-to-one relationship with God in vocabulary and images that lower God to one who is more of an erotic lover in the sky (or in the heart, as the case may be) than either a tender parent or a transcendent judge. In the past, one of the great problems of mass-appeal theology has sometimes been its overemphasis on judgment rather than love. In today's pop Christian theology, the confusion appears within the definition of love itself. In the Bible and in the better mystics (despite any other problems with mysticism as such) the relation of husband and wife, parent and child, and even lover and Lover were patently symbolic, never excluded sometimes clashing analogies, and always used the analogous relationship as a means of portraying *agape* love. In contrast, today's "contemporary Christian music," as it is called, rests in the eroticism of the relationship. In most contemporary Christian music, the eroticism undercuts all other concerns. Ironically, many who have capitalized on contemporary Christian music have characterized rock music as the work of

Satan. In reality, by exchanging the God of agape for Eros (or, by his Roman name, Cupid), Christian musicians (both performers and writers) have themselves turned the music of the Darkness—the music of Satan, in effect—into a multimillion-dollar business in the name of the Christ this music degrades and humiliates.

GOD AS THE HALLOWER

In the final analysis, God alone can hallow his name, and that hallowing—the return of his reputation among the nations—will come when he assumes his Reign once again over the entire creation. The role of the disciples is to let their light so shine before the world that the world may see the disciples' good works and glorify God. The hallowing of the Name comes by means of the disciples' witness, but it is not really their accomplishment. The disciples have been set free to bear testimony to the Light. Otherwise, they would still be in darkness. They have been set free so that, in the words of 1 Peter 2:9, words with which Matthew would hardly have disagreed, they might declare the"deeds of him who called [them] out of darkness into his marvelous light" (RSV). They have been created in Christ for good works that God might be glorified. God himself works for the hallowing of his name, then, by setting the disciples free; and they in their freedom are to bear testimony to that freedom by acts that manifest it.

CHAPTER 29

YOUR KINGDOM COME

The plea that God's kingdom come, that the Reign of God in all its fullness come quickly, is a plea for the immediate end of the Old Age and the ushering in of the New Age. It reflects an eager yearning that the transition period between the two conditions of life associated with the Old Age and the New Age be as brief as possible, that the return of Jesus be immediate. The plea of this line and the preceding one are closely related to the beatitude on hungering and thirsting for righteousness. As we have seen, that saying refers to those who long desperately for God to manifest his faithfulness to his promise and to restore us to faithfulness, as well. Both the beatitude and the plea reflect the intense hunger for the full transformation of the creation, a transformation into a condition of complete harmony with the Creator and within itself—outward faithfulness and inward integrity.

All three opening clauses of tne prayer are clear examples of the alternative to the prayer of the hypocrite. The hypocrite pretends to be praying for God to hear, while actually praying to be seen by others. These lines of the prayer, when translated more consistently with the Greek text, contain strict parallels among their components:

> Let your name be hallowed,
> Let your reign begin,
> Let your will be done—
> > just as in heaven, even so on earth.

(Matt. 6:9-10)

There is no question about who is to be the center of attention if the prayer is spoken honestly. All thought, all attention, is to be directed to God alone. These clauses, then, concern not simply the proper object of prayer, but the proper content of prayer, as well. The words to God are to be precise and appropriate to God as the one addressed. God does not reject honest praise that springs from the heart, but he will in no way be impressed with flowery words piled up simply for effect.

Both prayer as a means of attracting the attention of other people and prayer as a means of self-fulfillment are ruled out, as are prayer as an instrument for communicating positive ideas to other human beings as in some sort of auto-suggestion. The practice of prayer is not to be an attempt to achieve "prayer power." All such prayers—whether supported by the most sophisticated of theories, advocated as the most efficient technique of spiritual development, or acclaimed in the most popular of journals—are impersonations of genuine prayer. They are, in effect, a sort of spiritual technology and are to be utterly rejected by the assembly and by the disciple.

The plea that God's Reign come on the world is the plea that there never again be an Inquisition, a Hiroshima, a Wounded Knee, a slaughter of Ukrainian peasants, a My Lai, a Chernobyl, a Son of Sam, or a Helter Skelter. It is a plea that there never again be a Holocaust. It is a plea that the nuclear arms race be stopped in its tracks and brushed aside as even less than a memory.

It is a plea for the overthrow of all human governments, the uprooting of all human systems, the overcoming of all human institutions—the plea that there come at once that new order in which we no longer have either the common sorrows and pains of oppression, torture, illness, disease, and death or the common joys of family, friendships, hobbies, and professional achievements, but in which there is a new form of existence, the nature of which we have no idea whatsoever.

We plead, that is, for that full appearance of the New Age in which time and space are swallowed up and fulfilled in an existence that will not even be characterized by personality and identity as we now know them, because personality and existence, as we now know them, fully depend on time and space for their character and for our comprehension of them. We plead for that new Existence of which all we can say is, "when he appears we shall be like him" (1 John 3:2 RSV). We plead for that which is more mysterious than Death, but as certain as the Resurrection.

CHAPTER 30

YOUR WILL BE DONE

"Your will be done" is perhaps the most difficult line in the entire prayer to pray. We especially miss the profundity of it if we understand it to be a passionless, sentimental assent prayed in isolation from the world. The model for the genuine utterance of this line is Jesus in the Garden on the night of his betrayal (Matt. 26:36-46). In words that echo Psalm 46:5, 11 (the Greek text of the psalm and the text of Matthew use the same words), Jesus tells Peter, James, and John that he is in distress such as can be compared only to the distress brought by death. He then prays on three occasions that God allow the cup to pass from him. In the first prayer he prays that the cup itself (his passion) might pass from him, but, nevertheless, let God's will be done. In the second, and apparently in the third, he prays that if the cup cannot pass unless he drinks it, then let God's will be done. Many manuscripts of Luke's Gospel include in the Garden scene a note that Jesus prayed so fervently and in such agony that his sweat poured forth like great drops of blood (Luke 22:44), a note which even if not in the original Gospel does capture the intensity of the scene as Matthew, Mark, and Luke have described it.

For Jesus, then, "Your will be done" was not prayed in silent, unquestioning submission, but in the midst of a struggle with God himself. If Jesus did not lash out with the anger of Job, neither did he give in without resistance and pleading. It has been common in popular piety to assume that the truly righteous person argues neither with God nor with the Powers and Principalities. To question God has been viewed as blasphemy. To storm out against Death has been viewed as a lack of faith. Romanticizing Death as just a normal part of living and trivializing faith as some syrupy sort of assent, we have trivialized the cross itself. Paul, however, is entirely in keeping with the portrait of Jesus in the Garden when the apostle refers to Death as the last enemy to be destroyed. It is perfectly in keeping with authentic faith to curse Death with the words, God damn you, Death!

"Your will be done" (Matt. 26:42) came from Jesus' lips in the Garden not because of any lackadaisical attitude or because he knew he would be raised from the dead. He suffered and prayed not even certain that his death was the will of God. Otherwise, his prayer in the Garden makes no sense. "If it be possible, let this cup pass from me" (Matt. 26:39 RSV). The assent to God's will came despite the agony, despite the uncertainty.

"Your will be done" is not an assertion that in one way or another everything that happens is God's will. It is, in fact, a plea that recognizes that God's will is not done on earth. It makes no pretenses to knowing why God's will is thwarted, why God allows the defeated powers to wreak havoc, why the defeat of the powers, in the cross, did not put any end to their destructive capabilities.

To make the plea in its fullest sense is to stand stupefied before the chaotic explosions of history with no clearer answers to why than Jesus had to his "why" on the cross. To believe that God's will is ever done creates more problems than it solves, for if God does achieve his will at least now and then, why does he not always achieve it? Why did God abandon Jesus on the cross? Why does God remain silent in the face of genocide, starvation, death squads, the state murder of children, and the onrush of nuclear suicide? Why? Why? Why?

This why cannot truly be answered by the flip charts of simple-minded evangelism, the positive thinking of pseudo-Christian psychology, the hubris of self-styled Christian revolutionaries, the piecemeal crash fund-drives of church bureaucracies, or a conscience-salving theology of quietism. Every answer, from right, left, or middle, either assumes the rationality of the Darkness, attempts to play God in overcoming the supposed problems, or deprecates the depth of human misery and pain. Every effort to answer, to solve, to remove the mystery merely mirrors the Darkness from which it comes. Jesus' cry on the cross was a great, excruciating, Why? But the magnitude of its poignancy lies in it having been addressed to the one who was still "*My* God!"

CHAPTER 31

THE DAILY BREAD

In the desert, Jesus' response to Satan's suggestion that he feed himself by turning stone to bread was with a quotation from Deuteronomy: "Humanity does not live by bread alone, but by everything that proceeds from the mouth of God" (Matt. 4:4; Deut. 8:3). Jesus does not set bread over against everything that comes from God's mouth (paraphrased in most translations as "*every word* that proceeds from the mouth of God") in some dualistic or pseudospiritual sense, but includes bread as one of those things that come from God's mouth. We receive all things, including bread, because of God's Word.

The desert test was to see whether Jesus trusted God. It was a test to see whether he trusted the divine declaration made at his baptism: "This is my beloved Son." In two of the three elements of the test, the opening words are, "If you are the Son of God."

In Matthew's Gospel the heart of the desert test is repeated at the crucifixion. There, too, the words come: "If you are the Son of God." Whether the test is to create food lest he starve or to come down from the cross and save himself, the heart of it is for Jesus to show, by using the powers implied in the declaration to save his own skin, that he believes the declaration. In both instances, Jesus is left to endure the test, abandoned by God, sustained in his faith only by the divine promise.

The Deuteronomy passage Jesus quoted comes in the midst of a passage in which Moses is telling the new generation about to enter the Promised Land that the forty years of wandering in the desert has been God's way of testing them to see whether they would be faithful to God. During that time, God's protection and providence had been seen in the durability of their clothing and in the manna God provided them to eat. Manna, the bread of the desert, thus became one of the primary symbols of God's continuing provision for his people's well-being.

Later, bread became a symbol for the coming of the Messiah's reign, a symbol perceived in the great banquet to be spread for people from all directions as they come to join Abraham in the celebration of God's appearance—a symbol also perceived in several of Jesus' parables and in the multiplication of the loaves, indicating that the banquet already has, to some degree, begun.

The Last Supper was remembered, in the tradition on which the Gospel writers drew, as a celebration in which Jesus connected the meal with the appearance of the Reign of God, although the different authors bore different testimonies to the precise nature of that connection. The church was furthering the testimony when it began to understand the Supper as an anticipation of the great Bridal Feast of the Lamb at the end of history.

Jesus' words to Satan, therefore, when considered both from the standpoint of their origin in Deuteronomy and from that of their larger development in both households of the people of God, are not merely a flippant rejoinder to Satan, but are at the heart of the very significance of bread. Bread is that sustaining nourishment for the provision of which we are not to be anxious, because God knows that we need it (Matt. 6:32).

Bread was one of the symbols by which Israel was reminded of God's providential care in the past and was encouraged to look forward to his care in the future. Bread, however, is not simply that starchy food nutritionists regard as one part of a balanced meal. It is, in the final analysis, a symbol of all food. The blessing over a meal was originally either a blessing of the food by the head of the household (a blessing to acquire the benefits of the food for strength for the daily tasks) or a blessing of God (a blessing of God in response to God's bountiful goodness in all of life, as symbolized by the food).

Returning to Jesus' response to Satan, bread is properly received, acknowledged, and used only when it reminds us of the full scope of God's providence. Satan attempted to get Jesus to separate bread from its origin in God and from its intricate relationship with all that God does. Just as the serpent urged Eve to separate the acquisition of the knowledge of good and evil from the One who alone can declare what truly is good and evil, so the serpent's counterpart, Satan, urged Jesus to separate bread from the One who ultimately provides bread. Again, just as the serpent accused God of crass jealousy, Satan sought to raise in Jesus' mind the suspicion that God is not trustworthy. By refusing to accede to Satan's urging, Jesus maintained the tie between bread and all of God's other work on behalf of his creatures.

BREAD AND THE FALL

It is not sinful to desire food. God created us as creatures who become hungry. In the garden, Adam and Eve ate food provided by God himself.

They did not labor for food and did not receive food as reward for their work, but received food as a gift. Their caring for the Garden was not necessarily connected with receiving the gift. Outside the Garden, we must struggle for bread. We "eat bread in the sweat of our brow," not having wrested it from God, but having gained it in a daily struggle with the soil and with all those institutions, structures, and systems that control the soil in our day. Just as in the conquest of the Promised Land, Israel had to go in and take the land, although God gave it to them as a gift, so God is said to be the one who gives us bread because his command sustains the fallen world and its processes.

The plea for the daily bread is a plea that God continue to grant us sustenance. It is an acknowledgment that God is the source of our sustenance. It is also a plea that God overturn the consequences of the Fall and relieve us from being dependent on our ability to wrest food from the soil. There have been times when God intervened directly to provide food—times such as when he sent manna in the desert, when he sent ravens with food for Elijah, and when he provided food for the woman of Zarephath through Elijah. He also sent messengers to minister to Jesus after the testing in the desert. Such instances, however, have been specific interventions, not the ordinary condition of things.

Even the food that we wrest from the soil and from those institutions that control the soil comes, ultimately, from God's speaking. In Genesis 3:19, God's word to Adam about eating bread in the sweat of the brow, though usually translated with "shall," as though a command, is actually a declaration of what will be. Now Adam will have to struggle for his food. This is not a command, but a declaration. It does not mean that God will no longer be related in any way to food for his creatures, but that God will now allow them to eat only after they have struggled for their food. God will not take away food, but he will put barriers in the way of food, barriers with which they, and we, must contend. God both promises food and warns of the struggle.

The plea for food is a plea that God at least enable us to be victorious in the struggle for food, if not grant us food as an outright gift, that we might serve him without anxiety over food for today or tomorrow.

BREAD, THE FALL, AND MODERN AGRICULTURE

Most directly and clearly related to the symbolism of Genesis 3 is the activity of farming. Adam would now have to farm for his daily bread. Food would no longer be a gift unattached to Adam's involvement with the soil, but would be the fruit of his struggle with the soil. The soil would bring forth thorns and thistles, and Adam would have to combat the soil to force it to bring forth food.

The thorns and thistles which create problems for the production of food today are not the only problem, for the very tools we have created to wage the battle have become our enemy. Modern agriculture is engulfed by corporations and governments, by institutions and bureaucracy. Its problems multiply geometrically.

The plight of modern farming in the West is not, as some would have it, the result of farmers having forsaken a benevolent kinship with the soil, for, with one exception, that kinship has not existed between the soil and the human race since the Garden of Eden. The exception to this absence of kinship was when God gave Israel the Promised Land, made Israel the steward over that land, and gave torah for instruction on how to carry out that stewardship. Israel's conquest of the land, God's gift of the land as seen from the standpoint of Israel's own activity, was God's means of redeeming the land. It was a redemption that typified the eventual redemption of the entire creation, but which was negated by Israel's idolization of the land.

What has changed is the terms on which the struggle with the soil is waged. Until the advent of modern machinery, there was actually a kinship between the human race and the soil—a kinship of opposition. The human race carried on the struggle while respecting the earth, recognizing that the opponent belonged to God. The struggle was not a struggle to the death, but one that sought to preserve the opponent's fertility, even while wresting its fruit from it. Although the human race could not service the soil as Adam and Eve had serviced the Garden, neither could the race regard the soil as a godless enemy to be cursed and treated in just any way pleasing to the one who struggled.

The great change came, then, not when some supposed benevolent friendship was lost, but when the intimacy and kinship shared in competition and struggle with each other gave way to objective, rational manipulation of the earth. There was indeed a loss of the personal relationship, but it was the loss of a relationship of respectful combat and the substitution of a heartless, Godless view of the earth as simply a giant machine. Just as warfare between nations switched from hand-to-hand combat, in which it was possible to speak of the honor and courage of the enemy, to long-range combat (first, the long-range cannon, then the airplane, then the super bomber), so the combat between human and soil switched from the conflict of farmer and soil to that of agriculturalist and crop, then that to that of corporation and product. Just as the weapons of war became the TNT bomb, the nuclear bomb, and the neutron bomb, the weapons of farming became chemical fertilizers, chemical poisons, and genetic manipulation. The goal: the transformation of nature—the establishment of the creature as creator.

In brief, the human race, like Cain, sought to escape its punishment, sought to avoid the struggle with the soil, by enslaving the soil. No longer would we consent to the struggle. No longer would we consent to the sweat of the brow. We would end the struggle once and for all by weapons so powerful and so decisive that the soil would be unable to withstand them. We would become conquerors of the soil and bend its pride to our control. We discovered, however, that the only way to defeat the soil is to destroy it. This we have done. Consequently, we now must seek substitutes for the soil—synthetic foods, efforts at undersea farming—assuming in our pride that we can succeed where Cain failed: in circumventing the judgment of God. Just as Cain's line died out, we see the increase of Death in our bodies from food substitutes, poisons, and genetic manipulation.

Still, the earth brings forth food at the command of God. Although we have presumed on the prerogative of God, seeking to avoid the curse and even to displace the Creator by our own transformations of nature, God still keeps his promise. By his continuing providence, the season for raising food returns and the grain springs forth. The Chaos is held relatively in check. We are provided endurance in the midst of the disorder. The question is whether the full realization of the promise will be forthcoming only on the other side of international destruction.

THE PLEA FOR THE GIFT OF BREAD IN THE MIDST OF STRUGGLE

God's provision of food does not depend on our prayers or our piety. God not only knows what the disciples need, even before they ask; he also sends the sun and the rain, the two things absolutely necessary for growing food, on the good and the evil alike. There can be no implication in the Lord's Prayer, therefore, that the plea for daily bread is a prerequisite for God giving that bread or that God gives bread only to his chosen people. The human race receives bread as the outcome of struggle, not of prayer. Away, then, with arguments that poverty and hunger are God's punishment of the wicked or the lazy or those who do not pray. In fact, the wicked are frequently more abundantly supplied with food than are the righteous, because of the wicked's cheating, robbery, and double-dealing.

The plea for daily bread, then, is not an initiation of the gift, but a response to the gift. Seen in this light, the plea for bread is the way that disciples can profess that bread does come only from God. It is a way of acknowledging that we depend on the gift God bestows and that we do not live of our own strength.

Moreover, it is of great significance that the pronouns of the plea are plural, not singular. The plea, as is the entire prayer, is not a prayer for the individual in isolation. It is not "give *me* this day *my* daily bread," but "give *us* . . . *our* . . . bread." The individual may pray the prayer in private, but never with the assumption that he or she exists as a solitary Christian. Whether the assembly in which the individual finds his or her place be an institutionalized body, an informal gathering, or the church of the ages, the individual who prays the prayer must always pray it as one who is bound up in baptism with others of the assembly. The plea for bread is an acknowledgment that the assembly does not live by its own ingenuity or cleverness, but by the sustenance of God.

BREAD AND A STARVING WORLD

The plea that God give us bread, which means, "give the assembly bread," is not a self-serving plea that we be given food and that everyone else be ignored and allowed to starve. The plea, rather, is that God grant bread to the assembly so that it might faithfully carry on its task as the instrument of God's blessing on the world. The assembly bears testimony to the all-embracing love of God, God whose will is that nothing that he has created perish. The assembly, therefore, if it is faithful in its task of bearing testimony, will share its bread with those who have no bread. Indeed, it will give away its own portion of bread and will risk starving, if need be, to see that others are fed. To do less is to proclaim that God loves the world enough to suffer and, in Jesus Christ, to die for it, while undercutting our words by refusing to reflect God's character in our actions.

The question of why God, as a presumed God of love, would permit millions in Africa and elsewhere to die of starvation and malnutrition raises the problem of God's character versus God's power, as such questions always do, and there are no easy answers to the question in all its fullness. On the other hand, there is a point at which one must say that until we have been willing to risk death in order to see those starving people live, we raise the question to evade our failure to bear true testimony. We let people starve while we horde food that would feed them, but we blame God when they die.

The example of the widow and her mite was Jesus' illustration of what it means to profess God's ownership over all that we have, and in a starving world it speaks even more loudly of the way disciples should regard that which sustains them. In sermons we extol the woman, but in practice we are more likely to follow the example of those wealthy persons who preceded her.

In the Old Testament, both the acknowledgment of God's complete ownership of the soil and the food that came from it and an indication of God's care for the outsider are found in the instruction that a portion of the annual crop is to be left unharvested so that the resident alien might eat. The food was God's gift to the resident alien, but obtaining the gift required the cooperation of those Israelites who raised the food.

From the story and the instruction in tandem, we hear a testimony to God's care for those who hunger, to the expectation that God's people will share their possessions with those in need, and to the expectation that disciples will not take shelter in the legalism of a tithe, but will give massively of their goods to see that the hungry are fed, the naked are clothed, and the homeless are sheltered.

The plea for bread is correctly prayed only when it is spoken as a plea that we be given food in order that we might give food to others or be strengthened to help others. Any utterance of that plea simply for the sake of our own survival is a blasphemy born of the Darkness and leading to Death.

CHAPTER 32

RELEASE FROM OUR DEBTS

Forgiveness is release. Forgiveness says, "The chains, which bound you, are now loosened. You are obligated to make restitution no longer. Arise! Come forth!"

Several writers in recent years (John Howard Yoder and Sharon Ringe, to name two) have shown with great thoroughness the roots of the language of forgiveness in the Old Testament events of the Jubilee Year and the Year of Release. Exodus, Leviticus, and Deuteronomy call for certain years to be set aside as occasions when all debts are to be canceled among brothers and sisters in Israel, slaves are to be set free, and even the land is to have rest from planting. Whether and to what extent these instructions were observed is a matter of conjecture. They stand, nevertheless, as the Pentateuchal testimony to God's determination that any bonds that bind his people are not to endure forever. The occasions of release in Israel bear testimony to the liberating work of God—seen in one of its fullest expressions in the Exodus—and the call of God's people is to manifest that dimension of God's character by releasing one another. The Deuteronomic instruction for the Sabbath even makes the seventh day of each week a testimony to God's liberating activity. The head of the household is to observe the Sabbath so that the members of his household and his livestock may have rest from their labor just as God released Israel from labor in bringing them out of Egypt.

In the book of Isaiah, the motif is related to God's release of his people from exile. Just as Israelites were to have granted one another release (liberation) from debts and servitude and were to have granted momentary release to the land, so God brings liberation to the captives (Isa. 61:1).

This motif may also partially underlie the words of comfort in Isaiah 40:1-2, words that indicate Israel's release from a period of military service.

Apparently, Matthew has drawn on this motif for his calculation of the generations leading up to the birth of the Messiah. He counts three sets of fourteen generations from Abraham to the birth of the Messiah, giving us six sets of seven generations (Matt. 1:17). In each of the three sets of fourteen, the event of the final generation sets the stage for what follows. Jesse, the fourteenth generation from Abraham, gives birth to David, whose reign opens the second set of generations. Josiah is the fourteenth generation from David, and his sons are the ones in whose era the Exile takes place. The Exile then provides the setting for the third set of fourteen. Jesus is the fourteenth generation from the beginning of the Exile, and as Messiah he opens a new era. In brief, the era that begins with Jesus comes at the point where one expects to find the opening of the seventh set of seven generations. Jesus opens the seventh era, the era of release.[1]

This language of release and of Jubilee is important in the New Testament as the language of forgiveness. In first-century Judaism, human beings were generally regarded as debtors before God, either because of our inability (as finite human beings) ever to repay God for all his gifts or because of our failure to meet our obligations to God. Because of the latter, the same Aramaic word could mean either debt or sin.

The plea in the Lord's Prayer is that God release us from our debts. The use of "trespasses" two verses later, when the subject once again is forgiveness, indicates that the plea is for release from those debts that we incur by falling aside from the path in which we are expected to walk. When we do not follow the path God graciously lays before us, we fail to meet our obligations as God's people, and thereby we become indebted to God.

TRESPASS AS THE VIOLATION OF A RELATIONSHIP

To fail to live according to the way of life that God graciously lays before us is not properly understood if it is perceived primarily as the violation of a law code or of a set of rules and regulations. To view it in this manner is to view it impersonally, objectively, and legalistically. From this point of view, our sin or trespass is not the first thing to come between us and God; the instructions themselves have come between us already. In fact, there is a sense in which regarding the instruction as law code or regulations induces us to trespass, or fall aside, or disobey, or sin. The apostle Paul describes this in terms of Sin finding occasion in torah to lead him into the waiting arms of Death (Rom. 7:13-14). It seems less serious, less traumatic, at the moment at least, to break a rule, ignore a regulation, or violate a law than to

---

1. Of course, it is the fluidity of the motif that enables Matthew to combine the idea of Jubilee (eras of seven years leading to a fiftieth year) with the idea of the year of release (the seventh year).

disrupt a personal relationship. This is heard in that question people sometimes ask, Can I do this or that and still be a Christian? This is simply a way of asking, How much can I get away with under the law? It is an impersonal question that relegates God to some distant spot from which he may return someday to call us to account, but a question so bent on the moment that we assume we can cross that bridge when we come to it.

The debts we incur, however, are not legal debts written in some heavenly ledger, despite the popular portrayals of heaven that would have it so. Nor are they debts we can repay by doing more than some absent God has left instructions for us to do. Indeed, although our primary problem is our sins, our finitude alone would make it impossible ever to repay the goodness of the Transcendent God, even were we not plagued by Sin. Our debts, rather, are those unpayable debts that arise when a relationship has been violated.

When relationships are broken and we become aware of the horror of that brokenness, we cry out—either aloud to the other or silently to ourselves—wanting to know what we can do to restore the relationship. What can we do? What act can we perform that will make up for or overcome the offense? We must pay for what we did! And where the relationship has been genuine, the terrifying answer comes back: Nothing! Genuine friendships are neither created nor maintained by the simple act of doing something. Spouses who do not cherish each other do not create a cherishing relationship by gifts or deeds. A loving relationship with neglected children is not created by an outpouring of things. The gift given as a substitute for love is not a gift at all, but is an object of barter. The deed done in pretense of affection is a hollow act, cold and lifeless, leading only to despair. Where genuine affection and devotion exist already, gifts and actions may become the means of expressing and strengthening the relationship, but they have no power at all to create that which does not exist. Nor can they restore the relationship that has been ruptured. They can, in effect, become self-defeating as we exhaust ourselves, concentrating on deeds and gifts rather than on the other member of the relationship.

Broken relationships arise out of the Darkness of the Old Age. In our separation from God, we are left in the Darkness so that we cannot see clearly, if at all, the face of our fellow creatures. Once Adam and Eve had fallen away from their proper relationship with God, even before being expelled from the Garden, they fell away from each other and from the world around them. Adam pointed the finger at Eve.[2] Eve pointed the finger at the serpent. Later, in his anger at God, Cain kills Abel. In Israel, metaphorical adultery against God leads to physical adultery within Israel (Hosea).

---

2. The Hebrew text will not allow the popular emphasis on *you* in "the woman you gave me." Adam does not blame God *instead* of Eve, but blames both of them.

Broken relationships, between people and between people and God, are restored not by gifts or by deeds, but by forgiveness. The debt incurred by violating a relationship can never be paid. It can only be set aside. The only relevant act in the wake of a violated relationship is not a frantic effort at payment, but the humble plea for release, for amnesty.

Our own relationship with God is restored not by our deeds, not even by our repentance, but by God's accepting us and reclaiming us. In the cross of Jesus the Anointed One, God took the initial step of reclaiming and restoring. It is in that step that all human restored relationships are rooted. Our response is to accept that which has already been done, not to create something new.

Our actions toward others, our own outreach to reestablish broken relationships, then, are not acts by which we create a new relationship with others, but are acts that bear testimony to the persistent grace of God, testimony offered to God in the hope that through us he will bind up the deadly wounds of alienation.

RELEASE FROM ALIENATION

God has forgiven the world. He took steps toward reconciling the world even before the world asked (2 Cor. 5:19). That God takes the initiative in overcoming the alienation our offenses perpetuate is not a new idea in the New Testament, and the cross is not the first means God used in taking the initiative. In the first eleven chapters of Genesis, God makes several attempts to reestablish the world. He gives Adam and Eve a new son to replace the murdered Abel and the banished Cain, and he cleanses the earth with the flood and starts anew with Noah and Noah's family. When both these efforts fail to restore a sin-free creation, God calls Abraham to become the ancestor of a people who will be the means of the world's blessing, a means of reconciliation in the midst of the Darkness. Even the sacrificial system was given as a means of reconciliation, indicating that God was already reconciled to Israel and to the world. Forgiveness is not humanly induced, other than by sin, but is born of God's determination to overcome the alienation that springs up under the onslaughts of Death and the Darkness of the Chaos.

Such is the power of the receding Darkness, however, that even those whose lives are basically motivated and empowered by the Life of the New Age are not completely free from its influence. The relationship with God *is* ruptured. Relationships within the assembly *are* fractured. Consequently, the assembly and those within it must still repeat the plea, "As we here and now release from any obligation to us any who have offended us, please, Father, also release us from the consequences of any offense we have committed against you." This is no plea for forgiveness because the assembly has forgiven in the past. It is no plea, that is, for forgiveness as a reward, but is, rather, the recognition that just as others offend us and need our forgiveness, we too, being imperfect, offend God and need his forgiveness. The plea, when honestly prayed, is an abandonment of hypocrisy.

FORGIVENESS OF THE ASSEMBLY

The Lord's Prayer is a community prayer. It is a plea that God will release the assembly from those offenses it has committed as a body, each individual sharing the offense without regard to degrees of direct, personal responsibility. Even those individuals in the assembly who have opposed actions or attitudes that were offensive to God must acknowledge that, despite their opposition, they are a part of the assembly and, therefore, share its guilt.

Sad to say, the assembly that began as the agent of proclamation and reconciliation slowly but surely ceased trusting God to preserve the message through whatever means he chose and began to establish authorities, creeds, and doctrines designed as much to condemn as to reconcile. The assembly became a church. Those with interpretations of the gospel or the scriptures different from those in power could no longer be opponents in debate, but had to be shut out and, eventually, tortured and killed. The church became less a pilgrim people docile to God's work of reconciliation, preserved and protected by God, and more a citadel, guarding the Kingdom of Heaven and protecting God himself. The assembly under the cross became a city of executioners. Augustine called on the state to turn its weapons against the Donatists; hermits and popes in the Crusades rallied young and old as a series of mighty armies against the Moslems; theologians, monks, and bishops incited and turned loose the torturers and executioners on dissenters, Anabaptists, and Jews; frontier preachers blessed the European invaders of the North American continent; chaplains sought and won rank and authority in the military, thereby blessing—with parodies of the cross the Prince of Peace shining on their uniforms—the weapons of war. Past sins? Sins forgiven? When did the church repent of these? Indeed, does not the church, on the whole, acquiesce in their counterpart today?

The church has never, for example, confessed its primary responsibility, from the standpoint of human agent, for the Holocaust. For almost two thousand years the church had provided ideological support for the oppression and persecution of the Jews in Europe. Martin Luther is only one example of the way the church, through its leaders, sowed hatred and persecution of the Jews, an example for which no century passed without its counterpart.

To say that the church bears that responsibility in no way qualifies the assertion that the Holocaust was the supreme effort of the hosts of Darkness to destroy the human race and undo the creation. Rather, it simply indicates the extent to which the church in the West has served the Darkness rather than God.

"Release us from our debts." Until that plea is uttered in awareness of our complicity in crimes against humanity and, therefore, against God, it will be a mere formality, uttered in vain, that plunges to earth even as it falls from our lips.

DISCIPLES AND THE INITIATIVE FOR FORGIVENESS

God's release of his children from estrangement is closely related to the children's release of one another from estrangement and to the children's release of those outside the family.

It will be helpful to consider for a moment another Matthean text on forgiveness—the discourse in Matthew 18:15-35. When another member of the assembly offends a disciple, that disciple is to go to the offender and seek to work matters out between the two of them. If that fails, the offended one is to try again, accompanied by two or three others from the assembly. If that also fails, the offender is to be taken before the entire assembly, and if all these efforts fail, the offender is to be treated as though he or she were a Gentile or a tax collector.

This last step is not excommunication, but is the recognition that the offender is, at heart, not truly a member of the assembly, and, while in the community, is to be approached as one who has never responded to the gospel.

Peter's question in the wake of this does not ask how many times the other person is to be released in response to a request for release, but in response to sin. Jesus' answer is not that Peter should forgive as many times as the offender repents, but as many times as the offender offends! The steps that offended disciples are to take are not aimed at bringing the offender to account in the sense of some punishment or penalty, but mark the persistency with which the offended party is to seek reconciliation, thereby overcoming the rupture of fellowship in the community.

THE REFUSAL TO FORGIVE

Jesus returns to the topic of forgiveness at the close of the prayer (6:14-15). "If you release others . . . your heavenly Father will release you." The tense and mood of "if you release" indicate that Jesus is referring not to the practice of praying in general, but to a specific future event. "If in the moment of praying you release others from any offenses they have committed against you, then your heavenly Father will at that time wash the slate clean for you, as well."

The promise comes first! In keeping with the mood of the rest of the Sermon ("Here is the way we live," rather than, "Here are my orders that you are to obey"), Jesus is saying, "Here is the way the relationship works. You release others and acknowledge your sin, and God releases you in the same manner." This is not a threat, but is a description of the moment of genuine worship.

Verse 15 ("If you do *not* release . . . "), a warning, comes into play when there is some reason to believe that the way set forth for the assembly will meet with resistance. Should disciples refuse to forgive the offenses of others, God will not release disciples from the consequences of their offenses.

This is no bargaining arrangement between the assembly and God. It is the warning that if our release from the Darkness does not result in our spontaneously taking the initiative to forgive others, God will allow us to fall back under the bondage of the Darkness.

The discourse on forgiveness (Matt. 18, above) ends with a parable about a ruler who released a subject from a debt totaling more than fifteen years of wages, only to discover that the servant, in turn, refused to release a fellow servant from a debt amounting to about one day's wages. The ruler, in response to the servant's hardheartedness, reimposed the original debt and had the servant thrown into jail, sentenced to stay there until the debt was paid. The ruler did not forgive the debt in response to the servant having forgiven a debt, but simply out of mercy for the servant's inability to pay. The incarceration came when the servant showed no mercy to his debtors.

CHAPTER 33

TESTING AND DELIVERANCE FROM THE EVIL ONE

The Hebrew and Greek words translated "tempt" (Greek: *peirasmon*) mean "to test." Temptation, consequently, is a test or a testing.

Temptation has frequently been understood to be the rise of a desire or a question within us. Temptations, we are told, come to everyone, and "good people" or "good Christians" are expected to overcome temptation.

Such a definition of temptation makes it primarily a subjective phenomenon, a psychological event, a thought we must resist, overcome, and expunge. In the Bible, however, testing is not understood primarily as a subjective event that might be explained psychologically, but as an event rooted in an objective encounter and as one adequately understood only from a theological point of view.

The objective nature of testing can be seen in numerous passages in the Bible. Israel's generation of wandering in the desert was to test them to see whether they would trust God. Their physical situation was the test, the temptation. When God allowed Satan to rob Job of his children, livestock, and home and left Job with nothing but sores on his skin, an ash heap on which to sit, and a wife who mocked him, it was a test to see whether Job would continue to fear God even when there no longer seemed any reason for doing so. Job's condition was the test.

Testing occurs when we are confronted by events or circumstances that open to us the possibility of doubt or disobedience. To be faced with a situation in which one must trust or obey God or trust or obey something other than God—that is testing at its most basic. When the subjective response to the event is, "Shall I trust God?" or "Can God be trusted?"—even if the answer is yes—the test has, at least objectively, already caused me to fall away. That is, to the extent or degree that we subjectively entertain the possibility of trusting or aligning ourselves with someone or something other than God, we are not merely tested; we have succumbed.

THE TESTING OF JESUS

The Epistle to the Hebrews says that Jesus was in every way tested as we are, not meaning that he had all the subjective questions we have, but that he faced the same objective world we face and encountered events that had the potential of posing the same questions for him that events pose for us.

The testing of Jesus in the desert indicates the objective dimension of testing and is typical of all testing. In Matthew's account (Matt. 4:1-11), Satan approaches Jesus as the Master of Deceit and the Sower of Doubt.

Shortly before the testing, Jesus had heard the voice of God declaring him to be God's beloved Son. That event was followed by forty days of fasting in the desert; consequently, when Satan approached, Jesus was hungry. Satan recalled the voice at the baptism: "If you *are* the Son of God, command these stones to become loaves of bread." In other words, "See whether God can be trusted. If God means what he says, show that you are his Son by using your power to feed yourself."

An echo of this incident may be heard in Matthew 7:9, where Jesus assures his disciples that God is a loving Father who gives his children whatever good things they request, that is, good in that they are appropriate in light of God's plans. If one asks for bread, will God respond by giving a stone? That is, if one asks for that which is necessary for sustenance, will God respond by giving something irrelevant? If God is able to raise up from the stones children to Abraham (Matt. 3:9), certainly he can enable his Son to produce from the same stones bread with which to feed himself.

Although Jesus is later willing to use his power to multiply loaves for others who are hungry in the desert (Matt. 15:32-38), he refuses to do so when the purpose is to test God by feeding himself. Jesus will not confront God with an action taken to test God in some way. To do so would be to reject God's earlier Word.

In the second test, Satan again introduces his challenge with the words, "If you are the Son of God." It, too, is a challenge for Jesus to see whether God will validate his promise, this time by protecting Jesus from harm. In the psalm quoted by Satan (Ps. 91:11-12), God promises to protect and deliver the one who, in the midst of danger, trusts him to do so. The reference to the angels is reminiscent of the later passage (Matt. 26:53) in which Jesus says that were he so inclined, he could summon twelve legions of angels to deliver him from those who have come to arrest him. He rejects the possible help because the scripture must be fulfilled. God's plan must be followed to the bitterness of the cross. The God to whom scripture testifies is to be trusted without question or hesitation. In the desert, Jesus' response is that we are not to put God to the test, but are to trust him implicitly.

The third challenge does not begin with the words, "If you are the Son of God." It is an effort not to persuade Jesus to test God, but to persuade him to reject God as less beneficial than Satan. The test moves from one concerning God's truthfulness to one concerning God's sovereignty. The third test is not entirely unrelated to the other two, however, for if Jesus had affirmed Satan as the possessor of such authority without qualification, he would have been ascribing to Satan the status, power, and authority of God, or at least of a god. This would mean that God's dependability is qualified—not in terms of his truthfulness, but in terms of his power. It would not be a matter of whether he had been truthful in declaring Jesus his Son, but a matter of the relevance of that declaration.

This third test, heard in the context of John the Baptist's proclamation that the Reign of God is at hand, asserts Satan's reign over against the Reign of God. Satan is not trying to destroy Jesus, but is making a last-ditch effort to preserve his own power. If he can persuade the Son of God to join forces with him, there is a slight chance that God's Reign can be thwarted.

In essence, then, the three tests of Jesus are an attack on God's dependability—both from the standpoint of his truthfulness and from that of his power. Jesus, however, does not even for a moment have to struggle within himself to decide whether to accept Satan's offer. His response is immediate and to the point. "You shall not test the Lord your God!" The test occurs, but it does not raise the questions it was intended to raise. Jesus trusts God, without qualification, and aligns himself with God, without question or qualification.

After the testing, angels come and minister to Jesus. Those messengers of God, on whose assistance Jesus refused to rely in the second test, now come to his aid without him even asking.

TESTING AND THE WEAKNESS OF THE FLESH

Another passage helpful in understanding testing is Jesus' admonition to Peter to pray that Peter not enter into testing. "The spirit indeed is willing," Jesus warns, "but the flesh is weak" (Matt. 26:41). The meaning of this warning is provided by the context. Peter has just sworn never to forsake Jesus, even if loyalty leads to death (Matt. 26:33-35). Peter, however, is unable to stay awake and on guard even for an hour. "When the chips are down," Jesus sadly observes, "you will be unequal to the test, eager though you now are."

That test for Peter, later in the narrative, comes when he is identified in the courtyard as one of Jesus' followers. Its counterpart for Jesus is the cry of the crowd for Jesus to save himself.

There is a striking parallel between Peter's test and Jesus' test. Just as Jesus' test springs from the words at the baptism, "This is my beloved Son, with whom I am well pleased," Peter's test comes at the climax of a series of events that were initiated by God's words to the disciples: "This is my beloved Son, with whom I am well pleased. Listen to him." What Peter and the other disciples were to have listened to from Jesus were his words about the necessity of his passion, death, and resurrection.

The words of the crowd around the cross in Matthew's Gospel reveal that the crowd has become the instrument of Satan, for the words are the same as those of Satan in the desert: "If you are the Son of God . . . ."At the cross the challenge is for Jesus to test God by trying to come down from the cross.

Peter's test comes when he is recognized by members of the same crowd while he stands in the darkness as Jesus is tried. Peter has not truly listened to Jesus as God's voice admonished him to do, and now, in the Darkness, frightened and confused, he denies even knowing Jesus.

Just as Jesus had prayed that the cup of testing through suffering might pass from him without him having to drink it, so he had urged Peter to pray that neither might he, Peter, be tested. We are given no indication that Peter ever prayed that prayer, at least prior to the resurrection. In any event, it was not God's will that Jesus escape the events that lay ahead, and, likely, the response to Peter would also have been no.

The flesh is weak, no matter how eager the spirit. The will is not always able to follow through on good intentions. And it is objective events that provide the stumbling block. Despite the willingness of the spirit, there is always the danger that one occurrence or another will lead to the inner question and that, both in raising the question and in giving an inappropriate response, we will fail the test.

Even though testing originates in the outward, objective event and the arousal of a question or a doubt means we fail the test in one way, we should not conclude that how we respond is unimportant once the question or doubt is raised. The inner struggle with the raised question or doubt is one aspect of testing. Always, however, we are endangered by that smug heroism manifested as pride in having come out on top in the inner struggle. Although it may be relatively better to be victorious in that struggle, the struggle itself signals defeat in the initial confrontation.

DELIVERANCE FROM THE EVIL ONE

The language of the plea for forgiveness and the language of the plea for deliverance from the Evil One are closely related in the Bible. Forgiveness (release), as already discussed, has its origin in various occasions of release from debts and servitude. Deliverance's origins lie in deliverance from the enemy in time of war.[1]

---

1. The word *salvation* is simply another way of translating the Greek and Hebrew words of deliverance. Salvation, in the New Testament, is deliverance from the powers of Sin and Death and from the way of life produced by them.

The word *deliver,* in "deliver us from the Evil One," then, echoes the entire biblical drama of God coming to rescue his people as they lie in danger at the hands of those who would enslave or destroy them. In the plea of the prayer, disciples are to beg God to deliver them from Satan.

Most of the popular treatments of Satan and the demonic in modern fiction, movies, and certain religious groups, though seeking to affirm the danger of the demonic, actually do not take the demonic seriously enough. Satan is usually portrayed as a creature subject to magic and incantation, to humans who can manipulate cosmic power. Sacramental objects and holy ritual are reduced to the tools of magic powers, which human beings may wield against the forces of the Darkness. Even the cross becomes a magic amulet in stories such as those about vampires.

Such an understanding of the demonic and of human resistance not only is not biblical, but also is a type of idolatry the Bible specifically opposes. Whenever any object or set of words is perceived as containing an inherent power that mortals can wield against demonic forces, those objects or words have become idols. We have then become engaged not with faith, but with superstition and witchcraft. Conversely, any demonic power perceived to be subject to magic and to the inherent power of idols is thereby perceived as being less than the transcendent creature or power the biblical writers assert Satan to be. In the Bible, Satan is not subject to spells, incantations, or power-bearing objects, but is subject only to the power of God.

In the Bible, Satan is intimately related to Death. Satan is the instrument of Death's power, and, consequently, is susceptible only to the Word of God. The Lord's Prayer reflects this perspective in that Jesus instructs us to pray not for the power to defeat Satan, but for deliverance from Satan. This implies that though the Evil One, Satan, has already been conquered in the cross of Jesus Christ, he still, like some conquered nation whose governors continue to struggle and vex the conquering ruler, is able to wreak extensive havoc. The New Age, though having begun in the cross and resurrection of Jesus, has not completely obliterated the Old Age. The Light, though having burst forth as the dominating agent over the Darkness, has not obliterated the Darkness. Satan, though expelled from heaven in the death and resurrection of Jesus (Rev. 12:7-12), is still permitted to wage war against the people of God on earth (Rev. 12:13-17). Consequently, disciples are instructed to plead for deliverance from his attacks.

In the later literature of the Old Testament, it becomes clear that those efforts to undermine the work of God throughout the history of the creation had been manifestations of the demonic Powers. The serpent in the Garden of Eden, for example, was the instrument of the powers—the agent of Satan, the acolyte of Death.

In the era before Jesus and in the confrontation with Jesus himself (in the desert), the work of Satan, a work assigned by God, had been that of testing and accusation.

Satan's attack on Job in the Old Testament and the testing of Jesus and Peter in the New Testament are classic examples of the earlier role of Satan. Once Satan's authority was ripped away from him and his reign was snatched away in the cross, however, his work suddenly became more violent. In revenge for the defeat God had handed him, Satan sought to undermine and destroy the entire human race because it had been created originally in the image of God and God had been determined to restore that image. The place of attack was the people of God, the agents of renewal. The Prince of Liars became the Prince of Murderers. Christians and Jews were set against one another, and eventually both were set against the Moslems. As Christians increasingly identified with the secular government, thinking it possible to have two masters, international wars found brothers and sisters in Christ slaughtering one another in the name of secular ideals that had been baptized in the name of Christ. The Black Plague of Europe, the Inquisition, the economic suppression and various murders of the Jews in the Middle Ages—all were manifestations of the murderous Powers, all were manifestations that in the 1930s fell into the background as the Abyss spewed forth its fire.

It is for deliverance from these ravages of Satan and his hosts that we are invited to plead. We are to plead that the massive onslaughts of Powers not become for us a test of our confidence in God. We are to plead that the terrors of the Darkness that assails us not cause us, for a single moment, to turn aside from God. Argue, yes. Cry out in anger, yes. Fall mute in face of the Silence, yes. But turn aside? No! Simply plead for deliverance, and hang on even when abandoned.

PART EIGHT

THE LIFE OF TRUE FREEDOM

Do not store up for yourselves treasures on earth, where moth and worm consume and where thieves break in and steal, but store up for yourselves treasures in heaven, where neither moth nor worm consumes and where thieves do not break in and steal. For where your treasure is, there your heart will be also.

The eye is the lamp of the body; therefore, if your eye is sound, your entire body will be lighted, but if your eye is unsound, your entire body will be darkened. If then the Light in *you* is darkness, how great is the Darkness!

No one can serve two masters. He will either hate the one and love the other, or he will be attached to the one and disregard the other. You cannot serve God and Mammon.

Therefore I say to you, do not be anxious about your life—what you will eat or what you will drink, nor about your body—what you will wear. Is not life more than food and the body more than clothing? Look at the birds of the air: They neither sow nor reap nor gather into barns, yet your heavenly Father feeds them. Are you not more valuable than they? And which of you by centering your attention on it can add one cubit to your span of life?

And about clothing, why are you anxious? Look carefully at the lilies of the field, how they grow. They neither toil nor spin. Yet I say to you that not even Solomon, in all his glory, was arrayed like one of these. But if the grass of the field, which today is alive and tomorrow is thrown into the oven, God clothes in this manner, will he not much more clothe you, you of such meager faith?

Therefore, do not be anxious, saying: "What shall we eat?" or "What shall we drink?" or "What shall we wear?" For all these things the Gentiles seek! And your heavenly Father knows that you need them all. But you seek first his Reign and his faithfulness, and all these things, too, shall be yours.

Do not anxiously attempt to reach into tomorrow, therefore, for tomorrow will have its own anxieties. Each day's trouble is sufficient for the day itself.

Do not judge, lest you be judged. For the judgment you pronounce will be the standard by which you will be judged. And the measure you give will be the measure you get. Why do you see the speck in your brother's eye, but do not notice the log in your own eye? Or how can you say to your brother, "Permit me to take the speck from your eye," while there is the log in your own eye? You hypocrite! First, take the log from your own eye, and then you will see clearly how to take the speck from your brother's eye.

Do not give holy things to dogs, and do not offer your pearls to swine, lest they trample them under foot and turn to attack you.

Ask, and it will be given unto *you;* seek, and *you* will find; knock, and it will be opened to *you;* for *all* who ask will receive, and *all* who seek will find, and to *all* who knock it will be opened. Consider this: Who among you, if your child asks for bread, will give the child a stone? Or if the child asks for a fish, will give the child a serpent? If you, therefore, being corrupt, know how to give good gifts to your children, how much more will your Father in heaven give good things to those who ask him?

Whatever you wish people would do to you, therefore, do the same to them, for this is torah and the prophets.

(Matthew 6:19–7:12)

CHAPTER 34

COMPETING INVESTMENTS, THE LIGHT, AND COMPETING MASTERS

Gunther Bornkamm has argued persuasively for considering the portion in Matthew 6:19–7:12 as a sort of exposition of the Lord's Prayer. Moreover, 6:19-21 echoes the admonitions of all three earlier instructions concerning piety. Those who store up treasures on earth are those who seek to be seen by others, rather than concerning themselves with God's will. The reward of being seen and acclaimed by others, but losing the reward from God, is to lay up treasures that are consumed by moths and worms. The primary concern in both passages is the same—attention to God's will, rather than to that which establishes transient security or reputation among the children of the Darkness.

The treasure saying extends the piety sayings, however, to include all activities or desires that center on achievements in the present Age rather than on the Reign of God.

The saying on treasures parallels the plea that God's will be done on earth as in heaven. Earth, therefore, becomes more than a mere spot in cosmic geography. It is the Old Age counterpart to the earth of the New Age, which the meek will inherit. Just as the earth of that beatitude is the transformed earth of the New Age, the earth of the present saying is the corrupted, fallen world of the Old Age. Disciples are to set their minds—focus their attention, perspective, and will—on "things that are above, where Christ is . . . , not on things that are on earth" (Col. 3:1-2 RSV). They are not to let the world around them squeeze them into its own mold (Rom. 12:2, Phillips).

Such passages have been misinterpreted in much of the church's life because of the influence of dualism. That is, things on earth have been simply equated with physical, material reality, and things in heaven (or things above) have been equated with a subjective, inward piety. *Worldly* has been used to describe people who take material reality seriously. The element of accuracy in this has been that "earthliness" or "worldliness" frequently expresses itself in an attachment to property, money, clothing fashions, and the like. The flaw is seen, however, in the way the label has been used to justify callousness toward the poor, the hungry, and the homeless.

Jesus' instruction, properly understood, cuts across the line of separation that dualism assumes. To lay up treasures on earth may have nothing to do with physical reality; it can easily mean to cultivate human approval of things that dualism has called spiritual. The piety teaching on prayer is a good example. People whose primary or sole interest in praying is that others will recognize them as astute or articulate in praying, or will admire their piety, are people who are laying up treasures on earth. Conversely, people who use their physical possessions for the well-being of others because they are driven by God to do so may be said to be laying up treasures in heaven.

The heart of the assembly, and of the individual disciple, will be guided by the location of its investments. Indeed, what the heart truly longs for has become its idol.

It is here that the Western church most clearly reveals its essential atheism. Although the church has opposed and attacked many of the consequences of society's idolatry—poverty, drug abuse, the nuclear arms race, racism, pornography, and so on—the church has, at the same time, worshiped the same idols to which society has turned: power, prestige, comfort, and immortality. Moreover, the same justification used by governments and other power-seeking groups—corporations, labor unions, political parties, and others—is used by churches in their political and evangelistic ventures: "The world will be a better place if we are in charge." Of course, few put it that bluntly, but that is the common assumption. "Put us in power and we will usher in an age of peace and prosperity." Power is the key, power to change the world. Not to control the world in some obviously destructive or evil manner, but to control it for the greatest well-being attainable. The goals of the Darkness are attractive to well-meaning people because those goals often seem so humane. They are attractive to the wicked because they can be so easily propagated. Even the Nazis claimed to be working toward a better world—a fact that, rather than mitigating the evil they and their followers perpetrated, simply indicates the extent to which a desire for perfection can be a demonic desire born of the Darkness.

The desire for power gives rise to The Method—a deliberate, systematic effort to apply what we think we know about nature in order to achieve efficiency and predictability. The popularity of "how-to" books on every subject from cooking to being a parent to writing a sermon to taking charge of your own life is simply the popular manifestation of the underlying drive of the entire society, in fact, of the entire human race. The attempt to achieve power, or mastery, is the perennial expression of the original decision to eat the forbidden fruit. Eating it would give Adam and Eve power.

The quest for power through the increase of efficiency has no room for either the unpredictable or the unproductive. The latter creates a drag on the system; the former threatens to derail it. Those who impede or interfere with efficiency must be weeded out, and either relegated to the margins or eliminated. They must be identified (by achievement tests, aptitude tests, polygraph tests, personality analyses, drug tests, political oaths, and so forth), and then either pushed aside (through applying criteria for job qualifications, performance standards, continuing education requirements, salary manipulation, forced retirement, technicalities in contract clauses, and so on) or completely eliminated (by genetic manipulation, euthanasia, abortion, capital punishment, and so on). Considering themselves to be on the side of the universe, the Nazis relied on genocide, selective breeding, and thought control in their quest for a super race—a new human being who would embody what the Nazis assumed nature had intended all along. Modern governments and churches rely on propaganda, patronage, and legalism in the name of accountability and responsible planning.

Hitler was obsessed with Teutonic religion. Modern Western governments are driven by verbal allegiance to the god of all people (nature's god, god in general, the universal god, and others). The modern Western church is devoted to the god who brings prosperity to those who are willing to work for their reward, to the god who gives power, prestige, control, and immortality to those who show themselves worthy of power, to the god who places control in the hands of the elect, the elect being those who give evidence of their election by their desire for power. The recent passion to expose Satan worship has centered on rock music. It should also examine the worship of the ordinary Western church—liberal or fundamentalist.

THE CHURCH'S ADOPTION OF THE STRUCTURES OF POWER

This drive for power has resulted, in the case of the Western church, in regularly adopting the organizational structures of those components of society that wield controlling power. In the medieval period, the Roman Empire was the model. In the modern period, the republican model fostered by the Enlightenment has prevailed in Protestantism and now struggles for expression in the Roman Catholic Church. In more recent years, churches, sensing almost unconsciously the displacement of governments by corporations as the locus of national and international power, have increasingly come to reflect the corporate model in their structures, in their methods, and some even in their titles. In The United Methodist Church, for example, the officers responsible for overseeing the total life of the congregation once were called stewards ("stewards" meaning those who have a responsibility to take care of the landowner's or Lord's property). Now the affairs of the congregation are in the hands of an Administrative

Board with various members of the board representing the interests of the various components of the congregation and the stewards having been replaced by members-at-large (who represent the interests of the congregation as a whole). Even in the Roman Catholic Church and the churches in the Anglican Communion (churches that have maintained the outward forms of Roman imperialism), the bulk of the work of the church is carried on by a gargantuan bureaucracy. Perhaps the crassest expression of the mentality that has come to prevail in this respect was the motto widely asserted in American churches a few years ago: "People are our business!"

It can be argued, of course, that the acculturation of the church is a means of expressing incarnation theology.[1] Even if incarnation theology is granted in part, however, it should be noted that all New Testament references in support of it speak of the Incarnation not in terms of power, but in terms of powerlessness. No one has made a more persuasive case for incarnation theology than did Dietrich Bonhoeffer in *The Cost of Discipleship,* but throughout Bonhoeffer's analysis he speaks of incarnation as an acceptance of suffering. No sound incarnation theology can be used to justify the church's quest for power or the use of the church by individuals for personal power and prestige—uses such as may be seen in the so-called professionalization of the ministry. This professionalization is measured predominantly according to education (in which the bachelor's degree of the seminary becomes a master's degree, but without losing its elementary and intermediate content); job rights (which include study leave, vacation time, salary expectations, career opportunities, job advances, and so on); and respectability of title (which includes relatively simple or innocuous "Doctor of Ministry" programs that enable the pastor to match titles with holders of various and more rigorous academic and professional doctoral degrees in society). This is the vocation to servanthood?

Those in power in the church, of course, argue that power is necessary to serve. One church leader a few years ago was quoted as saying that if the church is going to serve society it must become a leader in society. This is precisely the view of messiahship that Jesus rejected. It is the triumph of the warrior messiah. It measures the effectiveness of the Servant of God by the values of Mammon and Caesar. It either ignores or denies the inevitable

---

1. Incarnation theology is that theology which moves from the Incarnation in Jesus Christ to assuming that the glorified Christ is incarnate in the church as his Body to assuming that the church must take on the forms of those societies in which it finds itself. To argue against incarnation theology is not to deny the legitimacy of any of these three assumptions, but is to deny the extent to which they can be identified with one another. That is, in Jesus Christ, God's Wisdom became human while remaining the divine Wisdom. In doing so, the Wisdom of God did not lack anything essential to human nature. An identical incarnation in human culture would mean that the church should adopt all elements of the culture in which it finds itself. The folly of such is obvious.

corruption of power into an instrument for self-preservation at the cost of those the servant is called to serve. Had God chosen to work according to the power-oriented values of human society, when the magi went to Herod's palace seeking the Messiah they probably would have had to look no farther. The Messiah would have been born in the palace without contradicting the expectation of a descendant of David, for were God's work done through human power, the Davidic line would not have been displaced. What God refuses to do, however, the church insists on doing—and in the name of God! Therein lies its idolatry and its practical atheism.

THE EYE, THE LIGHT, AND THE DARKNESS

The eye is the organ of vision. Despite their differences on many of the details of seeing, ancient theories of how we see generally agreed that light enters the body through the eye and enables us to see. Seeing enables us to organize the world around us; it is, in this respect, an organ of control. By seeing, I am able to put things in place. The clarity of the eye is crucial, therefore, if we are to order our experience accurately. With unclear vision, we mistake persons, objects, and spatial relationships. Although the blind person may expand other senses to an amazing degree, none of those other senses enables the organization and control that the eye enables.

Just as salt that has lost its savor is good only for being thrown out, and just as a light placed under a basket will be extinguished, the light which in the darkness is itself dark contributes to the darkness. Although the Light shines in the Darkness and the Darkness is unable to overcome it (John 1:5), those who are called to bear testimony to the Light must always take care wherein they stand, lest they fall (1 Cor. 10:12). They are not immune to the Darkness; the house swept clean of demons is always subject to the emboldened return of the demons, and in multiplied power.

Disciples who succumb to the Darkness do not simply fall away, but actually contribute to the power of the Darkness. Not that it is possible to escape all contact with and influence by the Darkness in the present life, but it is possible by grace to be basically motivated by the Light. Although the Light and the Darkness compete, and the Darkness will qualify the acts of those who serve the Light, there can be no dual slavery. One either serves the Light or is enslaved by the Darkness.

Jesus assumes that we are born with spiritual cataracts. Our eyes can permit the entry only of the Darkness. We behold the world only in distorted, blurry images, which we organize into a false world. The call of Christ, which sets the hearer free to respond, also sets the eye of the hearer free to see clearly. If the clarity of the eye thus established is rejected, the eye again is clouded and the Darkness returns.

To assert that the call of Christ brings liberation, however, does not mean that only those who hear and affirm that call have clarity of vision. The truth can be known only by those to whom it is given, but the gift is given to whomever God chooses, not only to those we approve. Grace is not confined to those who identify with the institutional church or with the historical or resurrected Jesus. The grace of the New Age is indeed centered in the death and resurrection of Jesus, but though it is set forth in that event, it is not confined to labels designated by humans. The task of disciples is not to protect a narrowly confined grace, but is to bear testimony to that grace which, though not universal, is not absent from any place where God chooses to pour it forth. The faith of the victims of the furnaces of Europe cannot be accounted for apart from the grace that bound them to the God in whom that grace was rooted, despite his silence.

If those who are to bear testimony to the Light succumb to the Darkness, then the Light which has come to them will be smothered, as when a lamp is placed under a basket. If even the Light of the torch-bearers is darkened, then great indeed will be the Darkness!

The subject of this passage, then, is not the salvation of the disciples, but the hope of the world. Through the disciples the Light is to penetrate the world. All manifestations of the Light have their origin and significance in the one who is the source of the Light. God's deliverance of the world is ensured because of God's dependability. Disciples are not to let this lead them into irresponsibility and laziness, however, for while acknowledging God's primary role, they must also live and act as though the future of the entire creation rested on the assembly's shoulders. Even though at the end the assembly will have to acknowledge that they are unprofitable servants, they must not view their role as responsible and faithful servants any less urgently, because the victory of the Darkness over the assembly enhances the power of the Darkness throughout the creation.

Disciples, therefore, must not turn their eyes toward the world or toward the Prince of this world, for turning the eyes corrupts the eyes. Just as the heart will be corrupted by the location of its treasure, so the eye will be corrupted by that toward which it casts a longing or assenting gaze. The antithesis on adultery has already warned of this.

Hans Dieter Betz, in an excellent article on this passage in light of ancient Greek thought, has given an exhaustive survey of the dominant theories on the physiology of seeing in the classical world and has observed that the passage leaves the reader or hearer with the unsettling question of how the inner light, once darkened, can be made bright again.

For all his help and accuracy in treating this passage, however, Betz has made what seems to me to be two mistakes, the correction of which is important for a fuller understanding.[2] One is the nature of the question posed by the saying. In light of the earlier sayings on salt and light, the question posed is not how the light can be restored, but whether it can be restored. In the salt saying, of course, the question is literally, How can unsalty salt be made salty again? but the warning that it is no longer good for anything but for casting out indicates that the answer to the question, How? is, In no way. If the question of the light is, How can it be made bright again? the answer is, It cannot be.

Betz' second mistake is in assuming that the light within is native to the body. That the concept of the inner light was common in Greek thought does not mean that the Gospels assumed the same "naturalness" about it. The light within of which Jesus speaks is not a light given at birth, but is the Light that comes in the ministry of Jesus. The Light has its own power to penetrate and clear the clouded eye and to lighten the body. As long as the eye of the assembly, or of the disciple, is fixed on the Light, the Light shines in the Darkness of the body. When the assembly turns its gaze toward the creation rather than toward the Creator, the eye is again clouded, and the Light that has entered flickers and dies because it is no longer sustained by the Light from without.

The saying, then, is a warning echoing the same theme as that on the storing up of treasures, but it extends that previous warning by saying that when the assembly centers its attention on the values and perspectives by which the fallen world is guided and motivated, it falls victim to those values and perspectives and is no longer able to bear the testimony it is called to bear. The mind is clouded (Rom. 1:20-21). The salt loses it saltiness. Freedom gives way to bondage. Something happens not merely to "the Christian Life" or to something called one's "spirituality," but to the entire world: It is left, potentially, to flounder in the Darkness, under the power of Death.

GOD VERSUS MAMMON

The opening of the instructions generally known as the Ten Commandments instructs Israel not to place other gods alongside the God who brought them out of Egypt. Although this matter-of-fact description of Israel's life was violated, it remained God's basic expectation for them. When Jesus was asked which of the commandments is the greatest, he responded by quoting the version of the expectation found in the Shema (Deut. 6:4-5): "You will be unqualifiedly devoted to God with all your heart, and with all your vitality, and with all your mind" (Matt. 22:37).

---

2. I am speaking of the meaning of the passage in its present context, not in any previous context. These meanings may or may not be the same.

The third petition of the Lord's Prayer is closely related to this commandment: "Your will be done." Not only *your* will in contrast to *my* will, as discussed earlier, but *your* will in contrast to Caesar's will or Satan's will or the will of anyone or anything other than God. In Matthew 6:24, it is God's will in contrast to Mammon's will.

This is one of only two passages in the New Testament that mention Mammon.[3] In the present passage, Mammon, as several writers (such as Karl Barth and Jacques Ellul) have pointed out, is portrayed as a Power.[4] It is a Power of the Darkness, taking its place alongside Beelzebub and Belial, the Principalities, and the Thrones and Dominions. Mammon is the name by which we identify those drives and impulses toward economic power. Of course, as assertive drives and impulses these elements of human nature can be quite adequately described in psychological, sociological, and perhaps even in biological and chemical terms. At the same time, however, and without our denying the analyses of the natural and social sciences, they are the manifestation, in our temporal, spatial life, of the seduction of the transcendent Powers of the Darkness. By the name *Mammon* we acknowledge that these drives and impulses are not mere human aberrations that can be corrected by human exhortation, developmental education techniques, threats of imprisonment, or shame alone. They are not elements we seek out and attempt to make a part of our character. They are drives and impulses to which we are subject, and we either assent to them or struggle against them.

Mammon, a servant of Death, gains entry at the point of our need for food, clothing, shelter, and certain aesthetic experiences; he twists those needs into omnivorous, insatiable cravings. The common description "luxuries become necessities" is true in a sense not often recognized. Luxuries do not simply become false needs that can be cast aside at whim. Mammon so reorganizes our hunger and thirst and so redirects our will that, in our deformity of spirit, we actually *need* the otherwise irrelevant, just as surely as an alcoholic needs alcohol because of a changed physiology. We are no longer satisfied with food that quenches the momentary hunger or that nourishes the body. Clothes that protect us no longer suffice. An

---

3. The other is Luke 16:9-13.

4. It is possible, of course, to speak simply of Matthew's personification of money or wealth—the usual translations of Mammon—but our tendency to do so grows partially out of our modern denial of the transcendent Powers and partially out of the absence, in other places, of the term as a designation for the Powers. Although John Calvin did not share the modern disdain of transcendent realities, he too interprets Mammon as riches. At the same time, he goes on to treat it as a metaphor for a wide range of attractions.

It might be argued that the parallels between the treasure and Mammon passages indicate that Mammon is to be considered mere earthly attractions, but this would be to overlook the larger context of the role of the Darkness (which is a topic in the passage immediately before the Mammon saying) as that which beguiles us and entices us to lay up treasures on earth.

income that provides the basic necessities no longer satisfies. We need extraneous food. We need fashionable clothing. We need a plethora of things that only an increased income can buy. We do not need these things in order to survive, but we need them to maintain and enhance the way of living that becomes an obsession.

The entire society becomes Mammon's realm and participates in his reign. New products that have no nutritional value or that are actually detrimental to health are devised. Clothing styles change rapidly among the poor as well as among the wealthy. Gimmicks for the household are introduced in blinding succession. Electronic entertainment equipment that is the apex of achievement becomes obsolete within a season. Advertising lures and persuades us of the value of items for either their nutritional advantages, their contribution to our comfort, their ability to provide sex appeal, their ability to convey power or the image of power, or their use in enhancing our social status or social acceptability. Science and medicine provide research for products that are nutritionally irrelevant at best, that promise to enhance our vigor and sexuality, or that claim they will enable us to live indefinitely. Churches place their stamp of approval on distorted food needs by elaborate social meals and by serving junkfood to youth at their meetings. Denominations and congregations prostitute the gospel by adopting the youth culture, just as they adopt the adult culture, as a tool of evangelism. Cultural forms are considered neutral and are not recognized as having theological implications in and of themselves, or if those theological implications are recognized, they are twisted into a supposedly hidden gospel. Church-sponsored colleges teach conspicuous consumption through their home economics and fashion merchandising departments. Television preachers must have every hair in place and must wear well-pressed, color-coordinated, well-cut clothes, and their followers share vicariously in their putative holiness by copying them. The spirit of the missionaries who forced African women to cover their breasts and African men to give up polygamy is inverted by evangelists who thrive on groupies and whose platform demeanor is more sexual than gospel. Image replaces substance. The cross is shrouded by the cloak of Dionysus and the gown of Aphrodite. The listeners and the watchers are oblivious to the fact that they no longer worship God, but Mammon in disguise. And they rejoice in the Darkness, thinking it to be the Light.

MAMMON AND CONQUEST

Those who are unable to afford the food and clothing of the middle and upper class are not thereby any less the prisoners of Mammon. They are lured by the same goods and enticed by the same images as are the rich. Mammon calls out to the poor in spirit with the same words Satan used in the desert: "Bow down and worship me and I will give you the world." What Marx correctly identified as the class struggle is not mere human perversity but is also a manifestation of Mammon's stealth, as Mammon—in league with the other Powers—seeks to destroy the work of God.

One of the major achievements of industry has been to produce cheap, imitation goods that can be afforded by even the poorer classes, provided the poor are willing to forgo certain things more crucial to their health. It is possible to imitate those with wealth, even if one is on the edge of poverty.

Capitalism has managed to avoid revolution in many instances by enabling the poor to adopt the symbols of success, even though those symbols are made from cheap material. Those too poor to acquire even the cheap symbols either fade away in despair, turn to petty crime, drown themselves in cheap wine, liquor, or drugs, or commit suicide. Underneath the surface, however, the resentment smolders. Recognizing the dangers, the authorities quietly, slowly transform the police into quasimilitary forces preparing for war. Thereby, the authorities reveal themselves to be simply another of Mammon's divisions, for the police become less the protectors of justice for all people and more the defenders of those with wealth and status over against those who are feared as the plunderers.

Under the lordship of Mammon, needs explode into an all-engulfing chain reaction. The original need for food, clothing, shelter, and aesthetics burgeons into a drive for conquest. Thus Mammon incites gluttony, hoarding, oppression, robbery, murder, legalism, and revolution. That which has been achieved must be protected. That toward which we aspire determines the means and provides the evaluation of the means by which we strive to reach the goal. And the goal is never reached, because the chain reaction is open-ended. We never have enough. Mammon is never satisfied.

CHAPTER 35

ANXIETY, SMALL FAITH, AND THE QUEST
FOR GOD'S REIGN

In the Sermon on the Mount, anxiety (Greek: *merimna*) is not a psychological term, but a theological one. Central to the meaning of the word is the orientation of the will and desire. *Merimna* is the centering of attention and concern on someone or something in doubt of its security or its reliability. Psychological anxiety may usually be present, but the root of the anxiety is the anxious one having turned away from or distrusted God. In 1 Corinthians 12:25 Paul contrasts the *merimna* that the Corinthians should have for one another with the discord that has erupted in the congregation. Though not identical with *agape* (complete, unqualified determination to seek the well-being of another), *merimna* does approach *agape* in meaning; for, theologically, *merimna* is commitment to someone or something.

The more common use of *anxiety* as a term in contemporary Western society is the psychological one, referring to feelings, or emotions. The degree of and the particular manifestation of psychological anxiety differs from one person to another. With one it may manifest itself as a rather cold, calculating determination. With another it may be a highly emotional obsession that results in various psychoses. Psychological anxiety is closely related to stress and can result in ulcers, baldness, blindness, heart disease, and even death.

From one standpoint, psychological anxiety is a consequence of theological anxiety over food, clothing, and mortality. From another standpoint it is the root of that theological anxiety. Ultimately, however, each feeds on the other as we are caught up in a circle of fear producing idolatry, idolatry reinforcing fear, and extended fear leading to an even more zealous idolatry.

The theological anxiety against which Jesus admonishes his disciples is that which is centered in preserving their own lives. This anxiety is rooted in and is a mark of the Old Age. Whether viewed as the root or as a consequence of psychological anxiety, the anxiety against which Jesus warns is a turning from the One True God and a turning to Mammon. In the midst of the New Age, it manifests the Old Age's effort, through Mammon, once again to enslave and to crush both those who have remained in the Darkness and those who have tasted the freedom of grace. This anxiety of the Old Age is the condition into which God has plunged us, corporately, abandoning us to our primal idolatry; it is also the source of individual anxiety for our survival as we seek to secure our future in the face of uncertainty.

Thus, anxiety over survival is both a symptom of the fallen condition of the creation and the means by which, as individuals and as an assembly of God's people, we compound and perpetuate our own involvement in that corporate condition. From this standpoint, anxiety for survival is intimately associated with Death. It is a manifestation of doubt—doubt evoked by the Power of Death, stimulated by temptation, and strengthened by pride. As a separation from God it is a concrete expression of Death rampant in the World.

FOOD AND THE ANXIETY OF EDEN

Even in the Garden, Adam and Eve needed food, as did the birds, the beasts, and the fish. These needs were a mark not of sin, but of creaturely limitation, of vulnerability, and of dependence on the Creator. There, God cared for Adam and Eve just as he now does for the birds, beasts, fish, and flowers. In the Garden, God provided the tree of life so that Adam, Eve, and the other creatures might live interminably, in good health and vitality. Upon their expulsion from the Garden, Adam and Eve and their descendants after them would retain the same needs they had in Eden, but God would now provide their food only as the outcome of Adam's and Eve's ingenuity, skill, and determination as they wrestled the soil. Now Adam and Eve would be confronted with Mammon.

In the Garden, Adam and Eve had lived by God's instructions as he taught them good and evil. The Powers, however, by means of the serpent, diverted Adam and Eve's attention.[1] They redirected their attention away from God's instruction and toward the possibility of self-instruction. Outside the Garden, because their food came through struggle rather than as mere gift, they were redirected in their attention. In the Garden it had been obvious that food was available. They had only to open their hands.

---

1. To speak of the serpent's role in this manner is not to say that the narrators of the Pentateuch intended the serpent as Satan or as a manifestation of the Powers. Likely, they did not so intend. The serpent's role in the narrative, however, is identical to Satan's role once Satan appears in the tradition, and the apostle Paul affirms a later insight when he identifies Satan with the serpent. My own concern is theological, not historical in the sense of mere objective facts.

Outside the Garden, God was still faithful, but since they now acquired food through struggle, it was only natural that they would become anxious about that food. Doubt had been sown by Satan. Now they continued in doubt. Rather than looking to God as the one who enabled them to gain their food through struggle, they looked simply to the food and to their own ability to win the struggle.

That this struggle for food resulted in anxiety is simply one way the Fall resulted in the impossibility of human beings turning to God by their own determination. All natural anxiety is the anxiety of the Darkness, the anxiety unto Death.

CLOTHING OUTSIDE EDEN

Although Adam and Eve needed food even while in the Garden, they did not need clothing there. Clothing masks our vulnerability, and before Adam and Eve aspired to be gods, or like God, they had no reason to consider their vulnerability. They were secure in each other's presence. Once they succumbed to the desire to be like God, knowing good and evil, they did, as the serpent promised, so become. But they also gained a second bit of knowledge they had not anticipated: They discovered their nakedness. They discovered their vulnerability. And they were ashamed.

God did not induce the shame. He did not impose it on them. Nor did he decree shame for their descendants. Shame over our nakedness is neither required by, respected by, nor approved by God. There are specific occasions in the Bible, of course, when God threatens to make people ashamed of something or other, and there are occasions when God threatens to do something that will result in the objects of the threat becoming ashamed. The shame that arises spontaneously, however, is a human-originated response to our vulnerability in the face of our pretensions of control and power.

When Adam explained that he was ashamed because he was naked and that this had caused him to hide from God, the only response that God made with regard to the nakedness was to ask Adam who had told him he was naked. God did not respond to the remark on Adam's shame, but to the offense that resulted in the shame—the offense of seeking to become gods or like gods. Adam's and Eve's shame was rooted in their pretense and aspirations.

The first clothes, then, were not for the purpose of hiding nakedness in and of itself, but were for the purpose of hiding Adam's and Eve's vulnerability from each other and from God. At first, Adam and Eve made their own clothes, from vines and leaves. Then God took pity on them and made for them more durable ones. He did so not to enable them to live with their shame, but to enable them to suppress their shame and to endure their vulnerability.

CLOTHING AS SYMBOL

Soon, clothing, which had been intended as a shield for human vulnerability, became a symbol of status, of prestige and lowliness, of power and impotence, of authority and subjection. Clothing, like food, was transformed from an object of legitimate anxiety, in the context of trust in God, into an instrument of the Darkness, a mark of our subservience to Mammon. Whereas Satan, through lies, sows doubt, Mammon, through anxiety, sows insensitivity, conquest, and cruelty. Clothing has become a means of asserting our own identity and of imposing identity on others—

- the use of uniforms in the military, in prisons, and in various educational institutions as a means of establishing order through the suppression of individualism;
- dress codes in high schools and universities, as well as the attack on these codes by those who resist the suppression implicit in them;
- the unofficial dress codes of age groups, usually most obvious among teenagers, but actually found with equal force among adults;
- the vestments of clerics and other church functionaries in medieval-oriented denominations and the unspoken dress code for ordained ministers in modern-day-oriented denominations;
- the expectations of how professional people will dress in medicine, law, and education;
- the conspicuous consumption of the wealthy by means of high fashion and the rush of the middle class to imitate in cheaper materials the fashion fads of the wealthy;
- the revolt against all the above habits by those who resist the depersonalization inherent in those habits;
- the use of styles as an instrument of rebellion by the young (a rebellion that contains within the ranks an intolerance of deviance even greater than displeasure or ridicule from adults);
- the advice lawyers give their clients on how to dress in the courtroom in order to have a desired effect on the jury;
- the ancient and modern practice of stripping naked prisoners of war and collaborators with the enemy, thereby emphasizing the prisoners' and collaborators' subjugation and powerlessness;
- the exposure of customarily covered parts of the human body in swim suits, strip shows, and certain clothing fashions as a subtle blend of assertion of independence, plea for attention, and denial of vulnerability (denying the vulnerability implied in nakedness,

challenging others by the power implied in denying vulnerability, flaunting restrictions as a means of distorting freedom, seeking personal identity and attention by casting off the anonymity imposed by clothing conformity).

In subservience to Mammon, we turn the gift of clothing as a shield for our vulnerability into a major weapon in the arsenal of pride. Clothing becomes a means of being both in and of the world. Even those who wear the name "Christian," beguiled by Mammon, view the Death-oriented uses of clothing as commonsensical, reputable, decent, and even "God's will."

It was not asceticism or some other distorted view of the body that led the early assembly to disparage ornamentation in their dress. It was the assembly's clarity of perception over the proper role of clothing. This is seen in examples as diverse as Jesus' charge to the disciples and 1 Peter's admonition on proper dress for women of the assembly. Jesus' instructions to the disciples as they went out to preach (Matt. 10:9-10) included the instruction not to take along extra clothing, because the people to whom the disciples were to preach would indicate their acceptance of the message and of the one from whom it came by their hospitality to the disciples (Matt. 10:40, 42). 1 Peter 3:1-6 portrays how the use of clothing to attract attention to oneself hinders testimony to the gospel of Jesus Christ; the same verses admonish female disciples married to husbands outside the assembly to bear testimony to the gospel by their character. The gospel, obviously, is not a matter of clothing, but a matter of character, and clothing can get in the way of character.

CLOTHING, NAKEDNESS, AND THE HOLOCAUST

Perhaps the most vivid example of the imposition with which we are familiar is that of the Jews in the death camps of Europe. The pretense that they were going to take a bath was not the only reason that the victims were forced to disrobe. Even if this were the conscious intent of the killers, the element of domination versus vulnerability hovered like a great vulture over the exercise. For those who had been starved, beaten, mutilated, and used for fiendish experiments in the name of medicine, being stripped naked before their enemies was the final humiliation—a humiliation in which the vulnerability implied in all the previous acts was emphasized by the primal symbol of vulnerability: nakedness.

In the midst of their humiliation, their agony, and their bewilderment over God's silence, however, the victims did not cringe. They did not give their murderers the pleasure of seeing them beg or cave in to their vulnerability. Cries of surprise, yes. Cries of rage, yes. The murderers could strip their bodies and lay bare their vulnerability, but because of the mysterious grace of the mysterious, Silent God, they could not stamp out their courage or rob them of their humanity. Those victims knew that the body is more than clothing, and they refused to act in any way that would testify otherwise, even in the ovens of Death and in the midst of Silence.

BIRDS, LILIES, AND HUMAN BEINGS

Human beings live not merely by bread, but by every act of God. To settle for food alone is to be lost in the Darkness. To be anxious over food is to give in to Mammon. Similarly, the body, in its vulnerability, requires more than mere clothing. It requires the providential care of God. Food is as necessary for us as it was for Adam and Eve, but so is the Word of God. Clothing is a gift of God, but in contrast to food, which builds and sustains the body, clothing simply masks the vulnerability of the body. What does a person gain by owning the world and all its kingdoms if life itself is forfeit? What is the advantage of owning huge, overflowing barns, if one dies in the dark of the night? Ecclesiastes, that sometimes underrated and unjustifiably maligned book of wisdom, saw the absurdity of concentrating on those things that provide us our economic security: "I hated all my toil which I had pursued under the sun, (for I saw) that I must leave it to the one who will come after me; and who knows whether that one will be a sage or a fool? Yet that one will be master of all for which I toiled and used my wisdom . . . . This too is absurd" (Eccles. 2:18-19).

Jesus' exhortation to give to those who beg from us is rooted not only in mercy, but also in this view of food and clothing. When people are in need, to hold back our own goods is to place our own well-being over against theirs and is also to give preservation of our own food and clothing the place that the Reign of God is supposed to have.

Were we not blinded by Mammon, we could learn from the birds and from the flowers of the field. Ever since the beginning of the world, God's power, his character, and his sovereignty have been evident for all to see—evident, that is, to any who are not blinded by the Darkness (Rom. 1:20-21). The Powers of the Darkness, however, have lured us into the realm of the blind, leaving us unable to see the work of God, deluded over the presence of the Powers, oblivious to our blindness, and disbelieving about the presence of the Darkness.

Jesus speaks the word of liberation. To the blind he says, "Look at the birds . . . Look at the lilies." Jesus brings the Light by which we can see. He opens our eyes. If we do not turn aside from the Light or close our eyes again, after a momentary blink, we can see the provision God has made for those creatures that cannot provide for themselves. The birds, though required to gather their food, do not sow and reap, but, like Adam and Eve, gather what God has provided. The lilies do not toil for their food or for their clothing. They have been sustained solely by the work of God.

The eye opened by grace, however, sees not simply a world in which God provides for the lower animals, but a world in which the Powers seek to disrupt that scheme. Nature is in disarray. Some birds multiply into destructive hordes; others have become extinct. The food chain has been disrupted, perhaps beyond recall, and every human effort to heal it is simply another disruption. God permits us, in our misdirected anxiety, to destroy those very things for which we are anxious. The worship of Mammon is the worship of Death, and in that worship we are destroyed. This disarray, however, does not negate Jesus' observations about God's ordinary care and sustenance of the world. The disarray reveals, rather, the alarming potential for destruction that God has permitted human beings to amass and to exercise. Just as God allows his creatures to hoard the daily bread he provides, so he allows them to destroy the cycles by which he has provided for the continuation of life. That birds do not have sufficient food to gather and that fields of lilies are scraped away in order to put down shopping malls or superhighways is not because God desires it so. It is because God permits Mammon, one of the conquered Powers, to exercise his destructive powers, even in the midst of the New Age and despite the subjugation of the Powers in the death and resurrection of Jesus.

The real question is multifaceted: not whether God exists, but why he is as though he did not; not whether God is powerful, but why he does not use his power to save the beauty of his creation; not whether God is love, but how love can watch the agony and suffering of the creation; not whether the agony and suffering of the world are the consequences of God's imposition of futility, but why God allows so much anguish; not whether God can speak, but why he is silent; not whether he abandons, but how long before he will again turn; not whether to abandon God, but how long before he will no longer have abandoned us; not whether God has a purpose in all that he does and all that he allows, but whether his purposes have room for him to permit his creatures to destroy the entire world. The question that can be raised with equal fervor by all the creatures of the globe is that of the Lord of the Creation as he hung on the cross: "My God, my God, why have you abandoned me?" But only those who are not Godless can raise the question. The unGodly can only mourn.

THE TWO QUESTS—THAT OF THE
GENTILES AND THAT OF THE FAITHFUL ASSEMBLY

Centering life's goals on food and clothing is idolatry in that it replaces God with Mammon. It ignores the fact that even the food for which we must struggle with the soil comes, ultimately, from God. It is apostasy, on the other hand, in that it turns aside to the way of the Gentiles. God knows that the Gentiles need food and clothing, just as he knows the needs of the birds and the lilies, for he made the Gentiles, just as he made all other creatures. Even when they do not acknowledge it, the Gentiles receive their food and clothing from him who is the source of all food and all clothing. Their quest for food and clothing as the central goal of life is a blind quest, one that understands neither the origin nor the fulfillment of their need. In their quest, the Gentiles testify to their own might—to the power of their own hands and the ingenuity of their own minds—unaware of either the Power that enslaves them or the One who feeds and clothes them despite their flight from him.

It is not to be so for the faithful assembly! The assembly is called to testify to the God who is the ultimate source of all life's benefits. The assembly is to bear this testimony by the focus of its attention. Whereas the Gentiles are anxious for food and clothing, the assembly is to seek the Reign of the God who gives food and clothing.

God knows the assembly's need. That is, God is on intimate terms with its need, not merely conscious of it or aware of it. Consequently, the assembly, if it embraces the invitation of its Lord, becomes free to put its need for food and clothing, and its struggle with the soil to attain these, into proper perspective. Since they are neither birds nor lilies, the disciples must exert themselves to wrest food from the ground and to spin thread from the wool of the sheep. As liberated human beings, however, they are enabled to engage in that struggle in the assurance that those things for which they labor are achieved because of the promise of God.

By its concentration on the Reign of God, the assembly bears testimony to a different way of life. By making God's Reign and God's faithfulness the central, dominating goal of its life, the assembly glorifies God. It becomes the bearer of the Light in the midst of the Darkness. By its confidence in God, manifested in its search for God's Reign, the assembly testifies that God is dependable, that God is faithful. This is not primarily a testimony to how people should live or to a cold, objective requirement that people seek God's Reign; it is, rather, a testimony to God's devotedness to his creatures and to his invitation of liberation to all.

The anxiety from which Jesus offers liberation is rooted in the perception that life is constantly threatened by Death. This is an accurate perception. It is also, however, the perception through which testing occurs. Those who embrace the grace of God respond to the test in meekness. Those who are blind to grace nurture ambition and self-determination. This is seen as clearly in institutional life as in individual life. The anxiety of the Gentiles is the condition of all nations, all governments, and all institutions, including the church. We can see the dynamics of such anxiety in the proceedings of those movements that spring up to alleviate various problems that plague society. The movement arises in compassionate response to the agonies of, say, the poor. It hurls itself into the fray in fear of God and love of neighbor. Then it becomes organized. It becomes an institution. Then Mammon appears. The organization needs money and members just as surely as an individual needs food and clothing. Anxiety for the poor gives way to anxiety for the institution's own survival. Awareness of the human dimension of its birth leads to the assumption that its survival depends on human ingenuity. It has become an organism and knows the fear of death. As a junior partner of Satan, Mammon promises survival and a modest degree of power if the organism will make him central to its anxiety. Those whose food and clothing were the purposes for which the movement began now become food and clothing to be consumed by the institution. Ends have become means as the institution becomes a devouring beast.

The history of all hitherto existing societies is the history of cannibalism.

When it becomes an institution, the assembly itself quickly begins to build the fire under the pots in which it will boil its victims as it prepares to consume them. The assembly can never hope to escape by programming or strategizing. Even the most astute process planning or management by objectives does nothing more than rearrange the firewood. The only deliverance from cannibalism is the transforming grace of God, as it transforms our appetite and creates a divine nausea over the menu to which the Darkness has accustomed us.

The assembly is given freedom to seek God's Reign and to escape the bonds of Mammon. The invitation carries with it the ability. The word translated "first" (*proton*) can mean either "the beginning of a series" or "central," "dominant," "primary." There can be no doubt that the latter is the meaning here. Jesus admonishes and invites the disciples to make the quest for God's Reign the dominant motivation of their lives. It is not a quest that can somehow be put aside after having succeeded; it is a continual quest. It would make no more sense to assume that the Reign of God can in one way or another be reached and then transcended than it would to assume that eating is something accomplished and then never done again. The Reign of God is to be the context for all other quests, determining the nature of those other quests.

THE PROMISE OF "ALL THESE THINGS"

The righteousness, or faithfulness, of God—by which his Reign is characterized—is manifested in his granting us those things essential for survival. Here, however, enthusiasm must not cause us to overlook the subtlety of this promise. Jesus does not promise that God will never let anyone starve. He does not promise that God will never let anyone go naked. The millions who have died in the famines and droughts of Africa and Asia, those who have suffered and died at the hands of tyrants and criminals, and the thousands who are, through no fault of their own, malnourished in both the East and the West in no way contradict this promise. They are a problem for those who believe in God, because they raise the question of God's silence in the face of horror, but the promise itself is confined to the admonition to seek God's Reign. The promise is a promise to those who are faithful disciples of Jesus. It is not a promise of luxury or even of convenience. Moreover, the promise is not correctly heard outside its tension with the beatitude on those who are persecuted on behalf of that Reign and righteousness over which they are anxious. The promise that all these things will be given to the disciples stands in ineluctable tension with the call to martyrdom. The promise of life is the context of the call to death on behalf of Jesus. Up to a point, but only up to a point, we can say that the promise is that, unless God wills our martyrdom, he will provide us the bare subsistence necessary to survive. This logical balancing of the promise and the call, however, does not finally solve the contradiction or resolve the tension; for, in the final analysis, to qualify the promise is to unravel the fabric of faith, and to qualify the call to martyrdom is to chip away at the cross.

The promise and the call, in their tension then, stand as absolute assertions, inescapable in their mystery, affirmed in the face of God's Silence, in Albert Camus' words, "affirming everything," lest, in our demand for logic, "we deny everything."

CHAPTER 36

ON JUDGING

To judge others when we are unable to see even our own condition clearly is to demonstrate our participation in the Darkness. Condemned to declare good and evil without assurance that our declaration and God's declaration are the same, we confuse good and evil. We tend to confuse the holy with the unholy. The beam in our eye makes such confusion inevitable.

Disciples are not called to judge. Should they find themselves in a position of judging, willingly or unwillingly, they should beware that they will themselves be judged on the basis of the same criteria that has guided their judgments of others.

There have been efforts to translate the verb rendered "judge" *(krinete)* in some other way, usually to emphasize the harshness of the judgment said to be intended. This effort has been made sometimes because of the passage's opposition to other New Testament passages where judging not only takes place, but is called forth, and sometimes because the passage is heard as a prohibition of decision making.[1] The efforts to squeeze a new meaning from the Greek text, however, results from ignoring the nature of the sentence. Jesus' words here are not an absolute command, but are a warning. If they are in any sense a command, they are so only in the sense of conditional command. Jesus simply warns that if the assembly is ever in a situation of judging, it must beware that its criteria will be turned on it.

JUDGING AND AUTHORITY

Judging is a function of authority. Even a beggar who, in his mind, judges a monarch thereby assumes that he is an authority on the matter at hand. From this standpoint, the deeper implication of the instruction in Matthew

---

1. An example of the former effort is the translation "Do not be excessive in your condemnation," as though condemnation is permitted in small degrees.

7:1 is the very nature of authority and how authority is to be exercised in the assembly.

A good example of authority wielded by rulers in the Old Age is Pilate's authority over Jesus. Pilate's ultimate authority is the authority to impose death. He has no authority to give life, but only the authority to impose or withhold death over his subjects. Even that authority is Pilate's only because God has granted it to him as a functionary of the Old Age.

Strikingly, the word used in the New Testament for authority *(exousia)* is a word that means "ability." In today's social sciences we usually distinguish between authority and power, but such distinctions are meaningless in biblical language. There, it is assumed that, if a person or a group has the power or ability to do something, it is because God has allowed it. Thus, God has authorized it, or given authority for it. This is not to ignore the fact that people usurp power not given by God. We would say that such persons have taken power without authority, just as we might point to people with certain titles that attribute authority to them, but who are people who have no power. Note, for example, the person who, though near the top of the bureaucratic scale, is not permitted to make decisions in keeping with his or her rank. Such a person, we say, has authority, but no power. On the other hand, someone near the bottom of the ladder, with no authority of which to speak, can wield enormous power.

In the New Testament, the question is never the theoretical one of whether power and authority coincide, for power manifests authority—that is, the expression of even usurped power indicates that God has authorized, or allowed, that usurpation. Pilate's authority was expressed in his power of death over Jesus.

Another example of the exercise of authority in the Old Age is found in the words of the centurion at Capernaum: "I am a man under authority, with soldiers under me; and I say to one, 'Go,' and he goes, and to another, 'Come,' and he comes, and to my slave, 'Do this,' and he does it" (Matt. 8:9 RSV). Authority in the Old Age is authority to bend others to your own will. The centurion, however, on approaching Jesus, knows that here is one who makes his Old Age authority meaningless. His first words to Jesus are "Lord, I am not worthy to have you come under my roof" (Matt. 8:8 RSV).

It is precisely this authority of the Old Age that Jesus rejects when he refuses to settle a property dispute (Luke 12:14). He does not say that property is evil or unimportant. He simply uses a parable to warn of what happens when, beguiled by Mammon, we make property the center of our anxiety. Jesus refuses to divide property because that is not his task. Personal property, whether used for good or ill, is a component of the Old Age, and Jesus' authority is not to be defined in terms of that authority. Even as the Son of Man, who will be judge on God's behalf on the day of judgment, Jesus will exercise a judgment that can be understood only in the appearance of the New Age. This is clear from the passages where, as the Son of Man, Jesus acts as the judge who heals and forgives rather than condemning and punishing (e.g., Matt. 9:1-18).

The authority of the Old Age and the judgment which that authority exercises carry with them—directly or indirectly, and to one degree or another—the same authority wielded by Pilate: the authority to impose or to withhold death. The authority of the Old Age affects our ability to find a job, to earn a living, to have control over our own lives, and to live as we wish in relation to others.

One of the characteristics of the authority of the Old Age is the power to judge. Parliaments and congresses; generals and presidents; monarchs and prime ministers; corporation officers and boards of directors; college trustees, presidents, and deans; faculty and student committees; parents and judges; bishops, regular clergy, and church bureaucrats, whether clergy or laity—all exercise the authority of the Old Age. Judicial decisions, military directives, labor settlements, college and university regulations, pastoral appointments, dormitory rules, parental directives—all are judgments by which the authority of the Old Age is exercised and manifested, no matter how necessary they be. They are the authority of "Go!" "Come!" and "Do this!"

AUTHORITY IN THE NEW AGE

Jesus does not eliminate authority among the disciples. On the contrary, he gives them the highest authority of all—the power of binding and loosing in heaven (Matt. 18:18). This is not the authority of the Old Age—the authority expressed by "Go!" and "Come!" and "Do this!"—but the authority of the New Age, authority characterized by humility and servanthood. The authority of binding and loosing is a *burden* of servanthood to be used for the glory of God and for the salvation of the world. Its primary use is to be for releasing. That whatever disciples bind on earth will be bound in heaven is a frightening warning with regard to judging. It is precisely because of the effect of our binding that we are warned that the criteria of our judgment will be turned on us. Whenever the assembly or a disciple exercises authority through "Go!" or "Come!" or "Do this!"—no matter how necessary it may be to speak that word and no matter who speaks it, bishop or freshly baptized layperson—it is no longer the free authority of the gospel, but is an authority forced or grasped in violation of and in contrast to the authority of service.

A good example of the authority of the New Age, the authority of freedom, is that which the author of Ephesians envisioned when he introduced the exhortation concerning relations between husbands and wives, masters and slaves, and parents and children with the all embracing admonition, "Be subject to one another out of reverence for Christ" (Eph. 5:21 RSV). Here, the roles prescribed by the Old Age are infused with the freedom of the New Age. Husbands are to be equally as subject to wives as wives are to husbands. Parents are to be as subject to their children as children are to parents. Masters are to be as subject to their slaves as their slaves are to them. Thus, the old wineskins of the society of the Darkness were to be filled with the new wine of the gospel. The church, however, was no more willing to stand for the bursting of wineskins than was the society in which it found itself; and when the end of slavery has come in various societies, and when the freedom of women has become a cause, the driving forces have been at least as much self-assertion and pride as expressions of genuine liberation. The revolutions of race, sex, and economic self-determination have not been true revolutions at all; they have been power struggles to steal the wineskins, not to fill them with new wine. And the church stands condemned for its complicity!

JUDGING, MERCY, AND HUMILITY

From one standpoint, the Sermon's passage on judging is a counterpart to the beatitude concerning mercy. If mercy is truly lived out, judging is automatically ruled out. Mercy as the steadfast, dependable love implied in the covenant relationship rules out, by definition, judging the brother or sister. In other words, the Reign of God sets us free from the Old Age with its alienation and its authority of Death. The Reign of God sets us free to live the merciful, reconciling life of the New Age. Whoever falls back into the authority patterns of the Old Age will be judged accordingly.

A passage in Matthew's Gospel, which seems on the surface to be in direct conflict with Matthew 7:1, is the discourse in chapter 18, a discourse sometimes erroneously said to concern church discipline, or the preservation of order in the congregation. The discourse begins with Jesus' words concerning becoming childlike, and this is immediately interpreted to mean "to exercise humility" (Matt. 18:4). Whoever practices humility is said to be greatest under God's Reign. This is not a prescription of how to become great under God's Reign, of course, for attempting to practice humility in order to be great would not be humility at all, but merely clever egotism. Jesus' words, on the contrary, are precisely in response to the question of who shall be greatest under God's Reign, and in effect they reject greatness as the world understands greatness. Just as the Lord humbles himself by taking on human form and submitting to humiliation and death, so also his followers are not to seek greatness, but are to humble themselves.

Chapter 18 then goes on to say that whoever welcomes "one such child"—that is, one of this kind of child, one who has become a child in the gospel—in Jesus' name welcomes Jesus himself (18:5). The discourse on disruptions in the congregation then comes in this context. Matthew has thereby described discipline in terms of humility. True discipline in the church is authority shaped by, supported by, and manifested as humility. Authority as rule and domination is a characteristic of the nations, the Gentiles. For Jesus' followers, authority is to be manifested as servanthood, just as Jesus' own authority is manifested in this manner (Matt. 20:25-28). In brief, the authority of the New Age is not a technique for service, but is expressed in service. One wonders what would happen in a denomination, a congregation, or a church-sponsored institution of higher education if those in authority were to give up all their socially derived trappings of authority and were to spend every minute of their day finding ways to serve.

AUTHORITY AND JUDGMENT

Authority in light of the Old Age automatically entails judgment. Authority in the Old Age can survive only by judging. Thus, in the Old Age—in a complete reversal of conditions—authority is the end and judging is the means. Those in authority exercise judgment in order to preserve their authority. Even the Christian who participates in organizations and institutions of the Old Age will discover again and again that the Old Age's exercise of authority through judging is unavoidable. No amount of wishing or of pretending that we are not judging will make it otherwise.

Matthew 18, on the other hand, is a discourse on authority as exercised under the Reign of God. That authority, characterized by humility, does not result in leading others to sin (18:7-9). Nor does it express itself in spite for the offender in the congregation, but in an effort to win the offender back into the full life of the assembly. It is not the Father's will that any of his children perish (18:14). The offended disciple, therefore, should first speak to the offender privately. The offense is not to be endured stoically, but it must be admitted that sin has invaded the fellowship. There is no need to wash dirty linen in public or even in the congregation, but when alienation has taken place, trying to grin and bear it is mere heroism. The freedom of the gospel is the freedom to approach the offender and say, "Come, let us reason together." Perhaps a private word will bring peace. If not, the offended party should take a witness along and try again. To ignore the offense risks allowing one's passivity to fester into pride and to enlarge into a martyr's complex. Failure to speak also allows the brother or sister to remain in sin and the assembly to remain fractured. A crowd is not necessary; the matter should be kept quiet. This is not the traditional legal requirement of two witnesses, for one other person may be enough. The entire assembly need not even know. Only when this use of witnesses has failed should the matter come to the attention of the entire assembly, and even then the purpose is to bring reconciliation. If the offender does not listen even to the assembly, then the offender is to be regarded as a Gentile or as a tax collector—as a candidate for conversion to the gospel (18:17).

Jesus does not call for the expulsion of the offender from the assembly, but for holding the offender in a new relationship. He does not say specifically what further action the assembly should take. He shows only how the offended party is to respond.

The assembly is to be guided by the presence of the resurrected Jesus, who is with the assembly whenever it gathers in his name (18:20). The assembly will decide how to deal with the matter, assured that God will allow it to make a decision that he himself will honor (18:19), for he has given the assembly the power of loosing and binding (18:18).

The last word on the subject, however, is not treating the offender as a Gentile and a tax collector, but forgiving the offender. It is not God's will that either the offended party or the assembly despise the offender. God himself does not despise, but seeks out—like a shepherd who, in order to find one stray, leaves ninety-nine sheep grazing, and who when he finds it rejoices over it more than over the ninety-nine that never went astray (18:13-14)! There are, then, to be no limits to the efforts of the assembly to "find the straying member" and no limit to the number of times the offended party is to forgive and accept reconciliation. This is the very purpose of the assembly's authority: reconciliation, release from the bondage of sin, not judgment.

The assembly is not to judge. It is not a matter of not being excessive in judgment, but of not judging at all unless we are prepared to accept judgment by the same criteria. Even the Son was not sent to condemn the world, but to be the means of its deliverance (John 3:17). The world was condemned already, before the Son came (3:18). The Son's appearance was for the purpose of lifting the condemnation for those who responded to him.

The disciples are set free from the need to judge. They are not to fall back into the Old Age and its version of authority, which makes judging necessary. Their authority as heralds of the New Age is an authority to serve, not to be served; thus they have no need to judge. God will judge. They must serve.

JUDGING AND FORGIVING

The words on judging in Matthew 7:1-5 parallel the plea for forgiveness and the warning about not forgiving that we find in the Lord's Prayer. The affirmation that, as we pray, we forgive others and the warning that if we do not forgive others our own prayer is corrupted and will not be answered are closely related to the warning that if we judge, our criteria for judging will be turned on us.

As already indicated, the authority of the New Age is the authority primarily to release others from the bonds of Death, and the authority to bind is to be regarded as a terrible authority—one to be exercised in fear and trembling.

None of this should lead us to assume that the assembly no longer has the responsibility to speak God's word of judgment on the Powers of the Darkness as they manifest themselves in public life. The assembly, as a prophetic community, does indeed have this responsibility. It has it, however, only when God gives it the word to speak. Speaking the word of God's judgment authentically can never be a matter of mere human insight, human wisdom, or human peeve. Only the reality of the gift verifies the authenticity of the pronouncement; even so, because God's word always has redemption as its ultimate goal, the assembly in speaking that word must speak it in anticipation of that redemption.

When the assembly truly speaks God's judgment, it does not itself judge, but proclaims a judgment not its own, one beyond its own authority to impose. The same is true of forgiveness. The assembly's authority to forgive is rooted in and expresses God's forgiveness. The assembly is an active agent, not a passive agent. It bears authority to forgive. That authority, however, does not bestow the innate power to forgive, but authorizes the assembly to pronounce, in God's name, forgiveness that is rooted in and comes from God.

The medieval church, of course, devised as a part of its ceremony the pronouncement of forgiveness, or absolution. In principle, this was perfectly consistent with and was an appropriate exercise of the authority granted to the assembly. The Lutheran and Anglican wings of Protestantism maintained the ordinance of penance, although they denied that penance is a sacrament, and Luther wrote vigorously of Christians as Christs for one another and of Christians' responsibility to remind one another of God's forgiveness. More radical and more pietistic groups, out of a basic misunderstanding of the pronouncement of forgiveness, abandoned the practice altogether. Ironically, however, numerous Protestant preachers, while rejecting the task of pronouncing God's forgiveness, eagerly and regularly pronounce God's condemnation of all sorts of personal and private practices and habits. They fail to acknowledge that just as only God can forgive, only God can condemn. They stand the authority of the assembly on its head, denying the authority to forgive, while asserting the authority to judge. All such preaching and pronouncement is the judgment of the Old Age—condemning and judging, with only the human decision to change asserted as hope. The word of judgment, however, when not rooted in grace, is a word leading only to despair and to Death. The word of freedom is not a warning of how the hearer must change his or her own life, but is a pronouncement of God's liberation of all God's creatures from the bondage of Death. Either judgment is pronounced with the aim of redemption or it is not of God, but is of the Powers of the Darkness.

CHAPTER 37

DOGS OF DARKNESS, SWINE OF SATAN

The assembly always stands in danger of being lured back into the Darkness. The New Testament staunchly assures the faithful that the difficulties they face will not be able to separate them from the love of God in Jesus Christ. It also warns, however, that it is quite possible for the faithful to turn aside from God's faithfulness. The assembly, therefore, is to pray that God will not put them to the test, but will deliver them from the snares of the Tester, the Evil One. In this parallel to the last plea of the Lord's Prayer, the disciples are warned of the danger of failing the test, of expressing their devotion to those creatures that are not God. The saying on holy things, pearls, dogs, and swine echoes elements scattered throughout the Sermon:

- meekness as trust in God,
- purity of heart as single-minded devotion to God,
- salt that loses its savor by being mixed with the customs and values of the Darkness,
- giving alms, praying, and fasting as properly performed with God in mind, not with other people in mind,
- turning the heart toward the world, rather than toward God,
- Mammon's challenge as an alternative to God,
- anxiety toward food and clothing.

In all these, the matter at stake is whether the assembly will keep its eyes, its heart, and its mind fixed on God as the sole giver and sustainer of life. Satan, the tester, attempts to shake the assembly from its steadfastness by sowing doubt: "Can God be trusted?" "Would God really ask you to do something so absurd?" "Bow down to me, worship me, admit that violence and Death are the real masters of this world, and the world will be your oyster. From that oyster will come pearls beyond value."

It is the same test manifested in the false prophets and prophetesses in the book of Revelation. In a time when the church was enjoying one of its relatively few occasions of relief from persecution (under Vespasian),[1] there were certain teachers and false prophets in the church who assured the members of the church that it was permissible to participate in religious ceremonies required by guilds for certain skills. Membership in the guilds was a prerequisite for permission to practice the skill or trade associated with the guild. The Revelation, however, regarded participation in such ceremonies as idolatry and deserving of death. It was the lure of the Darkness. The false teachers and prophets were the spawn of Satan, seeking to destroy the church from within. They were instruments of testing.

The Matthew saying under consideration is also concerned with false worship, or worship of false gods. Holy things are things that have been set apart and acknowledged as belonging to God. The verb that speaks of what is not to be done with pearls *(baleite)* is a word often used to mean "offer," in the sense of making an offering in worship.

Dogs and swine are associated with things that are alien to Israel. Dogs are scavengers. All dogs mentioned in the Old and New Testaments are violent, carnivorous, and if not wild, at least not truly domesticated. This association of dogs with violence and death lies behind the biblical designation of Gentiles as dogs. Gentiles are those rooted in the Darkness, in chaos, in violence. Swine, in the Bible, are the unclean animal *par excellence*. They, too, are associated with the forbidden, the evil, the Darkness.

To give dogs holy things and offer pearls to swine, then, is not simply, as some have suggested, a matter of confusion, though confusion it is. Nor is it a matter of inappropriateness, though inappropriate it is. Rather it is a matter of sin. The passage is a metaphorical expression warning of the consequences of succumbing to the enticements of Satan and Mammon. The gods of the Darkness are devouring gods, servants of Death. Consequently, when we are lured by them, we become not simply their servants, but, ultimately, the prisoners of Death. Sooner or later, our gods will turn on us and will either—like the werewolves of myth—make us like themselves, destroy us, or do both.

ANTI-SEMITISM:
THE CHURCH'S GIFT TO THE DOGS AND THE SWINE

The most devastating expression of the church's adoration of the Darkness, its captivity to the Powers, and its alliance with the world around

---

1. I follow a few nineteenth-century scholars and Vernard Eller here in assigning the book of the Revelation to the era of Vespasian, Domitian's father, rather than to the era of Domitian. The letters in Revelation 2–3 indicate that the primary threats to the church are not persecution, but the struggle with the synagogue and teachers who encourage church members to identify with certain elements of Roman culture.

it has been the church's acceptance and perpetuation of the alienation that arose in the synagogue between those who professed and those who denied Jesus' identity as the Messiah. The roots of the alienation are not clear. Perhaps it arose out of a combination of factors—the challenge of authority by followers of Jesus, the verbal attacks on Jewish leaders for complicity in Jesus' death, and other such factors. Whatever the causes, the church, once it had been completely separated from the synagogue, very quickly developed a polemic against the Jews. The hellish plague of anti-Semitism spread across Europe with deadly effects. Church fathers, scholastics, popes, and reformers who should have led the church in efforts toward reconciliation within the household of Israel, turned their minds instead to theological justification for economic oppression, social ostracism, political disenfranchisement, and eventually wholesale slaughter and attempted genocide. In Jews' ears rang words that evoked fear and horror: inquisition, pogrom, soil and blood. Certainly, among the greatest shames for the church was that by its sometime assent, sometime instigation of oppression and execution of Jews it was responsible for the central symbol of God's love for the world, the cross, becoming a sign to be feared among our brothers and sisters of Israel, the Jews. Whereas for the assembly the cross signifies the death of the son of God as a means of life, for the synagogue it came to signify the death of Jews at the hands of the church. Such is the consequence of giving holy things to dogs and offering pearls to swine, of laying our allegiance at the altars of the Powers of the Darkness.

CHAPTER 38

DOING UNTO OTHERS

The beatitudes on mercy and peacemaking and the antithesis on loving the enemy indicate that Jesus did not intend the assembly to manifest the character of God only within its own membership, but intended that it manifest it to the Gentiles as well. There have been several attempts to show that Jesus' words concerning love of the enemy were intended as a guide for community living, not for international living. None of these that I have seen, though articulately argued, are convincing to me. After all, for disciples to show contempt for Gentiles would imply that God holds the Gentiles in contempt. If God did not love the Gentiles, however, it would make no sense for him to send the sunshine and the rain on them as the means of sustaining life. To despise the Gentiles would be to not love the entire world, yet Jesus was not crucified for only a part of the world.

The present passage reaffirms the expectation that by its acts toward those outside, the assembly will bear testimony to the compassion of God for all his creatures. Following immediately on sayings that expound the Lord's Prayer, Jesus' words now reaffirm previous promises. Those who ask will receive (Matt. 6:12-14); those who seek will find (6:33). There is no reference in Matthew's Gospel to knocking, but in the teachings of the first-century rabbis, there are assurances that to those who knock in prayer God will open the door.

The passage opens with a promise and closes with an exhortation, the promise being rooted in a reminder of the goodness of God. As many commentaries point out, the passage encourages disciples to pray, promising that their prayers will be answered. The promise, however, is rooted in God's generosity to all who ask, seek, and knock. The assembly can be assured, therefore, that when it asks, it will receive.

The generosity of God is rooted in the character of God: God is good. Indeed, God alone is truly good. Such ascriptions are not philosophical points for speculation, but are testimony to what God has done in the life of

271

his own people, as well as in the life of the entire world—as seen, for example, in the previously mentioned gifts of rain and sunshine.

The exhortation that ends the passage is the real goal of the passage. Because God generously provides for the needs of all his creatures, including the assembly, the assembly is to be generous in its dealings with others—including those outside the assembly. In this way it testifies to the character of God. Moreover, such attention to those outside the assembly is not to be merely reactive, but is to be expressed in the initiative the disciples take in their relation to others—other disciples, Jews, and Gentiles—all. The Light does not wait for the Darkness to act, but takes the first step in illuminating the Darkness. Those who are bearers of the Light are to do the same. Disciples are not to do unto others as others ask, but as they, the disciples, would like to have others act toward them. Were the assembly to await the request, the request might never come, especially from the enemies of the assembly. The assembly is not to wait until the hungry ask for food, until the naked ask for clothing, or until the enemy attacks, to return good for evil. It is to seek the enemy's well-being even before the enemy acts. To do unto others as you wish them to do unto you is, in fact, to extend Jesus' exhortation "Love your neighbor as yourself" into "Love the outsider as you love yourself."

As the beatitudes make clear, following this exhortation will place the assembly or the disciple in a position of great vulnerability. The world, enslaved to the Darkness, does not manifest the character of God, but the character of Satan. No institutions—including, sad to say, the institutional church—do unto others apart from purposes of self-gain and self-interest. Furthermore, institutions will not long tolerate those within their circle whose actions threaten that self-interest. Anyone who calls for any government or for any other institution to feed and clothe its enemies or to offer to die that the enemy might live will receive ridicule, scorn, ostracism, persecution, and even imprisonment and death.

The rejection of Jesus' words on this point can be seen not only in the lives of nations and institutions, but also in the lives of individuals whose perspectives, attitudes, and consciences have been molded by the Powers that inhabit the institutions—even in the lives of those who wear the name of Christ. So-called Christian counseling and self-help enterprises, for example, commonly seek to engender in their clients and participants an ethos of self-fulfillment, self-assertiveness, and independence. The laity of the institutional church in the West has been inundated with church-sponsored courses in assertiveness training, aerobics, karate, and the like as means of building self-sufficiency and a sense of self-worth.

Certainly, characteristics of passivity, docility, and shyness born of fear or of a sense of worthlessness are neither virtuous nor desirable; nor are they emblems of spirituality. When they are rooted in fear or a sense of worthlessness, they are nothing more or less than manifestations of captivity to the Darkness. Self-assertiveness, self-sufficiency, and self-expression that lead us to meet the world on its own terms and that induce in us a self-centered approach to others are simply alternate expressions of that same captivity and are manifestations of the church's own seduction and imprisonment. They are ways a corrupted church panders to the worst in us. Jesus calls his assembly to meet the world not on the world's own terms, but on terms of the character and Reign of God. Only in that outreach to the world does the assembly know true freedom. Only in that approach does the disciple embrace and find sustenance in the Light. Only in that approach does the Darkness dissipate, Death give way to Life, and the creation find its fulfillment.

To take the initiative in doing for others what the assembly or the disciple desires for itself, himself, or herself is to bear witness to Light and Life in the midst of Darkness and Death. It is, in fact, to fulfill torah and the prophets. Just as Jesus, in his words and deeds, fulfilled torah and the prophets, so the assembly fulfills them by embodying them. Taking the initiative in acting toward others and doing for others as we wish they would act toward and do for us expresses in human life the divine ordering and restoration, which are at the heart of the entire body of torah and which underlie the ultimate goal of all prophetic proclamation. The assembly, by its life, serves as the means by which the divine order is set forth in the midst of the continuing Chaos.

NOT ALL THAT IS ASKED IS GIVEN

The promise that all who ask will receive does not include the assurance that just *anything* and *everything* for which one asks will be given. There are limitations.

Those who plead for entry into God's Reign on the basis of their prophecies and exorcisms, but who have not done the will of God, will not receive or find it opened to them (Matt. 7:21-23).

Those who claim to have forgiven, but have not, will not be forgiven (Matt. 6:15).

Those who seek answers from Jesus to questions intended as traps for him receive no answer (Matt. 21:23-27).

Those who seek signs as proof of Jesus' claims will receive no sign except the sign of Jonah (Matt. 12:39).

The fullest exercise of the disciples' authority depends on faith (Matt. 17:14-21).

God honoring requests on which two or three agree depends on those two or three having assembled in the power of Jesus' name (Matt. 18:19-20).

Moreover, the latter promise now appears in the context of the call for the assembly to go to great lengths in seeking to loosen, that is, to forgive and to be reconciled with the erring member of the assembly.

The promises related to asking, seeking, and knocking are promises about those things necessary for the assembly to survive and to operate as the faithful people of God. The support for the promises in the present passage refers to requests for those things that are essential for life. God will give good things, or appropriate things, to those who ask him (vs. 11), "good" meaning those things needed to enable those who ask to be and to do what God intends them to be and to do.

Moreover, that those who ask receive in no way means that those who do not ask do not receive. Were this the case, those who starve and those who do not ask would be the same people. Starvation would be a sign of impiety or atheism. The asking of which the promise speaks is to be understood in the context of anxiety. The Gentiles do not ask, but center their activities and efforts on grasping. They seek to establish life on their own terms and for their own purposes. God sends his sunshine and rain on them, as well. In their self-delusion, however, they deceive themselves into thinking that their success is owing only to their own anxiety-ridden works. Thus, they struggle in the Darkness, receiving, but ignorant of the one who gives.

All who seek God's Reign find it. All who knock at the narrow gate find it opened to them. God intends to spread his sovereign Reign once again over the entire creation. The very purpose of the assembly's existence is to serve as God's instrument in the triumph of that sovereignty.

Of course, those who knock at the wide gate find it opened also, but that gate leads not to Life, but to Death. On the day of judgment, those who cry out "Lord! Lord!" and are denied entry will be denied not because they did not knock, but because they knocked on the wrong door. God hides permanently from none who truly seek him, but those who seek the Darkness—even if they seek the Darkness thinking it to be the Light—will find the door shut in their faces.

There may be some reason, of course, why in one circumstance or another God so hardens hearts that people are unable to repent, unable to seek God. Isaiah described such a situation in the eighth century B.C., as did Amos, and Jesus interpreted the situation of the temple and the synagogue officials in his own day in light of the fulfillment of the Isaiah indictment. Such hardening, however, is always an act of judgment on God's part not for the purpose of completely destroying, but for that of leading through destruction to renewal. That God hides his face from time to time does not nullify his more basic characteristic of embracing all who truly seek his sovereign reign over their lives. Even the turning away must be understood in the context of reconciliation and return.

PART NINE

THREATS TO THE LIFE OF FAITH

Enter by the narrow gate. For the gate that leads to destruction is wide, and the path is spacious. Many are they who enter thereby. But the gate that leads to life is narrow, and the way is tight. There are few who find it! Beware of false messengers from God—those who come to you in sheep's clothing, but who, inwardly, are ravenous wolves. By their fruits you will recognize them: Are grapes gathered from thorn bushes, or are figs gathered from bramble bushes? Just so, a healthy tree bears edible fruit, but the unhealthy tree bears unedible fruit. A healthy tree cannot bear unedible fruit, nor can an unhealthy tree bear edible fruit. Every tree that does not bear edible fruit is cut down and thrown into the fire. Indeed, then, by their fruits you will recognize them.

Not everyone who says to me, "Lord! Lord!" will enter the Reign from heaven, but only the one who does the will of my Father in heaven. Many will say to me in that day, "Lord! Lord! Did we not prophesy in your name, and cast out demons in your name, and do many mighty works in your name?"

And I will assure them, "I never knew you. Depart from me, you torahless ones!"

Everyone, therefore, who hears these words of mine and does them will be like a wise man who built his house on the rock. The rain fell, the floods came, and the winds blew and beat on the house, but it didn't fall, for the rock was its foundation.

But everyone who hears these words of mine and does not do them will be like a foolish man who built his house on the sand. The rain fell, the floods came, the winds blew and beat against the house, and it fell. And great was its fall!

(Matthew 7:13-27)

275

CHAPTER 39

THE TWO WAYS AND THE PHONY MESSENGERS

The image of wide and narrow gates is created by the blending of two motifs common in Jesus' day—that of the narrow path that must be traveled to reach a desired goal, and that of the two ways. The motif of the two ways usually called for a decision on the way one would live; that of the narrow passage warned of the difficulty of living so as to attain the proper goal of life.

Good examples of the narrow entrance are found in 2 Esdras 7. One reference is to a narrow opening one must navigate in order to reach the sea. Another is a reference to a narrow mountain pass an heir must travel to reach a city he has inherited. In the second parable, on one side of the entrance is fire; on the other, deep water. A single misstep and one will either burn or drown. To come to the fulfillment of life, that is, one must endure danger. One may even have to face death.

Matthew and Luke are strikingly different in their versions of this motif in their report of Jesus' teaching. Whereas in Luke's Gospel Jesus emphasizes the necessity of deciding to enter, the limited time of the opportunity to enter, and the replacement of some of the originally rightful entrants with Gentile substitutes, in Matthew's Gospel he speaks of the necessity of choosing between two entrances—a broad one leading to Destruction and a narrow one leading to Life. Luke's version is concerned with who will be saved on the day of judgment; Matthew's, with the daily life of discipleship and the kind of life required for entry, as well as with the day of judgment.

In the final analysis, the daily decisions confronting every disciple are decisions of Life and Death. Just as Moses closed his discourse on torah by setting before the people of God the alternatives of life and death (Deut. 30:15-20), so Jesus, in his interpretation of torah, sets before the people of God in a later time the same alternatives. Discipleship entails daily choices on whether the assembly or the disciple will serve God or the Powers, and the Powers wear a multitude of faces. The Powers disguise themselves in the garments of Light; through the Powers, Death casts its net for the unwary.

THE DEMANDS, AND THE PERVERSION OF THE DEMANDS, OF DISCIPLESHIP

This is not the only passage in Matthew's Gospel in which the way of discipleship and the gospel and the way of Death are contrasted as, respectively, difficult and easy. In the interpretation of the parable of the sower in 13:18-23, for example, the work of the devil, persecution and tribulation, and the simple desire to be well off in the world are portrayed as obstacles of great proportion. In Matthew 19:24, the popular saying that it is easier for a camel to go through the eye of a needle than for a person of wealth to enter the kingdom also emphasizes the narrow path of faithful discipleship, and 16:24-26 reports the warning that true discipleship is a life of cross-bearing.

The warning that life under the Reign of God entails difficulty, of course, is open to the perversion of legalism. It may be twisted into an insistence on obedience to rules and regulations as the means of obtaining God's favor, molding our own character, and maneuvering our way into the New Age. It is equally easy, however, to arrive at the opposite perversion—the assumption that since our relationship to God depends on faith and cannot be purchased or merited, obedience is of little, if any, significance. The failure to recognize both the full scope of faith and the deeper dimensions of obedience in the New Testament has resulted, across the centuries, in a multitude of needless theological arguments. The assertion of the supposed differences between Paul and the Synoptic Gospels is only one example.

The difficulties mentioned in Matthew's Gospel are not a gauntlet to be run in order to earn God's love. Nor are they a series of tests by which disciples may earn a reserved seat in the congregation of the saved in the New Age. Rather, they are the inevitable dangers and difficulties that the assembly will undergo as it lives out the proper life that has begun to be realized within and among its members. The Old Age—with its values of wealth, power, authority, and esteem in the eyes of others—is a constant threat. The two gates are the entrances to the path of the New Age and to the path of the Old Age; and the Old Age, the Age of Death, constantly reasserts itself even for those who have chosen the narrow gate of Life. The assembly has come under the forward-reaching power of the New Age, but disciples are always subject to the enticements of the Old; and it is not necessary to retrace the steps of the narrow path to the point of entry in order to move from one path to the other. This is why we are to pray that we not be put to the test. We are to pray that events and circumstances not raise that doubt, but that they might be the occasion for a reflexive trust in God's power and love, with no room for the question ever to arise, no matter how overwhelming the circumstance. That the Lord's Prayer includes a request precisely for this protection indicates that the reflex of confidence in God is by no means a natural, innate capability we possess, but is solely a divine gift. The call to enter by the narrow gate is a call to exercise that choice which is not humanly possible, but which is a gift of God. It is an exhortation to use the gift that is given. It is a warning of what is stored up for those ungrateful enough, or blind enough, to reject the gift once it is given.

Of course, here lies a great danger that we must avoid. The warning about the respective characteristics of the two ways is not a mere moralistic observation to which we may successfully respond by following certain regulations and obeying certain laws. Instead, it is a wisdom observation about two orderings of life, orderings that have definite implications for action, but that in no way can be successfully reduced to a legal system. In fact, it is possible even to observe teachings related to the New Age, but to observe them as outward expressions of motives and ambitions rooted in the Old Age. For example, it is possible to refuse to enter into a divorce not on the basis of concern for each other or on the basis of a concern for the testimony to God's character, but simply out of fear of the fires of hell.

Participation in the New Age this side of the return of Jesus does not confer perfection of insight into what God wills as the proper way of acting. Only in the perfection of the New Age will torah be so perfectly written on the heart by the Spirit that simply to desire will be to express the will of God. For the present, the assembly must rely on the decision of God to make the written word come alive as the Living Word; the instruction of Jesus must stand in the inescapable tension between description and command. Because it describes the shape of freedom for those liberated from the Darkness, it is the word of grace—inviting, encouraging, enlightening. Because this side of the New Age the sojourn of the assembly remains in the world, however, the invitation will sometimes be a command. To compound the difficulty, the assembly, by its very relation to the Light, will constantly be a scandal and a threat to those whose lives are not merely lived in, but are dominated by, the Old Age.

THE TWO WAYS AND THE NATIONS

The alternative of the two ways is set not merely before the assembly and the individual disciples, but is set before all nations, all cultures, and all human institutions, as well. In appropriately rejecting the ascription of "Christian" to any contemporary nation or culture, we must distinguish between speaking of any nation or culture that has ever existed as having been Christian, on the one hand, and on the other hand, speaking of the possibility of a nation as a corporate entity repenting and glorifying God in Jesus Christ. On whatever grounds the adjective *Christian* is rejected with regard to nations, the assumption that nations are mere aggregates of atomistic individuals must not be one of those grounds. Biblically perceived, nations are corporate entities. They have creaturely lives of their own, lives in many ways distinct from the lives of individuals within them. As manifestations of the cosmic Powers, corrupted by Death, and as corporate entities in their transcendent dimension, the nations have been conquered already in the cross. Thus, all nations whether nominally viewed as Christian or otherwise, have been made servants of Christ. We do not yet see this servitude, or servanthood, because it is veiled in the mystery of God's ways, known only through revelation. The diversity of national attitudes toward the gospel may be accounted for, to some extent, in the same way that individual human responses differ within the framework of the corporate national response. Consequently, no nation can accurately be described as, in one way or another, either more or less a servant of God than any other. Theoretically, there is nothing to rule out a nation, a culture, or a people from becoming authentically Christian. It may even be argued that the West actually came close to being a Christian system, but that it failed because of its pride and that all current calls for a return to Christianity are calls to a return to what almost was, but what finally did not come about. It would also have to be pointed out, however, that all such calls are made with a misunderstanding of when and how the errors of the past were made. Contemporary calls for a return to something roughly resembling Christianity are expressions of nostalgia for a way of life that was not inherently gospel ethos, but was—for all its value and nobility—simply another expression of the Darkness. All such calls are calls for a return to idolatry.

THE ATTRACTIVENESS OF THE DARKNESS

The path that leads to destruction—whether for a nation, a people, or an individual—is attractive because the world of the Old Age is servant to realities beyond its ability fully to comprehend or to overcome. Failing to perceive the Light and the Darkness correctly, outside grace we declare the Darkness Light, and we are enabled thereby to love the Darkness as though it were the Light. Outside the influence of grace, our plans, our schemes, and our actions are subverted by the disguised Darkness, but since we mistake the Darkness for the Light, we are able to claim divine motivation and divine sanction for those plans and schemes and actions. Enthralled by the Darkness, our motives and intent shaped by the Darkness, we love the Darkness, thereby surrendering completely to massive self-love.

Apart from grace, we love the Darkness because we are one with the Darkness. Thus we live out our condemnation to declare good and evil.

Misunderstanding evil to be primarily a matter of morality, we declare good and evil on the basis of whether that which is named enables us to accomplish our own goals and desires. The accuracy of any human label of good and evil, however, rests on the extent to which what is labeled actually does coincide with God's own evaluation and declaration. There are not eternal principles of good and evil. Only God's persevering declarations determine good and evil. One can have eternal principles only if one denies the sovereignty of God over the creation. All efforts to affirm eternal principles of good and evil, consequently, are flirtations with practical atheism, affirmations growing out of a desire to bind God to our own values. Every such effort says, in effect, that there are eternal values sovereign over God, values God may have created, but which cannot be changed—values to which even God is now bound. Even the assertion that God freely binds himself to a body of principles he has created is, at heart, an attempt to bind God to our own theology. If God can be said to have established eternal principles of good and evil, then once we can determine what those principles are, we no longer have to take God seriously. At last we will have found a way to eat fruit of the tree of the knowledge of good and evil without dire consequences. This is one of the basic problems with the assertion that the written words of the Bible are themselves the Word of God without qualification, and it is why the Protestant reformers' insistence on the written words as the instrument of God's address is so important. Apart from the impact the Spirit alone can accomplish, any insistence on the authority of the Bible is idolatry in that it separates the text from God's free choice and attributes to it independent divinity.

THE FALSE MESSENGERS

It is precisely because the proper door and way can be known only by revelation that the difficulty of finding it is heightened by the presence of impostors posing as prophets. The Bible holds numerous examples of false prophets, men and women who claim to have had a revelation of God, but who either did not have such a revelation or had a deceptive revelation so that they might be unwitting instruments by whom God would lead the people to judgment.

In the New Testament, we read not only of false prophets, but also of false apostles. The precise nature of the prophets' activity in the early church is not clear, but by the beginning of the second century, the terms "false prophets" and "false apostles" could be used interchangeably. Their common factor was the false claim to speak a word from God.

There seems to have been a widespread belief in Judaism in the first century that by the time of Ezra, prophecy had ceased in Israel and that it would reappear only toward the end of the age, a belief that would account for those who viewed John the Baptist and Jesus as prophets, believing that the appearance of these two signaled the end of the Age. In this respect, it is appropriate, perhaps even to be expected, that the New Testament speaks here and there of prophets within the church. Paul viewed prophecy as one of the prime abilities granted by the Holy Spirit to individuals within the church. There is indication that the prophet might identify Jesus in public as the one in whom God's promises of a deliverer for Israel were fulfilled (Matt. 3:1-17; Luke 2:36-38); might foretell, under the Spirit's influence, certain events (Acts 21:10-11; 11:28); might seek to encourage a congregation (Acts 15:32; 1 Cor. 15:29-31); might empower an official (1 Tim. 4:14); and, even among the Gentiles, might evaluate the lives of his or her own people (Titus 1:12). The prophet might, as did the authors of the Shepherd of Hermas and the book of the Revelation, by reporting visions, proclaim God's involvement in the events during and immediately preceding his or her own time.

The false prophet, on the other hand, might perform great signs and wonders in an effort to lead people away from faith (Matt. 24:24; Acts 13:6-12; Rev. 13:11-17; 19:20) or might lead the faithful astray by teaching them to deny the human nature of Jesus (1 John 4:1-3). For Paul, the person who claims to be a prophet can be tested by whether he or she agrees with Paul's insistence that because God is not a God of confusion, but of order, the worship of God is to be orderly (1 Cor. 14:26-40).

Another writing from near the end of the New Testament period, *The Didache,* indicates that a prophet might teach, give ecstatic utterances (11:5–12:5), and even be the community's high priest—an identification especially striking in light of the assertion that anyone claiming to be a prophet, but staying longer than one day (or two, in cases of emergencies), is thereby identified as a false prophet.

These activities of the prophets in the early church are not noticeably out of keeping with what we know of the prophets in ancient Israel. Even the transient aspect of the true prophet's habits are reminiscent of the wandering prophetic bands around the end of the period of the judges and the beginning of the monarchy. The true prophet of the early church seems to have been assumed to speak by revelation under the influence of the Spirit and to identify for the hearers what God was doing or was about to do in the events of their daily lives. Even Agabus's prediction that a famine was about to come over all the world (Acts 11:28) is similar to predictions by prophets in the Old Testament, although we are not told what Agabus understood the importance of the famine to be.

False prophets, then, like true prophets, do not claim to speak the truth in general, but claim to bring a direct, specific word from God, a word they have been commanded to speak. It is not a problem of whose insights are more reliable, but of whether the one who makes such a claim has truly received the message from God. For us, this passage raises questions of whether God still sends prophets, whether the office of prophets is still a valid one, and how to recognize a person sent to fill that office.

THE DECEPTION OF SINCERITY

Not everyone claiming direct communication with God is to be trusted, and unfortunately, sincerity is no guarantee of authenticity. Impostors in any matter may deceive themselves at least as much as they deceive others. People have stolen, killed, and committed indescribable atrocities, firm in their belief that they are following an inner voice from God. It is hardly likely that all the false prophets in the Old Testament or all Paul's opponents in the New Testament were charlatans or that all those responsible for Jesus' execution were merely filled with hatred or blinded by fear.

How, then, in the ocean of competing claims, are we to recognize who, if anyone, truly speaks for God? Jesus warns that the way that seems easiest is likely the false way, that the way of truth is narrow and difficult. Although the difficulty of a path does not automatically rule it out as possibly a false one, the easiness of a path automatically marks it as one of which we should be at least suspicious. In Matthew's Gospel, Jesus is reported on at least two occasions to have warned his followers that the cost of discipleship is crucifixion. As Bonhoeffer so aptly put it, "When Jesus calls a man [or woman, we may add], he bids him [or her] come and die." Whereas taking up and bearing the cross is the price one pays for faithful membership in God's family, the false prophets proclaim a less expensive cost. In the antitheses of the Sermon, however, by removing the permissiveness some had associated with torah, Jesus removes all shortcuts around the will of God. The false prophets teach compromise for the sake of personal security, promising the saving of one's life by a means other than losing it.[1] They equate strict faithfulness with stubbornness and naiveté. In and of itself, of course, stubbornness is a characteristic of the fall and, as such, may be as destructive of discipleship as is any other scar from Eden. It can easily cause us to persist in a direction opposite the will of God, even when other factors suggest to us that our original sense of direction was mistaken. Stubbornness always masquerades as sincerity, and it can be worn sufficiently well to lead the naive to destruction. Nevertheless, taking up the cross does require determination and grit, and the divine gift of obedience may accommodate itself even to stubbornness.

---

1. There is, of course, a daily give-and-take by which one balances personal desires and ambitions over against the needs of others. Impostors, however, usually do not speak of balancing desires and needs, but of the reasonableness of accommodating God's will to what is practical and moderately successful by the standards of the Old Age.

DISCERNING THE IMPOSTORS

Matthew 24:11 speaks of false prophets who will arise and lead many astray—a reference that originally may have been related to the last days of the Old Age. In its present context, however, it refers to a period of time when "the end is not yet" (24:6), but which is "the beginning of the sufferings" (24:8). During this time, "The gospel of the kingdom will be preached throughout the whole world" (24:14a); afterward, "The end will come" (24:14b). These false prophets, then, are figures who appear during the messianic era, as do those in the Sermon on the Mount.

In Matthew, the key to recognition of false prophets is in 7:24. In comparison with Luke's parallel to this verse (Luke 6:47), Matthew's wording stands out sharply. In Luke it is Jesus' words in general that must be obeyed. In Matthew, "these words" can only refer to Jesus' words in the Sermon. The Sermon, for Matthew, is the definitive body of Jesus' teachings, not because it covers all situations the disciples will encounter, but because the teachings found there will include within themselves the method for interpreting all Jesus' teachings and a rationale on which to base daily decisions. The false prophet is one who rejects the validity and the crucial role of the teachings of the Sermon. The fruits by which the false prophet can be recognized are—

- the absence of mourning;
- less than complete commitment to seeing God's will accomplished;
- lack of concern for healing and reconciliation when the prophet's work creates alienation;
- the tendency to compromise the gospel by stressing its similarity to contemporary culture;
- equating subjection to human institutions with collaboration with those institutions;
- disparaging Jesus' teachings by an appeal to humanly designated realism;
- attention to one's image in the eyes of others for purposes of personal repute;
- assuming that God's will can be accomplished only if we make and are zealous to carry out decisions;
- viewing as being outside the kingdom people who do not follow our view of the truth, and treating such people as though they were not human;
- obsession with the faults of others and failure to respond to them in the mercy and kindness we desire for ourselves.

The false prophets are those who call for the destruction of the enemy; those who claim God's blessings on lies and broken vows; those who equate loyalty to any institution, including the church, with loyalty to God; those who deny the family of God by hatred and oppression of the Jews.

The false prophets are those who pedal the manipulation of emotions or the manipulation of the mind through psychological gimmickry in the name of Christian worship or evangelism.

That the assembly's response to Jesus and to the gospel does not render it completely impervious to danger from false prophets is seen in the warning accompanying the instruction on how to recognize them. Genuine caution against the easy path requires caution against those who, in a less than perfect world, try to persuade us either that the easy path is God's will or that God permits us to lavish a portion of our worship on Mammon.

The warning to beware the false prophets, however, is heard with complete accuracy only in the context of the prior warning against judging. Although God will judge—separating tares from wheat and destroying the tree that does not produce good fruit—we may not exercise that judgment for God. On the day of judgment, when God reigns over all, the false prophets will lay claim to participation in the New Age on the grounds that they have been prophets and exorcists in the name of Jesus. His power with them has been manifested in their ability to do "many mighty works." Even these words and deeds, however, will not suffice for lasting acceptance into the New Age. In response to the false prophets' greeting of "Lord! Lord!" Jesus will respond, "It wasn't I who empowered your work; it was the devil." When these phony prophets cry out "Lord! Lord!" Jesus will reply, "You have done the works of Darkness, even though they appeared to you and to those you deceived as the works of Light! Begone into the Darkness you have served so zealously and well!"

The false prophets will be identified then as those who have cast aside torah, thinking their prominence as orators and displays of healing miracles mark them as authentic messengers from God. Neither spectacular healings on television while praising the name of Jesus nor high-powered oratory that stimulates numerical growth is necessarily a manifestation of the work of Christ. It is unqualified blasphemy to couple supposed divine healings with the call to military action against the enemy—as is done day in and day out in Satanic religious programs that flood the channels of television in the name of Christ. The grace of God is undercut by denying Jesus' teachings. There is indeed a power present in such circuses of religion, but it is not the power of Christ. It is the Spirit of Darkness—it is Mammon, cohort of Satan, hypnotizing the audience and leading them unto Death.

THE PHONINESS OF SIMPLE ANSWERS

The false prophets are frequently quite sincere. Usually, they truly believe themselves to be God's messengers, called into service to do battle with the forces of evil. Usually, also, they assume that every problem has a simple solution, a single solution given them by God himself. Missing altogether in the false prophets is any sense of the mystery of God, any hint of the incomprehensibility of God. Taking the Bible as a combination almanac and moral rule book, they have a quotation for every occasion. If a disease such as AIDS sweeps the world, it is said to be God's way of getting at some unpopular group or some deviant nation. If someone dies in a horrible accident, it is said to be the will of God. Movie stars say they have become prominent because God blessed them; politicians say they have been elected because God gave them the victory; a business prospers, the owner says, because God has blessed it; a congregation or denomination suddenly grows by leaps and bounds, because it says God has given it growth; and so on. Whatever is, we are told, would not be were it not for God. So much knowledge! So much certainty! So little mystery! Such a trivial god!

A god who blesses our self-centeredness, who cherishes our vulgarity, who pulls our strings—a god whose thoughts are our thoughts, whose ways are our ways; it is a god all right: the god of Darkness! Such a god has an answer for everything—even for the Holocaust.

The God of Jesus Christ has no such easy answers. The written testimony of torah is vulnerable to objectivity, to manipulation, and to distortion; the Living Word, when spoken, gives no objective verification of its genuineness. The one who claims to speak for God can be tested only by fruits that sometimes are themselves ambiguous; and even the Son, as he hangs on the cross, suffers in bewilderment. The God of Jesus Christ upsets all our answers and forces us to ask the most disturbing of questions. The God of Jesus Christ chooses when to speak, but he also chooses when to remain aloof, when to abandon us, when to leave us to struggle with the experience of his Silence.

For the phony prophets, God is never silent. He constantly speaks to them in confidential revelations or points them to a simplistic text that can be quoted with a silly grin or a grotesque snarl. Their god is ever ready to accede to their most frivolous, most self-serving whims. How easy to serve such a god! How easy to gain a following from the masses who thrive on ego-building, simple answers! How easy to enter the wide gate and walk the spacious way! For the way of destruction, the way of Death, is not only easy; it is alluring.

The way of the God of Jesus Christ, however, is found through the narrow gate. The way is difficult to find, because the wide gate has all the best public relations experts. It is difficult to walk because it is the way of mystery, the way of the cross, and much of the time the way of the Silent God.

CHAPTER 40

THE TWO HOUSES

When the devastating forces of the Chaos, churning out of the Darkness, beat on the assembly or the disciple, threatening to devour like a mighty storm, the assembly or the disciple will stand firm only if all perception and all action are founded on Jesus' instruction in the Sermon.

The storm in the metaphor of the two houses expresses that Chaos in which all storms are rooted. The Chaos motif is integral to the ancient world's stories of the creation of the universe, and in Genesis 1 that Chaos is intimately related to the Darkness. In the beginning, when God created the chaotic Deep, that Deep was covered by the Darkness. God then brought order to the Chaos and created Light to banish the Darkness.

The rest of the ordering followed swiftly as God called the world and all within it into being. Finally, God saw all he had made, and it was just as he had intended it.

In response to human rebellion, however, God allowed the Chaos to reassert itself. The Darkness returned. Death was permitted to hold sway.

The Bible portrays the Chaos and its Darkness as manifesting themselves in the temporal realm in many and diverse ways. Psalm 46 portrays the manifestation in international warfare. The churning waters that roar and foam, threatening the earth, become real in history in the guise of the nations of the earth attacking God's order by waging war. The chaotic waters that God domesticated, by calming them into a river that "makes glad the city of God," seek to break loose. But God speaks, and the nations are brought to heel. The instruments of war are cast into a fire that all the waters of Chaos cannot quench.

Matthew's version of the Sermon emphasizes the foundations of the two houses, portrays the storm in elaborate detail, and emphasizes the fall of the house built on sand. The Chaos destroys the house because of the house's insufficient foundation.

Matthew also combines the chaos motif with that of wisdom. In his version of the Sermon, the two builders are, respectively, wise and foolish. The two houses are expressions of the "two ways" of traditional wisdom—a motif seen already in the two gates (Matt. 7:13-14).

For those who would be his faithful disciples, Jesus' instruction in the Sermon is wisdom. Wisdom, then—usually understood as insight into the deeper things of life, gained through experience and reflection—is seen here not as the consequence of experience, but as adherence to Jesus' instruction in the Sermon. Wisdom is revealed, not achieved by human effort. The world's wisdom is the wisdom of the serpent. The disciples are indeed expected to have that worldly, serpentlike wisdom (Matt. 10:16), but it is not to be the basis of their actions. Possessing both the wisdom of the serpent and the wisdom of God, they are to rely on the latter as the Light for their path.

The serpent's wisdom enables the assembly to fight the world on the world's own terms, if it so chooses. To do so, however, means accepting alienation, violence, and disruption as normative.

The wise assembly or the wise disciple is the one whose life is built not on the wisdom of the serpent, but on the instruction of Jesus. Such a person or such an assembly has a firm foundation. The disciple or assembly that abandons, ignores, or treats lightly that instruction has no solid foundation, and even the best constructed house, if it is not built on a solid foundation, cannot endure the chaotic forces that come storming out of the Darkness.

The foolish assembly chooses poor ground on which to build. It may have done mighty works in Jesus' name, may even have overcome those demonic forces that manifest the Chaos, may even have prophesied, but it has not done so by the power of God. It has been Satan divided against himself. The fruits by which true prophets are known are not their own power, but their adherence to the character of God as this is manifested in the instruction of the Sermon. Nevertheless, the person made wise by living in accord with the world's standards is not to be despised, but is to be seen as a prisoner of the Darkness, a prisoner whose liberation is the reason for the assembly's very existence. The contrast of the two houses does not indicate that the individual who is not a faithful disciple of Jesus is criminal, murderous, or despicable. Jesus has many sheep not of the institutional fold. Whether their nobility be a lingering shred of the original created order still preserved by grace—a wounded, but noble, conscience—or a sign of the resurrection implanted by grace, the sensitivity and compassion evident here and there in individuals is a sign of grace *despite* the Chaos, not a sign that the old order is not so chaotic after all.

The distinction Jesus draws is not between disciples and all others, but between those who hear Jesus' instruction and embrace it and those who hear it and ignore it. The words, in the final analysis, are words of promise on God's dependability and words of instruction on the manifestation of the character of God. Assemblies or disciples that ignore either also distort both, and they will perish. Since in the truest sense of the word *community* the individual is never overlooked, but finds true individuality in community, the instruction may be said to be for the individual disciple, but its primary intent is for the assembly as community.

The warning concerning the two houses is a warning to not follow the phony prophets and to not be phony prophets. The phony prophets will be cast aside, along with those who have followed them.

The phony prophets are wolves, even though they wear the clothing of sheep. At times, they may speak a worldly wisdom that has a certain worldly validity, and God may even use them occasionally to work wonders, but the ultimate consequence of their work is bondage to Death.

Psalm 1, a wisdom psalm on the two ways, can easily be heard, in the wake of the crucifixion and resurrection of Jesus, as a description of the assembly or the disciple who builds on the rock of Jesus' instruction, for Jesus' instruction is torah for the New Age. Blessed is the one who does not traffic with the ways of the Darkness, but who delights in Jesus' instruction, who meditates on it day and night. All that such an assembly or such a disciple does will prosper. It or he or she will receive the promised reward. Not a monetary reward. Not worldly prosperity. Those are the rewards of Mammon. The reward and prosperity of those who are faithful followers of Jesus will be that of bearing fruit, of being good salt, of glorifying the God who created everything and everyone.

The assembly that abandons Jesus' instruction focused in the Sermon has no foundation to support it in the Darkness. It will fall into the whirlpool of the Chaos.

The scandal of the institutional church in the West today is that it has chosen to make its home in the shadows cast by the Darkness, rather than in the shadow of the cross. Walking through the valley of the shadow of Death, it has embraced the shadows, mistaking them for Light, and consequently has become as much the bearer of Death as of Life and Light. The loss of church membership by traditionally moderate and liberal denominations— coupled with the popularity and increase of membership in cults, in Western distortions of Eastern religions, in pseudoreligious psychological movements, and in conservative and fundamentalist denominations—has been erroneously perceived by the shrinking churches as something that can be remedied by turning away from a concern for justice. Such churches believe it can be remedied by plunging into a preoccupation with a self-centered phony spirituality or with a pretentious, superficial, homogenizing gimmick called "church growth"; with dualistic, self-centered methods of autosuggestion in the name of spiritual formation; with the neo-Montanistic ecstasy and divine tête-à-tête of self-induced babbling mistaken for genuine speaking in tongues; and with numerous other heretical and pagan substitutes for a genuine—and, in the world's eyes, scandalous—encounter with the Word of God.

On the other hand, those same fluctuations of church membership are seen by those groups, cults, sects, and denominations that are mushrooming in numbers as evidence of divine favor on themselves and divine disfavor with those that are shrinking.

Actually, the increase or decrease of church membership says nothing about whether the church has been faithful to the proclamation of the gospel. Jesus' followers progressively dropped by the wayside as Jesus' words became harder and harder to bear. The church's greatest periods of growth have come both under persecution (as in the second and third centuries) and in times of national fear (as in the 1950s). Decline has come both in times of difficulty and in times of prosperity.

The institutional church in the West in our day has become a carbon copy of the religious institutions of Israel in the eighth century B.C. At that time, the prophets Amos, Isaiah, Hosea, and Micah warned that the two kingdoms were to be destroyed because of their unfaithfulness. No element of the two kingdoms came under greater criticism than the religious institutions. In both kingdoms the cult had become so thoroughly acculturated that the nations' corruption was the cults' corruption. Similarly, the entanglement of the church and the structures of power in czarist Russia and in pre-revolutionary France resulted in attacks on the church as violent revolutions overtook those countries. In France, even the Sisters of Saint Joseph, who dressed as widows in order to feed, clothe, and nurse the poor, were caught up in the turmoil, and many were executed.

Whatever the political or economic ideology of the nation, there is an inherent, inevitable tension between the goals of the state and those of the Reign of God. Any church that forgets this and aligns itself with the aims of the state thereby abandons the Reign of God, which destroys all human-made governments. Collaborating with democratic, republic, communist, socialist, fascist, or monarchical governments equally repudiates the Reign of God.

This is not to say that the individual disciple must never participate in the offices of government. When the disciple does participate in secular government, however, he or she must do so fully aware that the state operates on the basis of values and motives in conflict with the gospel and that it will be only a matter of time before the conflict between the two claims results in a crisis of decision making. On the other hand, the assembly as such, when it takes on a government role, is automatically forced to do so on the state's terms. The educational institution that relies on government funding for its buildings, research grants, endowed chairs, or any other element of its life must abide by the state's regulations. The church that accepts government funds to provide ministry in housing, food, or any other area must carry out that ministry on the state's terms. Of course, those regulations may be quite good in most instances, but the problem is that the church that agrees to the state's regulations is agreeing to allow the state, rather than God, determine its actions. As the book of Revelation makes clear, such entanglements will lead, in the long run, to a loss of all foundations. When the beast is destroyed, those who have relied on the beast for their sustenance are able only to stand and wail.

Nowhere is the warning against the people of God—viewed both in the Old Testament and the New as a holy *nation*—more clearly sounded than in the prophetic insistence that for Israel to enter into alliances with other nations is a breach of faith. It is an act that leads inevitably to homage to the gods of the partner nation. In the West, specifically in the United States today, alliance with the state in various ways leads automatically to the church confusing the generalized god exalted in the nation's symbols with the God of Abraham, Isaac, Jacob, Deborah, Esther, and Jesus. It is an equation as complete as was that of Yahweh with Baal in the days of Hosea.

The metaphor of the two ways, coming at the end of the Sermon, closes Jesus' discourse in a manner parallel to the way the book of Deuteronomy ends. The assembly of God's people is warned that before it lie the alternatives of Life and Death. The exhortation is to choose Life. The warning is of the consequences of choosing Death.

The assembly or the disciple that treats Jesus' words lightly, seeing them as in some sense for the "next world," as impractical because others do not live by them, or as culturally conditioned and, therefore, easily explained away, and those who seek to qualify the stringency of Jesus' words on the basis of human frailty or meticulous hairsplitting, are those who unbind, or loosen, the instruction. Loosening the instruction, they loosen the structure of the house. Sharing society's foundation—the shifting sands of transient human opinion—that assembly or individual, in the onslaught of the stormy Darkness, is swept into the oblivion of Death.

EPILOGUE

When Jesus finished these words, the crowds were thoroughly stunned at his teaching, for he taught them not as their scribes, but as one having authority.

(Matthew 7:28-29)

The crowds, though not Jesus' immediate audience, have heard his instruction and are disoriented by the authority he displays. Matthew is quite clear about the reason for this astonishment. The crowds are accustomed to hearing torah interpreted by scribes who do not display such authority.

The scribes of first-century Judah were, for the most part, also the lawyers of Judah. Logically, who was in a better position to know what torah says than were those who spent their lives copying torah, producing new manuscripts for the preservation of torah? A scribe, however, usually could not settle an issue for an inquirer simply by quoting torah from the Pentateuch, for torah in the Pentateuch does not cover all possible situations. Interpretation and application were required. Moreover, the scribes with whom Matthew was familiar could not unilaterally interpret and apply torah, but had to rely on precedent—in much the same way that a judge in a lower court today must rely on precedent and superior court rulings. The scribes, in other words, were authorities only in the sense that they knew where to go for authoritative help in finding solutions.

Jesus, however, in Matthew's Gospel, does not rely on precedent or on some other authority. He himself has authority. He stuns the crowds not only by ignoring certain precedents of jurisprudence, but by countermanding other precedents, as well. The Greek verb that describes the crowds' reaction indicates being struck as though momentarily numbed physically by a heavy blow. Their minds are numbed by Jesus' apparent audacity, for he assumes God's own authority.

THE ORIGIN OF AUTHORITY

The Greek word translated "authority" *(exousia)* is made up of two separate words *(ex ousia)*, which, translated as literally as possible, give us "from essence," which suggests self-sufficiency, or self-derived ability. Obviously, such a literal translation misses the idiomatic usage of the word, but it does help us understand why in different contexts the word can mean such various things as authority, power, ability, right, and even freedom of choice. When used to speak of authority, it can refer to the authority itself, to the one bearing authority, to the realm of authority, or to the source from which the authority comes.

In the Bible all authority ultimately comes from God, either by permission or as an outright gift. God alone has authority "from himself," or self-generated authority. All authority, whether earthly or heavenly, other than God's authority, is provisional and limited. Indeed, even the authority of Jesus as resurrected and transformed Ruler of God's creation, though all-encompassing, is from God (Matt. 28:18).

JESUS' CONTINUING PRESENCE AND AUTHORITY

As the one who bears all authority on God's behalf, this transformed Jesus continues with his assembly until the end of the Old Age (Matt. 28:20), as the assembly extends its circle throughout the world. The assembly makes new disciples and instructs those new disciples in those things in which the original disciples themselves have been instructed—the instruction of the Sermon, along with that of the discourse on forgiveness and reconciliation (Matt. 18) and that of the discourse on how to await Jesus' return (Matt. 24–25).

For the assembly there can be no determinative authority other than Jesus—parents, spouse, employer, government officials, military superiors, priests or other church officials, denominational founders, noted thinkers, or any other. Any other claims to determinative authority arise from the Darkness and are to be resisted. The centuries of the church's life have seen eloquent examples of such resistance: Luther (in his early years), the Anabaptists, Roger Williams, Ann Hutchinson, the framers of the Barmen Declaration, and a multitude of other women and men whose names are known only to God.

At its purest, this resistance to the authority of human institutions has not been slavish obedience to a code of ethics, or even to conscience, but has been exactly the opposite. It has been the insertion—into a world of demands, regulations, and restrictions—of genuine freedom. It has been the exercise, over against the tyranny of the Darkness, of that freedom and integrity which God holds forth to all creatures. Imposed regulations and restrictions, though often helpful in preserving a relative order in the world of Darkness, are nevertheless a mark of the Darkness.

THE PURPOSE OF JESUS' AUTHORITY

Jesus' authority is not unbridled, directionless authority aimed at confining us to a narrow, rigid, miserable life of denial, but is authority for loosing and binding—loosing us from Death and binding the power of the Darkness. It is the authority to release us from Sin (Matt. 9:6).

In various discussions of earlier versions of portions of this book, someone has usually responded: "You have shown us the Darkness, but how do we reach the Light?"

My reply can only be that the attempt to reach the Light is itself an effort born of the Darkness. To assume that we must reach the Light—not to mention the assumption that we *can* reach it—is to have fallen victim to the Darkness's lie that God does not truly love us with an unqualified Love, that God does not take the initiative toward us, but that he demands that we take the first step before he will turn to us. This is also a denial of Jesus' authority, however, for it denies the very thing Jesus' authority is given him to accomplish, the liberation of the creation from the Darkness.

If we live under the assumption that God waits for us to take the initiative, the consequences will not be simply setting up for ourselves certain requirements as techniques for ascending into heaven, but setting them up for others, as well—and in God's name. If Jesus is viewed as having authority in that case, it will be authority not to deliver us from the Darkness, but the authority to destroy.

The effort to reach the Light is like the effort to swim by fighting the water: It results in being engulfed in that which you are fighting. The sense of needing to do something for one's own eternal security is Satan's way of posing as God in our conscience.

The call of Christ itself is the liberating event. His invitation liberates us from the Darkness. We no longer have to reach out for the Light. Walking in the Light we will hear in the Sermon on the Mount a depiction of our true freedom, life lived spontaneously as a testimony to the character of God. Living in that freedom, we will take up the cross and, empowered by the Light, go forth into the Darkness, that the world might be brought to glorify God.

REPRESENTATIVE BIBLIOGRAPHY

This bibliography is far from exhaustive, but is of a broad spectrum of treatments of the Sermon on the Mount. A few titles have been included that, though not on the Sermon as such, treat the Gospel of Matthew in its entirety, portions of the Sermon, or topics closely related to the Sermon. The list is confined to works originally in English or translated into English.

Albright, W. F., and C. S. Mann. *Matthew*. Garden City, N.Y.: Doubleday, 1971.

Allen, W. C. *A Critical and Exegetical Commentary on the Gospel According to St. Matthew*. Edinburgh: T. & T. Clark (Reprint), 1957.

Augustine. *Our Lord's Sermon on the Mount According to Matthew*. Trans. the Reverend William Findlay. Revised and annotated by the Reverend D. S. Schaff. Vol. VI of *A Select Library of the Nicene and Post-Nicene Fathers*. Ed. Philip Schaff. Grand Rapids: Wm. B. Eerdmans Publishing Co., 1979.

Betz, Hans Dieter. *Essays on the Sermon on the Mount*. Philadelphia: Fortress Press, 1985.

Bonhoeffer, Dietrich. *The Cost of Discipleship*. Trans. R. H. Fuller. Rev. ed. New York: Macmillan, 1959.

Bornkamm, Gunther. "The History of the Exegesis of the Sermon on the Mount," *Jesus of Nazareth*. Trans. James M. Robinson. New York: Harper & Brothers, 1960.

Bornkamm, Gunther, et al. *Tradition and Interpretation in Matthew*. Trans. Percy Scott. Philadelphia: Westminster Press, 1963.

Bultmann, Rudolf. *The History of the Synoptic Tradition*. Trans. John Marsh. New York: Harper & Row, Publishers, 1963.

Calvin, John. *A Harmony of the Gospels of Matthew, Mark, and Luke.* Vol. 1. Trans. A. W. Morrison. Grand Rapids: Wm. B. Eerdmans Publishing Co., 1972.

Campbell, Will D., and Bonnie Campbell. *God on Earth: The Lord's Prayer for Our Time.* New York: Crossroad Publishing Co., 1983.

Chrysostom. *Homilies on the Gospel of Saint Matthew.* Trans. the Reverend Sir George Prevost. Revised with notes by the Reverend M. B. Riddle. Vol X of *A Select Library of the Nicene and Post-Nicene Fathers.* Ed. Philip Schaff. Grand Rapids: Wm. B. Eerdmans Publishing Co., 1979.

Davies, W. D. *The Setting of the Sermon on the Mount.* Cambridge: Cambridge University Press, 1964.

Dibelius, Martin. *The Sermon on the Mount.* New York: Charles Scribner's Sons, 1940.

Ellul, Jacques. *Money and Power.* Trans. LaVonne Neff. Downer's Grove, Ill.: Intervarsity Press, 1984.

Fox, Emmett. *The Sermon on the Mount.* New York: Harper & Brothers, 1938.

Guelich, Robert A. *The Sermon on the Mount.* Waco, Tex.: Word, 1982.

Hill, David. *The Gospel of Matthew.* Grand Rapids: Wm. B. Eerdmans Publishing Co., 1981.

Jeremias, Joachim. *The Sermon on the Mount.* Trans. Norman Perrin. Philadelphia: Fortress Press, 1963.

———. *The Lord's Prayer.* Trans. John Reumann. Philadelphia: Fortress Press, 1964.

Johnson, Sherman. "The Gospel According to St. Matthew: Introduction and Exegesis," *The Interpreter's Bible.* Vol. 7. Nashville: Abingdon-Cokesbury Press, 1951. Pp. 231-625.

Jordan, Clarence. *The Cotton Patch Version of Matthew and John.* New York: Association Press, 1970.

Kierkegaard, Søren. *Christian Discourses.* Trans. Walter Lowrie. Princeton: Princeton University Press, 1971.

Kissinger, Warren S. *The Sermon on the Mount: A History of Interpretation and Bibliography.* Metuchen, N.J.: Scarecrow Press, 1975.

Luther, Martin. *The Sermon on the Mount and the Magnificat.* Vol. 21 of *Luther's Works* (American ed.). St. Louis: Concordia Publishing House, 1956.

McArthur, Harvey. *Understanding the Sermon on the Mount.* New York: Harper & Brothers, 1960.

McKenzie, John L. "The Gospel According to Matthew." *The Jerome Biblical Commentary.* Englewood Cliffs, N.J.: Prentice-Hall, 1968. Pp. 62-114.

Montefiore, Claude G. *The Synoptic Gospels.* Vol. II. 2nd ed. New York: KTAV Publishing House, 1968.

Petuchowski, Jakob J., and Michael Brocke, eds. *The Lord's Prayer and Jewish Liturgy.* New York: Seabury Press, 1978.

Prabhavananda, Swami. *The Sermon on the Mount According to Vedanta.* New York: New American Library, 1972.

Schweizer, Eduard. *The Good News According to Matthew.* Trans. David E. Green. Atlanta: John Knox Press, 1975.

Stendahl, Krister. "Matthew." *Peake's Commentary on the Bible.* 2nd ed. New York: Thomas Nelson and Sons, 1962. Pp. 769-98.

Trible, Phyllis. *God and the Rhetoric of Sexuality.* Overtures to Biblical Theology series, no. 20. Philadelphia: Fortress Press, 1978.

Weil, Simone. "Concerning the Our Father," *Waiting for God.* Trans. Emma Crauford. New York: Harper & Row, Publishers, 1973.

Wesley, John. *Explanatory Notes Upon the New Testament.* Naperville, Ill.: Alec R. Allenson, 1958.

Wilder, Amos N. "The Sermon on the Mount," *Interpreter's Bible.* Vol. 7. Nashville: Abingdon-Cokesbury Press, 1951. Pp. 155-64.

Windisch, Hans. *The Meaning of the Sermon on the Mount.* Trans. S. McLean Gilmour. Philadelphia: Westminster Press, 1951.

Yoder, John H. *The Politics of Jesus.* Grand Rapids: Wm. B. Eerdmans Publishing Co., 1972.

INDEX

This is a topical index. Occasionally, it locates topics or themes rather than specific words. The faithfulness of God, for example, will sometimes be the essence of a passage, though the term itself does not appear. On the other hand, the terms "the Darkness" and "the Light" are so pervasive that they are simply marked *passim,* which means "throughout (the book)."

299

Constantine, 48
contemporary Christian music, 29-30, 212-13
Corinthians, First, 131, 150, 159-60, 176, 245, 251, 282
Corinthians, Second, 131, 228
cross, the, 15, 31, 33, 38-39, 54, 61, 63-64, 103, 105, 113-14, 164, 181, 191, 201-2, 216-17, 228
crucifixion. *See* cross, the
Crusades, 229
cult (temple), 125
cynicism, 59-60, 62, 73

Daniel, 67, 83
Darkness, the, *passim*
David, 226, 245
Declaration of Independence, 96
Deuteronomy, 125, 130, 143, 151, 165, 174, 180, 209, 218-19, 225, 277, 291
devil, the. *See* Satan
Didache, the, 282
divorce, 159-64, 279
Donatists, 229
drug abuse, 60
dualism, 71, 241-42

Ecclesiastes, 190, 256
Eden, 126-27, 171
Elijah, 220
Ellul, Jacques, 50, 248
Ephesians, 98, 125, 263-64
Esdras, Second, 277
Esther, 83
Eusebius, 48
Eve, 24-25, 126, 130, 162, 171, 219-21, 227-28, 243, 251, 253, 256
evil, 43, 67
exile, 22, 35, 52, 55-57, 60, 73, 76, 81, 83, 191, 225-26
Exodus (book of), 130, 142, 143, 151, 174, 225
exodus, the, 68, 132, 184, 225
Ezekiel, 22, 35, 89, 101, 151
Ezra, 281

faithfulness of God, 21, 36-37, 47-48, 53-55, 61, 67, 70-71, 77, 93, 105, 117, 125, 127, 141, 149, 151, 157, 162, 163, 166-67, 169, 189, 218, 222, 228, 234, 246, 258, 259, 268, 288
Fall, the, 24-25, 32-33, 55, 60, 61, 66, 69, 74-75, 92, 100, 104, 126, 130, 145, 146, 164, 166, 173, 176, 181, 211, 219-22, 227, 252
fasting, 58, 196-98

fear, 31, 43, 55
flood, the, 100-101, 104
forces of Darkness. *See* Powers, the.
Former Prophets, 66
freedom, 26, 27, 33, 36, 38-41, 62, 67-69, 71-73, 87, 91, 103, 105, 135-36, 139, 158, 162, 164, 166, 168, 170, 176, 213, 255, 263, 264-65, 275, 279, 293
freedom of speech, 171

Gandhi, 197
Gehenna, 147, 149, 158
Genesis (book of), 100-101, 104, 153, 159, 175, 208, 220, 228
genetic counseling, 26
gnosticism, 95, 205
goddess worship, 206
good and evil, 24-25, 75, 126-27, 130, 252-53, 261, 280-81
government, 75

Hagar, 153
Hare Krishna, 95
Hebrews, Epistle to the, 233
Hitler, Adolf, 31, 243
Holocaust, the, 31-34, 215, 229-30, 270, 286
hope, 21, 54, 61-62, 65, 70, 82, 149, 246
Hosea, 85, 106, 132, 151, 227, 290, 291
Hutchinson, Anne, 293

ideology, 110-11, 114, 116, 124
idolatry, 28, 57, 60-61, 92-98, 127, 206, 210-12, 236, 242, 251, 269, 280, 281
Incarnation theology, 244
Inquisition, 237
insanity, 43-44, 54
institutions, 65, 68, 74, 86, 97, 107, 110, 114, 123, 173, 215, 259, 265, 274, 279, 284
Isaiah, 21, 35, 47, 52, 55, 84, 89, 92, 101, 105, 109-10, 122, 144, 205, 225, 276, 290
Islam, 189

Jeremiah, 89, 101, 133, 149, 151
Jews, 32, 47, 72, 82, 195, 202, 229, 237, 255, 270, 285
Job, 49, 58-59, 62, 190, 216, 232
John Chrysostom, 198
John, First Epistle of, 135, 215, 282
John, Gospel of, 39, 58, 97, 107, 122, 125, 134, 245, 266
John the Baptist, 21, 282
Jonah, 67, 197
Joseph, 83

DATE DUE

JUL 2 6 1991		
3/10/95		
MY 10 '96		
JA 02 '08		

DEMCO 38-297